Sir Thomas Lauder Brunton

The Bible and Science

Sir Thomas Lauder Brunton

The Bible and Science

ISBN/EAN: 9783337033767

Printed in Europe, USA, Canada, Australia, Japan

Cover: Foto ©Lupo / pixelio.de

More available books at **www.hansebooks.com**

THE
BIBLE AND SCIENCE.

BY

T. LAUDER BRUNTON, M.D., D.Sc., F.R.S.,

FELLOW OF THE ROYAL COLLEGE OF PHYSICIANS,
ASSISTANT PHYSICIAN TO ST. BARTHOLOMEW'S HOSPITAL,
AND LECTURER ON
MATERIA MEDICA AND THERAPEUTICS IN ST. BARTHOLOMEW'S HOSPITAL SCHOOL;
FORMERLY BAXTER SCHOLAR IN THE NATURAL SCIENCES IN THE
UNIVERSITY OF EDINBURGH.

WITH ILLUSTRATIONS.

London:
MACMILLAN AND CO.
1881.

The Right of Translation and Reproduction is Reserved.

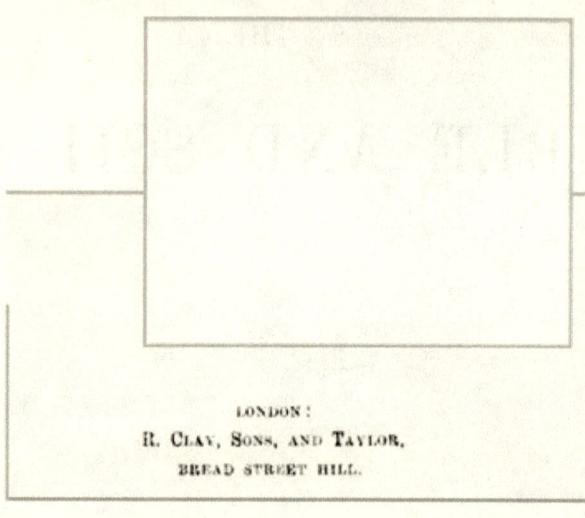

LONDON:
R. CLAY, SONS, AND TAYLOR,
BREAD STREET HILL.

TO

JOHN HUTTON BALFOUR, M.A., M.D., LL.D.,

F.R.SS. LOND. AND EDIN.,

LATE REGIUS PROFESSOR OF BOTANY AND MEDICINE IN

THE UNIVERSITY OF EDINBURGH,

THESE LECTURES ARE RESPECTFULLY DEDICATED BY

HIS ATTACHED FRIEND AND FORMER PUPIL,

THE AUTHOR.

PREFACE.

Many people consider the doctrine of evolution, or, as it is not unfrequently termed, Darwinism, as necessarily atheistic, and regard it with horror mingled with fear. They look upon it with horror, because they think that its spread will be injurious to religion and morality; and they fear it, because they see that every year its adoption is becoming more general, and that, notwithstanding their dislike to it, they are unable to stop its progress. In addition to this, some have a lurking dread that the doctrine may be true, and that they may by and by be forced, in spite of themselves, to acknowledge its truth, and to give up the cherished religious beliefs which have been their joy and strength. Feelings of this sort induce some people to remain wilfully ignorant, both of what the doctrine of evolution really is, and the arguments that may be adduced in support of it; while others refuse to see the force of the arguments; and others, again, are rendered most unhappy by their inability to deny their truth. The objects of the present work are to give a brief and popular sketch of the data on which the doctrine is founded, and to show that instead of being atheistic it is the very reverse, and is no more opposed to the Biblical account of the Creation than those geological doctrines regarding the structure and formation of the earth's crust which were once regarded as heretical and dangerous, but are now to be found in every classbook, and are taught in every school.

The plan adopted has been to give a brief account, first, of the living things both animal and vegetable which now exist on this earth and of their relation to one another; and, secondly, of the forms of life which existed in the early ages of the world's history, and their relationships to one another as well as to those of the present day. After this follows a discussion of the question how these various forms of life, past and

PREFACE. ix

present, came into existence, whether by sudden creation or gradual evolution.

The three introductory chapters may seem at first sight to have but little connection with those which immediately follow them, but they have a direct bearing upon the questions discussed in the later part of the work. They are intended to illustrate several subjects which might not be readily understood if no examples were given, while the examples could not have been so conveniently introduced afterwards.

The countries of Egypt and Palestine have been described as typical specimens of countries where the climatic conditions were entirely different, so that abundance prevailed in one while famine desolated the other, and drove a starving people to one of those wholesale migrations which have played so important a part in the world's history.

Life in ancient Egypt has been described in order to fix attention on this ancient civilization, and make it a landmark in the world's history, so that the long centuries which lie between then and now might serve as a measure of geological time. Egyptian funeral ceremonies have been described at some length as having a bearing on the possible site of Paradise.

The influence of similar external circumstances in producing a similar character in different races is exemplified in the Fellaheen of modern, and the Israelites of ancient Egypt, while the effect of different external circumstances upon the same race is seen in the comparative bravery of the desert-born Israelites and the cowardice of their helot fathers.

The hereditary transmission of qualities is illustrated by the conduct of Joshua and his Arab coadjutor Caleb, although a still better illustration might have been given in the constancy with which the love for "jewels of silver, jewels of gold, and raiment,"[1] manifested by the Israelites on their departure from Egypt has been transmitted to their descendants at the present day, as well as the dislike to manual labour, which they no doubt carried with them from the land of bondage.

I know of no book which affords illustrations of subjects like those I have just mentioned so

[1] Exodus xii. 35.

readily as the Bible, and other examples might have been advantageously introduced were it not that they would have unduly lengthened the introductory chapters.

As the object of the work is not to present new discoveries to the reader, but only to describe well-known facts and show their bearing upon certain opinions, it seemed unnecessary to illustrate it by new woodcuts. Indeed it seemed advisable rather to take them from well-known text-books to which the reader could refer if he wished for fuller information on the subjects cursorily treated of in this work.

The books to which the author is chiefly indebted for woodcuts are Flower's *Osteology*, Gegenbauer's *Comparative Anatomy*, Geikie's primers of *Geology* and of *Physical Geography*, Hooker's primer of *Botany*, Huxley's *Physiography* and his *Physiology*, Sir John Lubbock's *Metamorphoses of Insects*, Oliver's *Botany*, St. George Mivart on the *Common Frog*, Wyville Thomson's *Depths of the Sea*, Waterton's *Wanderings*, and White's *Selborne*. Some illustrations have also been borrowed from *Nature*; and figs. 164, 165, 166-173, and 180, 181 have been copied by the courteous permission of Messrs. Kegan Paul and Co. from Hæckel's *History of Creation*.

I take this opportunity of returning to the authors and publishers of these works, as well as to other friends who have assisted me in the preparation of this work, my most hearty thanks for their kindness.

I cannot here name all the friends and authors by whom I have been helped, but I ought to mention that the facts and arguments on pages 341 and 342 are reproduced, as nearly as my memory enabled me, from a lecture which I heard delivered by Professor P. G. Tait nineteen years ago.

CONTENTS.

LECTURE I.
INTRODUCTORY—BIBLE LANDS—EGYPT 1

LECTURE II.
INTRODUCTORY—THE EXODUS 25

LECTURE III.
INTRODUCTORY—BIBLE LANDS—PALESTINE 42

LECTURE IV.
NATURAL HISTORY—PLANTS AND TREES—THEIR STRUCTURE
AND GROWTH 50

LECTURE V.
PLANTS AND TREES—MODE OF CONTINUING THEIR RACE OR
REPRODUCTION 72

LECTURE VI.
PLANTS AND TREES—NUTRITION AND GROWTH OF THE
INDIVIDUAL 96

LECTURE VII.

PLANTS AND ANIMALS 115

LECTURE VIII.

GENERAL SKETCH OF THE ANIMAL KINGDOM—INVERTEBRATA 143

LECTURE IX.

GENERAL SKETCH OF THE ANIMAL KINGDOM—VERTEBRATA 163

LECTURE X.

GENERAL SKETCH OF THE ANIMAL KINGDOM—VERTEBRATA—COLD-BLOODED ANIMALS—FISHES—AMPHIBIA—REPTILES 179

LECTURE XI.

GENERAL SKETCH OF THE ANIMAL KINGDOM—WARM-BLOODED ANIMALS—BIRDS 200

LECTURE XII.

GENERAL SKETCH OF THE ANIMAL KINGDOM—WARM-BLOODED ANIMALS—MAMMALS 214

LECTURE XIII.

GENERAL SKETCH OF THE ANIMAL KINGDOM—MAN . . . 238

LECTURE XIV.

DISTRIBUTION OF PLANTS AND ANIMALS IN TIME 255

LECTURE XV.

GENERAL SUMMARY 301

LECTURE XVI.

THE MOSAIC RECORD AND EVOLUTION . . . 337

LECTURE XVII.

DEVELOPMENT OF INDIVIDUALS 368

INDEX . 403

LIST OF ILLUSTRATIONS.

PLATE I. . . . . *To face page* 14
PLATE II., FRONTISPIECE . . . . *To face title*

FIG.		PAGE
1.	The lotus	51
2.	Netted-veined leaf	54
3.	Parallel-veined leaf	54
4.	Forked-veined leaf of fern	54
5.	Germination of a dicotyledon (mustard)	55
6.	Germination of a monocotyledon (wheat)	56
7.	Diagram of a cross-section of the stem of a dicotyledon	58
8.	Diagram of a cross-section of the stem of a monocotyledon	59
9.	Longitudinal section of vegetable tissue, showing cells and vessels	61
10.	Diagram of a cell	63
11.	Multiplication of a cell by subdivision	65
12.	Growing point of a stem, showing the mode of growth by subdivision of cells	65
13.	Cell imperfectly filled by protoplasm	67
14.	Cellular tissue of pith	67
15.	Cells with thickened walls from the stone of a stone-fruit	67

LIST OF ILLUSTRATIONS.

FIG.		PAGE
16.	Elongated cells, with their walls thinned here and there so as to form pits	68
17.	Pitted cells united to form a vessel	68
18.	Diagram representing a common arrangement of the tissues in a fibro-vascular bundle	71
19.	Fungus, showing growth by subdivision of cells, which remain attached to one another	73
20.	Creeping stems and roots of couch grass	75
21.	Mushroom, showing stalk or filleus, on the gills of which the spores grow	79
22.	Hair moss	79
23.	Fern	80
24.	Part of fern-leaf, bearing clusters of spore-cases	81
25.	Lycopod	82
26.	Lesser club moss	83
27.	Female flower of yew	84
28.	Vertical section of flower of hypericum	85
29.	Growth of ovule of celandine	86
30.	Single stamen of mallow with 1-celled anther	86
31.	Anther after dehiscence	86
32.	Staminal scale of Scotch fir	87
33.	Scale of Scotch fir-bearing ovules	87
34.	Vertical section of flower of China primrose, showing ovary with ovules	88
35.	Scale of cypress with naked ovules	89
36.	Transverse section of ovary, enlarged, showing ovules attached to placenta	89
37.	Pollen grains of buttercup	89
38.	Diagram representing pollen grains on the stigma of a carpel of buttercup, which have developed their tubes reaching to the micropyle of the ovule	89

LIST OF ILLUSTRATIONS.   xix

FIG.		PAGE
39.	Pollen grains of buttercup on the stigma, with their tubes extending	89
40.	Longitudinal section of ovule of heartsease	90
41.	Male flower of nettle	92
42.	Flower of spotted orchis	93
43.	Single pollen-mass of spotted orchis, with its caudicle and gland	93
44.	Section of a flower of orchis, showing a bee standing upon the lip, with its head touching the sticky gland to which the pollen-masses are attached	94
45.	Fragment of epidermis with a stoma	105
46.	Spiral vessels with cellular tissue on each side	105
47.	Longitudinal section through the extremity of a root-fibre of buttercup	106
48.	Tea-plant with exposed stamens	108
49.	Section of flower of periwinkle, with the stamens protected by the tube of the corolla	109
50.	Sundew	111
51.	Dionæa, or Venus fly-trap	112
52.	An amœba figured at two different moments during movement	120
53.	A foraminifer with extended pseudopodia which pass through the pores of the multiloculate shell	125
54.	Transverse section of a foraminifer, showing the arrangement of the separate chambers in the shell	126
55.	Grains from a piece of chalk, showing the cases of foraminifera	127
56.	Actinosphærium, a rhizopod	127
57.	Diagram of the digestive cavity of one of the Infusoria	128
58.	A sponge	130

LIST OF ILLUSTRATIONS.

FIG.		PAGE
59.	Diagram to represent the first differentiation of the organism into ectoderm and endoderm, and the formation of a digestive cavity	132
60.	Syncoryne, with a number of budding medusæ on it at different stages of development	136
61.	A portion of a colony of hydroid polyps with budding medusæ	137
62.	Sea-anemone or actinia	138
63.	Section of sea-anemone or actinia	138
64.	Diagrammatic section of an island surrounded by a fringing reef	140
65.	Diagrammatic section of an island surrounded by a barrier reef, with intervening lagoon	140
66.	Diagrammatic section of a coral island, or atoll, with central lagoon	140
67.	Coral island with central lagoon	141
68.	The gastrovascular system of a cydippe	142
69.	Diagrammatic representation of the water-vascular system of a starfish	144
70.	A starfish	145
71.	Stone-lily or crinoid	146
72.	Tape-worm	147
73.	Nervous system of insects	149
74.	Diagrammatic transverse section through the hinder half of the body of a sandworm	151
75.	Diagram of the circulatory system of a lobster	152
76.	Insect, showing the three segments	154
77.	Diagram of an ascidian	157
78.	Cephalopod	161
79.	Single vertebra seen from above	163
80.	Diagrammatic view of the human body	164

LIST OF ILLUSTRATIONS. xxi

FIG.		PAGE
81.	Diagrammatic view of the human body	166
82.	Diagrammatic representation of the limbs in mammalia	167
83.	Ditto	168
84.	Diagram of the fore-limb of an amphibian	169
85.	Manus of a marsupial	169
86.	Skeleton of the manus or hand of various mammals	170
87.	Hinder extremity of a larva of salamander	171
88.	A front view of the pelvis	172
89.	A front view of the sternum	173
90.	Bones of the upper extremity with the biceps muscle	174
91.	Red and white corpuscles of the blood magnified	177
92.	Amphioxus lanceolatus	181
93.	Diagram of an ascidian	183
94.	Lepidosiren annectens	189
95.	Axolotl of Mexico	191
96.	The Proteus	191
97.	Tadpoles in different stages of development	192
98.	Lizard	195
99.	Crocodile	195
100.	A mud-tortoise (*Trionyx*), showing the dorsal plates	197
101.	Skeleton of pterodactyl	198
102.	Skeleton of the foot of a reptile	201
103.	Hinder extremity of bird	202
104.	Hesperornis regalis	205
105.	Jaw and vertebra of ichthyornis	206
106.	Compsognathus longipes	207
107.	Haunch-bones and legs of bird, dinosaur, and crocodile	208
108.	Woodpecker	209
109.	Foot of a woodpecker	210
110.	Nightingale	211
111.	Vulture	212

LIST OF ILLUSTRATIONS.

FIG.		PAGE
112.	Ostriches	213
113.	Ventral surface of innominate bone of kangaroo	216
114.	Great ant-bear	219
115.	African black rhinoceros	212
116.	Bones of the manus of pig, rhinoceros, and horse	224
117.	Foot of deer	225
118.	Stomach of an antelope	226
119.	Section of cow's horn	227
120.	Fore-limb of young dolphin, showing how the bones are modified to form the so-called fin	230
121.	Polecat	231
122.	Rat	232
123.	Hedgehogs	234
124.	Monkey	236
125.	Convolutions of the brain	240
126.	Sketch of a battle between reindeer	242
127.	Celt or axe-head of flint, rudely chipped	257
128.	Lance-head of finely-chipped flint	258
129.	A flint lance-point, showing two sides and edge	258
130.	Celt or axe-head of polished stone	259
131.	Geological map of Egypt	261
132.	Quarry in sedimentary rocks	266
133.	View of contorted strata	267
134.	Vertical strata	268
135.	Fossils	273
136.	*Sigillaria* attached to stigmarian roots	276
137.	*Stigmaria ficoides*	276
138.	Section of a part of the Cape Breton coal-field	277
139.	Section of tooth of labyrinthodon	278
140.	Cycad	279
141.	Skeleton of ichthyosaurus	281

LIST OF ILLUSTRATIONS.

FIG.		PAGE
142.	Skeleton of plesiosaurus	281
143.	Skeleton of pterodactyl	282
144.	Microscopic section of chalk from Sussex	283
145.	Atlantic ooze from a depth of 2,250 fathoms	283
146.	Compsognathus longipes	284
147.	Hesperornis regalis	285
148.	Palæotherium magnum	287
149.	Glacier descending into the sea and breaking off so as to form icebergs	289
150.	Floating icebergs	290
151.	Boulder deposited from an iceberg	291
152.	Boulder planed and scarred by glacial action	292
153.	Glacier of Zermatt	293
154.	Skull of old man of Cromagnon: vertical view	294
155.	,, ,, ,, profile	295
156.	,, ,, ,, front view	296
157.	Bones of the old man of Cromagnon	297
158.	Sculptured bone handle representing a reindeer	298
159.	Mammoth carved in ivory	299
160.	The mammoth	300
161.	Hinder extremity of bird	309
162.	Skeleton of the foot of a reptile and a bird	310
163.	Frog developed in egg, without undergoing metamorphosis	311
164.	Development of an ascidian	312
165.	Development of amphioxus	313
166.	Embryo of tortoise (4th week)	316
167.	,, fowl (4th day)	316
168.	,, dog (4th week)	316
169.	,, man (4th week)	316
170.	,, tortoise (6th week)	317

FIG.		PAGE
171. Embryo of fowl (8th day)		317
172. ,, dog (6th week)		317
173. ,, man (8th week)		317
174. Recent equus		322
175. Pliocene pliohippus		322
176. Protohippus		323
177. Miocene miohippus		324
178. Mesohippus		324
179. Eocene orohippus		325
180. Embryos of four vertebrates		347
181. Ditto		348

ERRATA.

Page 107, line 19, *for* "stems" *read* "stamens."
,, 161, ,, 1, ,, "paelozoic" *read* "palæozoic."
,, 194, ,, 10, ,, "vertebrata" *read* "mammalia."
,, 218, ,, 1, ,, "Hyracordia" *read* "Hyracoidea."
,, 252, ,, 12, ,, "Euthocomi" *read* "Euthycomi."
,, 306, ,, 9, ,, "teleostian" *read* "teleostean."
,, 395, ,, 23, ,, "Ackerman" *read* "Eckermann."

In the frog barometer mentioned at p. 394, the animal is stated in the last edition of the *Encyclopædia Britannica* to sit at the bottom of the vessel in bad weather and to mount in good weather. I am unable to discover whether my original German informant or the writer of the article in the *Encyclopædia* is correct, and have therefore left the statement as I got it.

THE BIBLE AND SCIENCE.

LECTURE I.

BIBLE LANDS—EGYPT.

In going along the streets of a town, one's ear can hardly fail to catch the cry, "Papers! Papers!"; and at every stationer's shop we are struck by the great number of new periodicals which are exposed in the windows for sale. In no age of the world's history has the saying of the wise man, that "men shall run about, and knowledge shall be increased," been more thoroughly verified than in the present. When we compare the general diffusion of information to-day with what it was five and twenty years ago, we are surprised at the change that has taken place within the limits of a quarter of a century. Nor is it merely in the extent of general diffusion of information that this change has taken place. It has occurred also in depth and variety.

In taking up one of the daily papers, we find that it contains news from every part of the world—from Afghanistan to the United States, from Kaffir Land to Baffin's Bay; and the news conveyed in the papers excites in the minds of those who read it a wish to know something of the appearance and productions of the lands of which they read, of the stature and physiognomy of the inhabitants, as well as of their manners, customs, and general mode of life. To supply this craving for knowledge, we have all sorts of magazines, pamphlets, books, and lectures, so that every individual in this country, whether living in a large town, a retired village, or an isolated cottage, has an opportunity of becoming acquainted, more or less accurately, with countries and peoples of whom his parents had not even heard. The acts of these peoples, their wars and treaties with us and with others, the names of their rulers, and their doings generally, come under the head of *history*, but their stature and strength, their powers of endurance, their mental capacity, the character of their soil, its fertility or its barrenness, the height of their mountains, the width of their passes, the depth, rapidity, and course of their rivers, all come under the *natural history* of these peoples, although they would influence to a great extent the events of the history of these races, by determining the numbers of their armies, their power of fighting or strategy, and their relations with others. The term "natural history" is a very comprehensive one, for it includes, in its widest significance, a description and explanation of everything that we see around us.

Under this title we may discuss the appearance of the earth on which we tread, its colour, its consistence, the outlines of its mountains, the depth of its valleys, the superposition of the different strata which are laid bare by a stream as it cuts for itself a deeper and deeper channel; the appearance of the trees which fringe its banks, the plants and flowers which carpet the meadows at its sides, the names and characters of the birds and beasts which live around it, the fishes which swim in its waters, the insects, worms, and slugs, which swarm around its banks; the sea-weeds, crabs, and other marine productions which any one who follows its course to the ocean would meet with at the sea-shore; and all the marvels which he would encounter in his visit if he were venturesome enough to proceed to the lands beyond the sea.

But the term "natural history" includes more than a mere description of animals, plants, and minerals. It embraces the relations of the different kinds of plants, animals, and minerals to each other; their distribution over the world's surface; the mode in which they live; the conditions by which they are influenced;

their succession in the world's history; and even the place of the world itself in space, its age, its development, its future. This subject is so wide that it is impossible for any one to become acquainted with anything more than the mere rudiments of the whole of it, and it has accordingly been divided, both for the purposes of instruction and research, into several departments. The appearance and composition of the different kinds of earth and rock are treated of under the head of mineralogy, the succession of strata under that of geology, the distribution of land and water under geography, the rainfall, the temperature, and the direction and force of winds under meteorology, the description of plants under that of botany, of animals under zoology, of the different races of man under ethnology, and the functions of life, and the modes in which men, animals, and plants manifest a life of their own, are treated of under physiology.

Day by day each of these branches of knowledge is extending. The number of facts included in each, is becoming greater and greater, until it is impossible for any one man to master all of them, although, like Solomon, his wisdom excelled the wisdom of all the children of the east country, and all the wisdom of Egypt, and though he were wiser than Ethan the Ezrahite, and Heman and Chalcol and Darda the sons of

Mahol[1] whose names have come down to us as marvels of learning. How much of our present knowledge we owe to these learned men it would be impossible to say, for the story goes that Aristotle, to whom we are indebted for a great deal, borrowed largely from the stores of Solomon. When Alexander was passing through Palestine on his career of triumphant conquest; Jerusalem at once opened its gates to the victor of Tyre, and the High Priest placed at his disposal all the treasures of the Temple. Amongst these were said to be a number of manuscripts containing the sayings of Solomon regarding plants, from the cedar that is in Lebanon to the hyssop that is upon the wall. These MSS. were sent by Alexander to his tutor Aristotle, who is said, though with what truth I know not, to have made free use of them, and thus, indirectly, we at this moment may have in our possession much of the wisdom of Solomon.

The news we get in the daily papers from far-off countries awakes our attention, and excites our curiosity regarding them, but to many a one these events, happening in distant lands, even although we receive news of them on the very day of their occurrence, seem much less read, and awaken much less interest, than the events which took place thousands of years ago, but which are narrated in the Scriptures. These, having

[1] 1 Kings, iv. 30, 31.

been read and re-read by us in our early youth, seem almost like a part of our own lives, and the actors in them seem like personal acquaintances.

Which of us has not pictured to himself, over and over again, the scene of Rebecca meeting Eleazar at the well, with his line of camels behind him, patiently waiting until some one should draw water for them? Or the long caravan which brought the aged Jacob to meet his long-lost son Joseph in Egypt? Or the lion standing beside the disobedient prophet and his ass, having neither torn the ass nor mutilated the man? Or the bears which destroyed forty and two children who had mocked the prophet Elisha? Which of us has not longed to visit the scenes where these various events happened? To see with our own eyes the exact spots where they took place? To tread with our own feet the same paths which the patriarchs trod? And to view mentally the whole drama in the very places where it was enacted!

Twenty or thirty years ago, but few people could gratify their desire to visit Bible lands, but now they go in great numbers. We see personally conducted tours by Cook or Gaze advertised at the beginning of every winter, and although it can hardly be very agreeable to join one of these large parties, there can I think be few pleasures greater than that of travelling, either alone or with one or two friends, in the East. Not only is there the purely physical delight of an unclouded sky above, a clear, warm, dry atmosphere around, giving strength, energy, and activity to the body, and buoyancy and joyousness to the spirits, but there is the mental pleasure, of moving backwards, as it were, through many centuries of the world's history, and seeing before one, day after day, buildings, paintings, and sculptures, as fresh as if they had come only yesterday from the hand of the architect or artist, although those who designed and fashioned them have mouldered into dust for thousands of years. At every step you seem to get new light thrown upon passages of Scripture with which you have been familiar from childhood, but which until now have never been thoroughly understood. On landing in Egypt, for example, and passing onwards through the Delta towards Cairo, you notice the miserable hovels of the Fellaheen, looking more like large mud bee-hives than anything else; you see their occupants later on, toiling from early morning till dusk, with no covering but a cloth around the loins, and with no reward except food barely sufficient to keep body and soul together, and you no longer wonder that the Israelites, after centuries of similar toil, had no thought beyond their daily bread; and would willingly have again bartered their liberty for the fish which they did eat in Egypt freely, for the onions and the melons and the leeks.[1]

[1] Numbers xi. 5.

You walk through the streets, and see carriages driving along through the crowd, preceded by a lightly clad runner, armed with a stick, with which he admonishes such animals as may stand in the way, while he cries "To the right!" "To the left!" "Make way!" and you at once perceive the humility of Elijah, when he voluntarily assumed the position of a running footman before Ahab's chariot, immediately after his triumphant victory over the priests of Baal. On riding some miles out from Cairo, you come to a grove of palm-trees, inclosing a green open space in the centre, on which stands a solitary obelisk. Here and there are mounds of broken bricks, made of clay mixed with straw and burned in the sun. Never in my life do I remember a pleasanter moment than when I sat down on one of these, and looked at the scene before me, for this was the realization of my childhood's dream, this was the spot where Joseph had lived. Yonder might have been the granaries where he received his brothers; here, in the neighbourhood, stood his house, where he returned, weary with his day's work, and was received by his lovely and loving wife Asenath, whose gentle care had obliterated from his mind, not only all the sorrows and trials of his early life, the hatred of his brothers, his slavery in Egypt, his temptations in Potiphar's house, and his long imprisonment in the dungeon, but had almost made him forget his dead mother, the kind old father who had loved him so well, and the little brother Benjamin to whom he had been so deeply attached, so that he called the name of his first-born son Manasseh, "For God," said he, "hath made me forget all my toil, and all my father's house." Here he rested and was at peace; though from time to time no doubt he was called to journey over the length and breadth of the land to inspect the crops and regulate the taxes. It may be interesting to dwell for a moment on the scenes that met his gaze, the products of the country which were paid to him in tribute, and the peoples who were either subject to him, or came in their distress to ask corn from him as a favour.

Fancy then to yourself a country shaped like an enormous capital letter Y, with its arms pointing towards the north, and its leg towards the south. The boundaries of the country are abrupt ridges of yellow limestone hills, and the leg of the Y, and the space between its arms, are filled in with perfectly flat, rich, dark soil, covered with vegetation, and watered by an immense river, which flows as a single, mighty stream, through the valley, and spreads out into many branches when it reaches the triangular space between the arms of the Y, which, from its resemblance to the Greek letter, has received the name of the Delta. The whole of this fertile country, inclosed as it is by the barren limestone hills, on which not a blade of grass grows, and beyond which stretch sandy deserts, is emphatically the product of the river. Rising in the far south, it carries with it rich soil from the countries through which it flows, and in the course of ages has not only deposited this rich mud over the surface of the barren sands in the valley between the hills, but has formed at its mouth a bank which has gradually pushed back the waters of the Mediterranean until the Delta is now about 120 miles both in length and breadth. Every year the river gradually rises, and covers the whole of this fertile tract, and again, gradually subsiding, leaves behind it the rich, soft mud, in which the seed sown will, after a month or two, spring up, yielding fruit a hundredfold. Both the rise and fall of the river are watched by the natives with the utmost anxiety. For if it fall short of its usual rise even by so little as two cubits, so flat is the country that a great part of it is left uncovered by the fertilising flood, and drought and famine is the consequence in Upper Egypt. If on the other hand the waters rise even a cubit too high, they overflow the fields destined for the autumn crops and devastate the Delta, invading the slight elevations on which the houses are built, covering the meadows and starving the cattle. The river slowly begins to rise at the beginning of June, attains its greatest height in the first half of October, and then begins to sink. In February the waters have retired within their banks and the fields are drying up.

Let us, in order to form an idea of the country, suppose Joseph at this time of the year to be starting on a tour of inspection, and let us in thought accompany him.

He has said farewell to his wife and children. His chariot and horses are at the gate, he springs up, and, accompanied by his attendants, drives onwards towards the southern point of the Delta, just where it joins the Nile valley. At first he proceeds amongst shady trees, bounded on either side by fertile gardens, but as he rides on, his path lies through a strip of hard, sandy desert, in crossing which, the hind legs of one of the horses ridden by his attendants suddenly becomes paralysed, the animal sinks upon his haunches, and the horseman falls backwards. The Cerastes, or horned snake, a little viper only about a foot long, lying concealed in the sand, which it resembles in colour, irritated by the passage of the cavalcade, has bitten the horse's heel. Immediately the poison spreads up the leg, paralysing it, and, when it reaches the spinal cord, paralyses it also, thus destroying the power of both hind legs, and causing them to give way under the weight of the animal. Only within the last year or two have we learned the exact manner in which such a poison as this acts upon the body, but centuries ago its general effect was well known, and no more vivid description of it could be given than that of the dying Jacob, who compared his son Dan to "an adder in the way, a serpent in the path, biting the horse's heels, so that his rider falleth backwards."

But, hardly delayed by such an incident as this, let us suppose the *cortége* again moving on. To the right spreads the green carpet of the Delta; in front rise the ends of the limestone ranges which inclose the Nile valley. Close under the western range, and built on a projecting shelf which juts therefrom, rise three pyramids of enormous size, whose solid blocks of gigantic stones rise tier upon tier, forming a huge mass which has resisted the wear of centuries, and which seems likely to last to the world's end. Joseph's course lies past the pyramids, but the river intervenes between him and them. Quickly flows the muddy tide between high dark-brown banks fringed with palms among which run little channels for conveying water from the river to the belt of herbage and plants which extends from the bank to the foot of the hills. For the hot sun quickly dries the moist mud left by the inundation, and, unless the vegetation upon it were watered artificially, it would soon be withered. The surface of the river lies sunk several feet below the level of its banks, and the water must be raised by devices, which are of exactly the same kind as those which were made use of by the Israelites in Egypt. Upon a short upright post is balanced a long bar, which has a bucket at one end, and at the other a heavy mass of clay. The Fellah who works it, just as the captives of the Egyptians formerly did, pulls down the bucket, fills it with water, and then, suddenly letting go, the heavy mass of clay at the other end descends, and thus raises the full bucket, which is then emptied into a little channel. These channels are very shallow, and have numerous branches, into which the water is allowed to flow or is cut off at pleasure by the foot of the labourer breaking down or building up a slight dam of mud at its entrance. To the Fellah, to-day, the language would be as appropriate as to the Israelite of old: "The land of Egypt, which thou waterest with thy foot."

A little further on he may have seen some weary brickmakers labouring in hard bondage, some breaking up the hard mud with picks, others bringing water from the river or a neighbouring pool to soften it, others working it up to a proper consistency, while others moulded it to the proper shape, as we see in this picture taken from the tomb of one of the Pharaohs who lived at a time not far remote from that of Joseph.

To those of us who think of stubble such as we get in our own fields it may have seemed very extraordinary that the Israelites could get enough to make bricks with. But the Egyptian mode of reaping was not always like ours. Some kinds of grain they cut down as we do, and threshed it out by the feet of oxen. But of other kinds they only cut off the ears, leaving the straw standing on the ground, and this no doubt was the stubble which the Israelites collected. The corn, after being winnowed, was taken to the barns and there measured, each measure being carefully noted by a man who was placed there specially for the purpose. Into such granaries as we see figured here (*vide* Pl. I.) was the tribute paid by the Egyptians to Joseph, and from these was corn sold to them when the famine was sore in the land. But it was not only from Egypt that people came to buy corn or to acknowledge the power of Pharaoh and seek his aid or friendship. From the far south they came bringing ostriches, giraffes and monkeys, and so the land of Egypt was enriched, net merely with its own agricultural wealth and the manufactures of its inhabitants, but with all the choicest products of all surrounding countries.

And of all the riches of this wealthy country, the best was Joseph's.

Connected by marriage with one of the noblest of Egyptian princes, the high priest of On, and, as prime minister of the king, second only to Pharaoh himself, Joseph no doubt inhabited such a house as we find from pictures on the monuments was inhabited by the

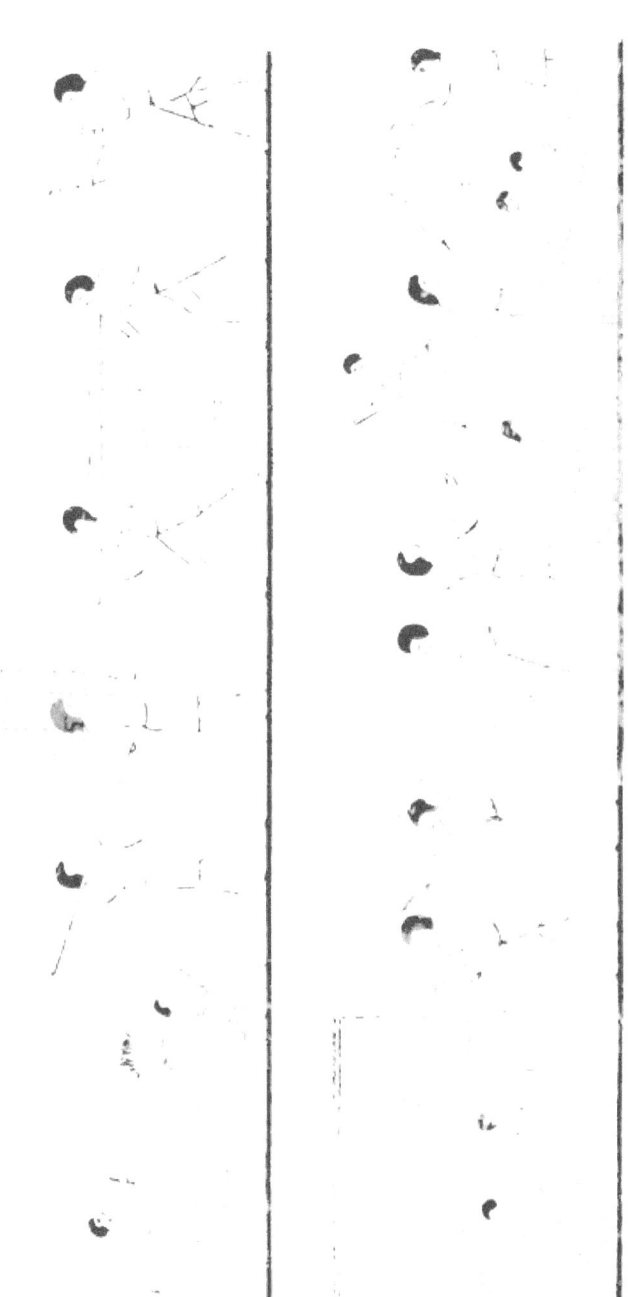

PLATE 1.—FROM CAILLIAUD'S "RECHERCHES SUR LES ARTS ET MÉTIERS DES EGYPTIENS."

At the right hand side in the upper part of the plate labourers are seen carrying corn to the threshing floor, and at the left hand side the process of treading out the corn by oxen is represented. At the right hand side in the lower part the process of winnowing is depicted, and further to the left the corn is being stored in vaults and its quantity is registered by a clerk. These pictures are peculiarly interesting as being probably painted at a period near that of Joseph, the tomb in which they are contained being said to be that of the father of Aahmes, a naval officer who helped to expel the Hyksos.

Egyptian nobles. Through a high gate, with flagstaffs on either side, he entered a paved court-yard, round which extended an open shed, the roofs of which were supported on wooden columns, and which served for stables, chariot-houses, and dwellings for the slaves. In the back wall of the court was a second door, leading to a large garden, with beds of flowers, aromatic plants and vegetables, groups of shrubs, and rows of fig-trees, pomegranates, tall palms, and shady sycamores and acacias.

Here and there were trellises, covered with vines, from which hung clusters of juicy purple grapes, and in the centre was a large tank, filled with clear water, from which the garden was watered, and where the children were occasionally allowed to angle for the fish with which it was stocked. On one side of the garden stretched a long, one-storied house, with an open verandah running along its whole length, and from which the doors of the sitting and sleeping rooms all opened. At the further end, a row of store-rooms extended out at right angles, in which were kept all the food and goods necessary for the household. The floors of the sitting-rooms were covered with rich carpets, chairs and stools of graceful shape and brilliant colour stood about the rooms, which, during the day, were partially darkened by heavy blinds and shutters to keep out the noon-tide heat. In the garden, near the tank, was a summer house, in which Joseph and his wife were accustomed to sit during the cool of the evening, while the children played around them, and refreshed themselves with the fresh juice of grapes newly plucked from the neighbouring trellises.

But it is not probable that the life of Joseph and his wife was entirely free from those bereavements which fall to the ordinary lot of man. In the course of nature the father of Asenath would in all likelihood die before them, and they probably stood around his death-bed. As soon as the last breath was drawn, they and the rest of the family would break out into loud lamentations, renewed from time to time, and continued not only while they remained in his house, but in the streets as they passed from it to their own home, and on their way they would throw dust upon their heads as a further sign of grief. For three days this was continued, and the body was then sent to the embalmers. These removed the brain by inserting a curved iron instrument through the nostrils, and, an incision being made in the side, the intestines were drawn out, washed with wine, and covered with spices, and, the belly being filled with myrrh, cassia, and other aromatics, the body was sewn up again and kept in salt for seventy days. It was then washed, wrapped up in bands of fine linen, smeared with gum on the inner side, and placed in a wooden case somewhat in the form of a man. It was then restored to the friends, who, all this time, had kept up their lamentations at home, by neglecting bathing and the care of their garments, in order to show that their intense grief was too absorbing to allow them to attend even to their most ordinary duties. During this period, too, the tomb was being prepared for the dead (generally on the other side of the river). When ready, special notice was sent out to forty-two judges, and afterwards a public announcement of the day was made, the mummy case was carried out of the house and placed in a hearse upon a sledge, and the funeral procession commenced. First were servants, carrying tables loaded with eatables of all sorts, and animals for sacrifice. The next group carried warlike implements; and the third, furniture, and a chariot, followed by the charioteer, with horses yoked to another car, which he drove on foot; next came plate and jewellery, rings, collars and necklaces, and after them came the sacred boat and the eye of Osiris, while others carried small images of the god, and of the bird which was the emblem of the soul. After these were carried flowers, and bottles for libation, and then came hired mourning women, throwing dust upon their heads, beating their breasts, and lamenting the dead. Next followed the hearse, drawn by oxen and men, and in it stood at either end of the sarcophagus, the nearest female relations of the deceased. Beside the hearse walked the high priest, and behind it came the male relatives of the departed. Some, with downcast eye and saddened look, stepped along in solemn silence, while others gave vent to their grief by beating their breasts. Arrived at the river-side, the forty-two judges were found ranged in a semicircle, and, near at hand, boats were waiting ready to convey the funeral party across. The judges now proceeded to judge the dead, and grant or deny to him the honours of sepulture, according as he seemed to deserve. If the decision were favourable, the funeral company would cross the river to the tomb, while if it were adverse, they must return home with grief and shame. The judges summoned all those who had anything of which to accuse the deceased to stand forward, but if his life had been just, no valid accusation could be brought, and those who had envied his greatness, and might, through ill-will, have wished to cast ignominy upon his memory, were deterred from making false accusations by the remembrance of the penalties which they knew would follow if their assertions were found to be untrue. The judges having pronounced the dead worthy of sepulture, the bearers of food and furniture embarked in a large boat, which was followed by a small one holding cakes, fruit, and green palm-branches to throw before the hearse on its way to the tomb. Next followed the men with flowers and plate; and then two other boats, in which stood the male and female mourners, beating their breasts and lamenting loudly. Last came the hearse, surrounded by the chief mourners, in a consecrated boat, with an altar at the prow, from which the high-priest burned incense. Arrived at the opposite shore, the procession disembarked, and the sledge was drawn across the sandy desert to the tomb. This consisted of a number of chambers, hewn in the solid rock of the Libyan hill, and the walls were decorated with pictures illustrating the ordinary occupations of the deceased and his family, painted in colours which, even at this day, remain almost as vivid as when freshly applied, and show us the ordinary mode of life of those who lived fifty centuries ago. Arrived at the tomb, the mummy was taken out of the hearse and placed erect in one of the chambers, and his wife, embracing it, burst out into a loud wail, and called upon all her friends to join with her in praises of the deceased. In the meantime the high-priest poured out libations and offered up incense, while all around joined in the lamentation, and threw dust upon their heads, after which the tomb was closed and they all returned to their homes.

In Egypt the concerns of a future life beyond the grave occupied the thoughts of the living more than in any other country, ancient or modern; and it is therefore all the more surprising that not only the books of Moses written after leaving Egypt, but all the earlier parts of the Old Testament, should contain no reference to any future state. From their silence on this subject it has been inferred that the Israelites of old, like the Sadducees in later times, had no belief in a future existence; but it is exceedingly difficult to imagine that they could leave Egypt without a belief of this kind. Especially is this the case when we find that their funeral feasts remained so important, that, when an Israelite brought his tithes to the temple, he had solemnly to affirm that he had not eaten thereof in his mourning nor given aught thereof for the dead. (Deut. xxvi. 14.)

But let us now turn again from the private to the public life of Joseph.

Forced by the famine which prevailed not only in Egypt but in the surrounding countries, deputations came to beg for leave to buy corn in Egypt, the granary of the ancient world. With them they brought the products of their country as presents to gain them grace in the eyes of Joseph. Amongst others came the brethren of Joseph, and they carried down from Canaan with them balm and honey, spices and myrrh, nuts and almonds. When they arrived, he spake to them by an interpreter, for although the rulers of Egypt at this time were derived from the Semitic race, allied in blood to the inhabitants of Canaan, their long residence in the country had probably so modified their forms of speech that it was no longer intelligible to the children of Israel, although when Abraham visited the country no such interpreter seems to have been necessary.

The customs of the higher classes also appear to have been modified by the feelings of the people. The King and the ruling race at this time are supposed to have been the Hyksos, or shepherd kings of Egypt, who, originally a pastoral race, had invaded the land and driven the former rulers out of the Delta and far up the Nile valley. This invasion by a pastoral people had rendered the very name of shepherd obnoxious to the Egyptians, and although the rulers belonged to this race, they seem to have yielded to the popular prejudice, and Joseph's brethren were set at a table apart from themselves. On the arrival of his father and brethren, Joseph led them up to Pharaoh, and after permission to dwell in the land of Goshen had been granted, Pharaoh commanded Joseph, if there were any men of activity amongst his brethren, to make them rulers over his cattle. How this command was fulfilled we learn incidentally from a curious passage in the Book of Chronicles, from which it appears that some of the sons of Ephraim were killed in an attempt to recruit their stock from their neighbours' herds without asking leave. The following is the passage:—"And the sons of Ephraim . . Ezer and Elead, whom the men of Gath that were born in that land slew, because they came down to take away their cattle, and Ephraim their father mourned many days."[1]

After the death of Joseph, a quarrel arose between the king of Lower Egypt, who demanded from the king of Upper Egypt—a descendant of the regal race which before the foreign invasion had ruled the whole country—a valuable spring, which the latter refused to give up. In consequence of this a war broke out, which, after lasting for nearly eighty years, ended in the expulsion of the foreign race, and the union of the whole of Egypt under one king. Naturally enough the new rulers were suspicious of the Hebrews, a people more numerous than themselves, allied in race to the foreign conquerors, and bound to them by ties of gratitude and affection for numerous favours received at their hands.

To expel them in a body, by open violence, was impossible, and besides, it would have been ruinous, for they were skilful herdsmen and agriculturists. They had been dwelling a long time in the Delta, they knew what embankments were needed to protect the towns, and what canals were necessary to fertilize the country. The people belonging to the conquering race, hitherto penned up within the narrow regions of

[1] 1 Chron. vii. 22.

Upper Egypt, would barely have sufficed to carry on the work, even if they had been so inclined, which apparently they were not. It was, therefore, to some extent necessary to retain the great body of the Israelites in the country, although part of them, it would seem, had left their land along with the remnant of the Hyksos, whom, probably, they had aided in their struggle with the Egyptians.

But on the other hand, should the Hyksos again return to invade the country, the numbers of the Israelites who in all probability would join their standard would render their success a matter of great probability if not of actual certainty. It was not impossible, too, that they might combine amongst themselves, either to win back part of the country as their own, or else to migrate from it and seek to conquer territory for themselves elsewhere. Thus the Egyptians ran the risk, either of having a second civil war, or of losing their skilful labourers and servants, and being compelled themselves to undertake distasteful and menial work. It was therefore not in a spirit of cruelty, but, as they thought, of wisdom and self-preservation, that the new king said to his people "Behold, the people of the children of Israel are more and mightier than we; come on, let us deal wisely with them; lest they multiply, and it come to pass, that, when there falleth out any war, they join also unto our enemies, and fight against us, and so get them up out of the land." At first, then, as we are told, they set over them taskmasters to afflict them with their burdens, and made their lives bitter to them with hard bondage and forced labour in making sun-dried bricks, and building treasure cities, Pithom and Raamses. By the abstraction of so many labourers from their ordinary occupations, the work of those who were left was enormously increased, and the mortality amongst those engaged in the works was in all probability enormous, if we may judge from what has been observed, even in the present day, in the construction of the Suez Canal. Such work as brickmaking, carried on under the rod of the taskmaster under the burning sun as we see it depicted on the monuments, was well calculated to destroy many of the Israelites, and to break the spirit of the survivors. Nevertheless, it was ineffectual, and the Egyptians were forced to have recourse to the more direct mode of lessening the numbers of the Hebrews by drowning the children.

LECTURE II.

THE EXODUS.

WE all know the story of Moses, and how he was drawn out of the water, and brought up as the son of Pharaoh's daughter; but we do not, I think, all realize how much is implied in this, and also in the verse—" And Moses was learned in all the wisdom of the Egyptians." From Josephus we learn that, in his royal capacity, he led an army into Ethiopia and vanquished the Ethiopian king, whose daughter became his wife. It is possible that, proud of her royal rank, she somewhat slighted and despised Aaron and Miriam, who, unable to bear her scorn, may have been thus induced to combine against Moses as we read in Numbers xii. 1. As he was learned in all the wisdom of the Egyptians, Moses knew the true signification of the complicated worship in which the common people were made to adore birds, beasts, and creeping things. He knew that all these were simply symbolic of the attributes, such as "All-seeing, All-knowing, All-creating," of the one God, who is over all, and in all, and around all, in whom in a very definite sense indeed, they lived and moved and had their being, and were, as a Greek poet, who had possibly derived his idea from the Egyptians long afterwards said, " His offspring." From Him they came, of Him they were, to Him they returned. (Acts xvii. 28.)

Of geometry, astronomy, and possibly of chemistry, Moses had no mean knowledge, for the Egyptians had fixed, very nearly, the proper length of the year; they were able indeed to rectify, by observation of the stars, all its inequalities, and compute time accurately, and it seems not improbable that the Pyramids were intended to serve as astronomical observatories, as well as tombs for deceased kings. All his knowledge, and all his warlike service, made him, however, only more dangerous. When it became known to Pharaoh that he had taken the part of the oppressed Israelites, he was forced to flee across the desert to the eastern side of the Red Sea, and there to dwell in some oasis with the chief of a wandering Arab tribe. At last Rameses the Second died, a man of great mental power and iron will; the oppressor of the Israelites, the mighty conqueror, who had not kept them alone in hard bondage, but had ruled his Egyptian subjects also with an iron hand, and taken from the country many of its best and bravest, to perish in the foreign wars which he had waged against the tribes of Syria and Palestine, and the Greeks of the Archipelago. Rameses was probably the playmate of Moses in childhood and his fellow student in youth, for Seti, the father of Rameses, caused him to be educated along with other young nobles of the country. The knowledge which Moses and Rameses would thus acquire of each other's abilities and character would lead them to fear as well as respect one another, so that Rameses dared not have Moses residing in Egypt, and Moses knew that any attempt on his part to return from exile would cost him his life. Under the reign of his feeble successor, Menepthah the First, Moses dared to return to Egypt, and then, under his leadership, as we know, the Israelites left Egypt, after an unwilling consent had been wrung from the king by the twelve terrible plagues with which his country was visited. Amongst these was one which used to puzzle me not a little, the plague of "darkness which might be felt." Why, I thought, did the people all remain in the dwellings? Why could they not take lanterns with them and move out? But a day which I once spent at Port Said showed me what was probably the reason. On waking in the morning it seemed to me that everything had been turned into pea-soup. Above, around, and on every side, was a thick yellow mist, darkening the air like a London fog, but differing from it in this respect, that it was darkness perceptible; a darkness that might be felt, and painfully felt too, for it was caused by a storm of sand, driven by the wind, and every particle stinging the skin like a needle. It was the khamâsîn, and while it was blowing those who were wise all stayed in-doors.

After leaving Egypt, the Israelites did not take the short way to Palestine, as this would have brought them in a few days into collision with the warlike Philistines, against whose well-trained and well-armed bands a mob of slaves, mostly unprovided with arms and unskilled in the use of those which they might have, would have had no chance of success.

Therefore it was that a long and toilsome route was chosen; and through the wilderness, over the sandy desert, stopping now and then at an oasis, the children of Israel journeyed under the leadership of Moses.

Shortly after crossing the Red Sea they came to the wells of Marah, and there an incident occurred which illustrates the value of the information regarding that region which Moses had acquired during his long residence in it. The water of these wells was so bitter that the people were unable to drink of it; but when Moses had "cast" a tree into the water it became sweet. This incident has puzzled some commentators, who have supposed that it was some acidulous fruit which

Moses cast into the water, and thus rendered it palatable; but such an explanation is untenable, both because no such fruit is to be found in any quantity near the wells of Marah, and because no acidulation would render the water sweet. The true sense of the passage is obscured by the word "cast" having been used instead of "put" by the translators. It ought to have been "a tree, which, when he had *put* into the waters, the waters were made sweet." The way in which the tree was put in and the waters rendered sweet, is shown by Josephus, and by some modern writers acquainted with the district where the incident occurred. Along the shores of the Red Sea there are springs where the water, as it gushes up when one digs into the sand, contains salt but in quantities so small as to impart no unpleasant taste. When this water stands in a pool for a short time it becomes more and more concentrated by evaporation, until it is so salt as to be quite undrinkable. If this bitter water be now drawn off and thrown away, the water which springs up in its place on digging into the deeper layers of sand below is quite sweet. In place of digging at the waters of Marah, Moses seems to have extemporised a kind of Artesian well by driving a wooden pipe into the sand; for Josephus tells us that he divided a piece of wood lengthways in the middle, and put it into the well. He then set the strongest men among them to draw up water, and when the greatest part was drawn up, the remainder became fit to drink.[1]

From Marah the Israelites went onwards until they came to Sinai, and thence, after the giving of the law, they turned northward, towards the borders of the land of Canaan. Arrived at Kadesh, they sent messengers to spy out the land, and these, with one consent, brought back a favourable report of the fertility of the country, describing it as a land flowing with milk and honey, and bringing grapes, figs, and pomegranates in evidence of the truth of their statements. But while they all agreed regarding the desirability of possessing the land, ten of them were faint-hearted, and described its conquest as an impossible task. They had seen there the giant sons of Anak, in whose sight they seemed, and in whose presence they appeared to themselves, as grasshoppers. Only two, Caleb the son of Jephunneh, of the tribe of Judah, but who, as we learn from Josh. xiv. 6, was really a Kenizzite, and Joshua, the son of Nun, an Ephraimite, whose ancestry, as we have already seen, had been engaged in border warfare, felt confident of their power to dispossess the inhabitants of the country, and take possession of it. Unable to persuade the people, however, they, as well as Moses and Aaron, narrowly escaped being stoned by the mob, who wished to return to Egypt, but, shortly afterwards

[1] Josephus, *Antiq. of the Jews*, bk. iii. ch. 2.

changing their minds, resolved to attempt the conquest of Palestine, although the leaders refused to go with them. The consequence was that the Amorites and Hivites utterly routed them, and pursued them with great slaughter. After this unsuccessful attempt, they spent nearly forty years wandering about in the wilderness until the cowardly and vacillating slaves, whose spirit had been broken by hard labour under the rod of the taskmasters in Egypt, had died out, and their offspring, born and bred in the desert, and likely to be a better match for the warlike Canaanites, had risen up in their place. Avoiding a contest with the Edomites, who were nearly allied to them in race, they vanquished Sihon, king of the Amorites, and Og, king of Bashan, and overran their country.

Forty years they wandered, until all but three of those who had left Egypt were dead, and then, on the borders of the Promised Land, Moses himself called the tribes together, and after some touching words of advice and farewell he walked forth alone to die.

And now the leader was gone who, careless of his own comfort and regardless of fatigue, would sit the whole day judging between man and man, until reminded that his work might and should be done by deputy. The whole company, saddened by his loss, descended the steep declivity of the Moab hills into the Jordan valley, and travelled along until they came to the brink of the river, which, swollen with the early rains, was rushing like a mill-race into the Dead Sea, a few miles lower down. As soon as the feet of the priests entered the turbid stream, we read that its waters stood up as in a heap towards the city Adam, while those which flowed towards the Dead Sea were cut off, leaving the channel dry. One of the puzzles of my childhood's days was to imagine the condition of the waters thus cut off, for I fancied to myself the river Jordan, like such streams as I had been accustomed to, flowing through a small channel with level meadows stretching on either side. How then, I thought, did the waters stand up as in a heap? I could picture to myself a steep, glassy wall of water running across the channel itself, but was there likewise a level wall along each bank, or did the waters flow over the meadows on either side? On seeing the Jordan, however, I at once discovered the solution of my childhood's difficulty. The Jordan valley itself is a huge furrow, like that of the Nile, about ten miles wide,[1] inclosed between steep hills, stretching away to high tablelands on either side, and in the middle of this runs the river, within its double channel. The one channel, which it may possibly have filled long, long ago, when much larger than now, is, at

---

[1] The numbers given here are all rough estimates, formed by the writer in the course of a day's ride over the country without any measurements.

the place where the Israelites are supposed to have crossed, about 100 yards broad, and some 60 feet deep. Within this is the present channel, about 30 yards broad, and eight or nine feet deep. The bottom of the larger and outer channel, between its banks and that of the river, is covered with thickets of brushwood, which formerly afforded cover where wild animals could hide in comfort so long as the river remained within its proper channel, but when it became swollen with the rains, and overflowed its ordinary banks, though still remaining within its outer channel, the waters, invading their lair, drove out the lions which, in anger,[1] went to the higher grounds, and there made havoc among the cattle.

Within this larger or outer channel, then, confined by its bank on either side, the waters of the river might become filled up as a heap. Here was an answer to one inquiry of childhood. There were no invisible or glassy walls, indeed, at the sides to prevent the waters from running over the surrounding country. Was there, then, one to dam them up in their channel, and thus to cut them off towards the Dead Sea, or was the dam here simply of earth? On standing at the river's brink, the whole scene appeared to pass before me. The country around is highly volcanic. Earthquakes occur with great frequency, and, during such

[1] Jer. xlix. 19.

convulsions of nature, we know that the relations of land and water becomes greatly altered. In the earthquake of Lisbon, for example, the sea seemed to recede more than a hundred yards, and then appeared suddenly to return to its former height. This was due, not to any change in the water, but to a change in the ground, which first underwent a sudden upheaval and then sank again to its original level. Here, I thought, we have the method by which the Israelites were able to pass over dry-shod. If the bed of the stream at this place underwent a sudden upheaval at the time of their passage, the consequences would be exactly those which are described in the Book of Joshua. The waters would rise up like a heap, filling the channel far up the valley, and those flowing down to the Dead Sea would be cut off.

To some this explanation may seem mere fancy, but it appears to be the one accepted by the Psalmist, for, in the 114th Psalm, we find "Jordan was driven back; the mountains skipped like rams, and the little hills like lambs." "What ailed thee, O thou sea, that thou fleddest, thou Jordan that thou wast driven back? Ye mountains that ye skipped like rams, and ye little hills like lambs? Tremble, thou earth, in the presence of the Lord, in the presence of the God of Jacob." Here the Psalmist seems to ask the question why Jordan was driven back, and to give us indirectly as an answer that the earth trembled, or, in other words, that there was an earthquake.

The Hebrew word translated tremble in this passage is not the word usually employed to denote an earthquake, and it signifies a prolonged convulsive effort rather than a sudden shiver. This distinction makes the expression of the Psalmist describe the occurrence which we have supposed to take place even more graphically than if he had employed the ordinary word for earthquake.

Some two or three miles from the Jordan's western bank, and a couple of miles from the foot of the steep, almost perpendicular, ascent which bounds the flat Jordan valley, lay Jericho, after the wonderful siege of which the Israelites sent up spies to the city of Ai. To any one who has toiled up that weary ascent, the words of the spies are wonderfully expressive, "Let not all the people *labour* unto Ai." But the unfortunate issue of their first attempt to take the city made it necessary for all the people to join in the assault. There they found themselves high above the Jordan valley, and could now see what the Land of Promise was like. It was not like the land of Egypt, which they had "watered with their feet," but a land of hills and valleys, a land of corn and wine, a land of oil-olive, and honey. For here from Bethel, which stood a little to the west of them, ran

D 2

eastward to the deep trench of the Jordan valley a number of parallel valleys with intervening ridges like the teeth of a comb; near this was the spot upon which Abraham had pitched his tent shortly after his entrance into Canaan, and his selection affords us a curious instance of the slight alteration which has taken place in the habits which have passed down from father to son, to his descendants the Arabs of the present day, and at the same time of the exactness of the descriptions which we find in the Book of Genesis. The Arabs now generally camp at the upper end of the valley, sending their flocks downwards along its course to browse through the day, and again bringing them up at night. They do not, however, camp on the top of a hill, as that would be both inconvenient and uncomfortable. Knowing this fact, I had been a little astonished at the statement that Abraham pitched his tent upon a hill between Bethel and Ai, but a look at the hill itself at once removed my difficulty. The hill here is, as I have already said, like the back of a comb, with ridges, which answer to the teeth running eastward from it. In one of the valleys lying between them, no doubt Abraham camped in exactly the same way as his descendants do now, and yet the words of the text are most literally exact, "He pitched his tent upon a hill which lay between Bethel and Ai." Shortly after the siege of Ai, occurred that remarkable event which had such a powerful influence upon the fortunes of the Israelites, raising their spirits and utterly disheartening the people of the land who had gathered together to oppose them, and thus rendering the conquest of the Promised Land a matter of comparative ease. This remarkable occurrence has been a great stumbling-block in the way of those who could not possibly see how the events narrated in the text could be brought into harmony with the so-called laws of nature. So long as the view was held that the sun and moon were practically large lanterns, suspended in the sky for the purpose of giving light to the earth, and travelling round it in twenty-four hours, it was not at all surprising that these should suddenly stop in their course for several hours. But when it became known that the apparent motion of the sun and moon was due to the diurnal revolution of the earth, with, roughly speaking, a velocity at its surface of one thousand miles an hour, the apparent standing still of the sun and moon became much more difficult to believe. For in order to produce the phenomenon we must suppose that the earth had been suddenly arrested in its course, and that this arrest was continued for several hours, after which it resumed its motion. We all know the shock which results from the sudden application of the break to a railway train, even when going little more than twenty miles an hour, and the tendency which every person and thing in it has to fall forwards, continuing their motion after the train itself has stopped. Now fancy the disturbance that would be created by stopping an enormous train moving at the rate of one thousand miles an hour. The same disturbance would take place if the motion of the earth around its axis were arrested. People and things upon it would all tend to fly off, the waters of the seas would rush out of their beds with tremendous violence, and carry destruction far over the continents, even if the solid crust itself did not crack under the strain. Such difficulties as these some years ago led an Italian, whose name I have now forgotten, to scrutinize more closely the meaning of the text, and to see whether the significance popularly attached to it were the correct one. The literal meaning of the Hebrew words translated "stand still" in Joshua, is, I believe, that given in the margin, "Be dumb," and is the same as that which is differently translated in Leviticus, where Aaron is said to have "held his peace" after the death of his two sons, Nadab and Abihu. The point of the question, then, according to this Italian commentator, lies in the translation of the somewhat ambiguous phrase, "the sun and the moon were silent." He translates it "be dark," instead of "stand still," and considers the darkness to have been caused by a total eclipse of the sun. The difficulty in regard to this interpretation is that the text seems to indicate that both sun and moon were visible. But when the moon is close to the sun, as it is before an eclipse, it is rendered invisible by the sun's brightness. The words of Joshua, "Sun, be thou dumb upon Gibeon, and thou moon in the valley of Ajalon," may only refer, however, to the true position of the moon, and not to its visibility, for they indicate that the sun and moon were close together, and that the moon was to the west of the sun. For in order to see the sun in the midst of heaven over Gibeon at all, the spectator must have been standing at some point to the northward of it, and to one in that position the words "standing over the valley of Ajalon" would exactly convey the idea of the moon being in the heavens close to the sun and a little to the west of it, for this valley runs down only a little to the west of Gibeon.

Now this is the very condition under which a total eclipse of the sun takes place. First, the western edge of the moon gradually covers the whole disc of the sun, and then apparently leaves the latter at its eastern edge.

The effect of such an occurrence as a total eclipse of the sun, even upon civilised peoples, is very extraordinary. In the battle which was fought between the Medes under Cyaxares, and the Lydians under Croesus, the eclipse of the sun which took place during the fight struck such terror into both armies that the conflict was suspended. Supposing that it had been known to the one army and not to the other, and that, moreover, it was regarded by the one as a token of the divine interposition in their favour, and by the other as an evidence of the wrath of the Deity, we can fancy what an enormous advantage it would give to the one side over the other. If we consider, too, that the Israelites had hitherto by no means shown themselves to be a very courageous people, no less than 12,000 of them having but a short time previously been routed by the inhabitants of the small town of Ai; and that during a great battle the combatants do not watch the progress of time or calculate its lapse with great accuracy, so that it might be several hours before they noticed that the sun was not going down as usual it seems not unnatural to conclude that a total eclipse would be very much more beneficial to them, by striking consternation into their enemies, than such a prolongation of the day as would simply allow them to slaughter a greater number of the scattered fugitives. We read, too, that at the Creation the morning stars sang together; and if this be taken as a poetical equivalent for shining, we may perhaps reasonably be inclined to think that the Italian interpretation of the words "Be dumb" as meaning "Be dark," is nearer the truth than the one in the English translation, "Stand still."

CONQUEST OF PALESTINE.

After this victory the children of Israel, flushed with success, went southward, taking cities and destroying the inhabitants until their victorious career was stopped by the southern desert, and, again turning north, they continued to vanquish the peoples of Canaan as far as Mount Hermon and the Valley of the Lebanon.

LECTURE III.

BIBLE LANDS.—PALESTINE.

AND now let us take a nearer view of the Land of Promise. It has played such a large part in the world's history, that one is inclined to look upon it as a large country, whereas in reality it is very small, its greatest length being little more than 150 miles, and its breadth about 90 or 100 miles. This strip of land is bounded on the west by the Mediterranean, and on the east by the great Syrian desert. But, small though this country is, the Palestine in which the great events of Scripture history were enacted is much smaller still, for all that part of the country which lay to the east of the Jordan, which was divided between the tribes of Reuben, Gad, and the half tribe of Manasseh, only comes incidentally into Bible history, and the tribes to which it was allotted were amongst the first to be carried away into captivity. This part of the country forms a high table-land, and is divided from the other and more important part by the deep Jordan valley.

This part, the land beyond Jordan, as the Israelites on the way from Egypt were accustomed to term it, is that to which we will at present confine our attention. It forms a long, somewhat irregular triangle, with a ridge of high land running down its centre, and falling upon the one side abruptly down into the Jordan valley, and on the other shelving more gently towards the Mediterranean shore.

On the other side of the Jordan the high table-land of the Haurân again rises abruptly to an equal level with the hills of Palestine, so that the Jordan valley seems, as I have already said, like an enormous groove, hewn out by some vast chisel so as to separate Palestine proper from the continent of which it would otherwise have formed a simple continuation.

On each side the central ridge of Palestine is furrowed by valleys more or less parallel to each other, so that one may compare it to a double comb, the teeth of which are the ridges intervening between these valleys, and the alternate spaces the valleys themselves, which run towards the Jordan or the Mediterranean and convey thither the water which falls upon the country during the former and latter rains.

Not only does the country slope less abruptly towards the Mediterranean than towards the Dead Sea, but the heights sink down before they reach the sea shore, and leave between them and the sea a strip of fertile plain, which here and there sends prolongations into the heart of the country. This plain, throughout a great part of its extent, bore the name of the Plain of Sharon, and its northern continuation was known as the Plain of Esdraelon. This level fertile tract of rich land, as well as the bottom of the various valleys, was well adapted for raising crops of grain, and so the land might well be called a land of corn.

The hillsides strike a stranger now visiting the country, and especially a visitor from England, as very barren, being steep and exceedingly stony, so that in many places one would say that the average was about three stones to one blade of grass, but even amongst these stones one still sees the olive tree flourishing, and a visit to the valleys of the Lebanon, where the hillsides are well cultivated, at once shows the wonderful capacity and productiveness of the country. Throughout the greater part of Judea the hillsides are simply covered with stones. The terraces which formerly rose tier upon tier upon them have been broken down, and the trees and plants which grew there have utterly died out; but in the Lebanon one sees a whole hillside covered with a series of terraces such as those with which one is familiar on the banks of the Rhine, each terrace only a few feet broad and raised by a wall five or six feet high from the one below it. Each terrace is planted with maize or vines, and along its edges grow fig-trees and mulberries, planted alternately, with sometimes vines hanging in festoons from their boughs. The corn or maize supplies the inhabitants with bread, and with fodder or litter for their cattle. The fig gives them most nutritious food, which when dried is a useful and agreeable addition to their ordinary fare. The mulberry yields food for the silkworms, the cocoons of which are sold for money, and the vines produce wine, which though often at present very poor in quality, only requires a little more care in its cultivation, to bring it up to a pretty high standard. On those parts of the hills which remain unterraced grow the olive-trees, either singly or in groves, and the oil extracted from their berries forms a substitute for butter. In addition to this we sometimes find, close to the houses, rows of beehives, and the wildflowers which grow plentifully around not only yield honey to their occupants, but also to colonies of wild bees which form their nests amongst the rocks. One could hardly, therefore, give a better description of this country than that which is contained in the Book of Deuteronomy.—"For the Lord thy God bringeth thee into a good land, a land of brooks of water, of fountains and depths that spring out of valleys and hills. A land of wheat and barley, and vines, and fig-trees, and pomegranates, a land of oil-olive, and honey." It was also, as the passage goes on to say, not like the land of Egypt, which was dependent for water on the Nile, but was watered by the rains of heaven.

During the winter, the weather is sometimes very cold, with snow, frost and hail, and occasionally winds have been noticed of such a piercing character as to be almost beyond our belief. It is narrated by Dr. Thomson, in *The Land and the Book*, that on one occasion a party of travellers were about to cross the Jordan valley, a distance of only a few miles. Shortly after they started, a piercing wind came down from Hermon; so exceedingly cold was it, that although most of them turned back at once and tried to reach the village from whence they had started, several of them fell dead, chilled through and through, before they could regain shelter. We are accustomed to regard the climate of Palestine as very warm, and to forget the description of the Psalmist, which is so very true.—"He giveth snow like wool; He casteth forth His ice like morsels; who can stand before His cold?" As spring advances, the weather becomes warm and pleasant. The early rains moisten the earth, and in the more fertile parts of the country the grass springs up forming a green carpet. The almond trees are covered with blossoms, so that they look like solid masses of snow tinged with rose colour, and at once show the significance of Solomon's comparison to the hoary head of old age.—"And the almond tree shall flourish, and the grasshopper shall be a burden, and desire shall fail." The beautiful cistus, which may dispute with the autumn crocus the title of Rose of Sharon, throws out its large rosy blossoms, and on the hills of Judea, one may see, thickly covering the ground, the white flowers of the Star of Bethlehem. The melting snows on the high hills, such as Hermon, swell the Jordan until it overflows all its banks, and the smaller streams, which at other times of the year are either dried up or shrunk into narrow beds, are likewise flooded, so that they become dangerous to ford, or utterly impassable, as the Canaanites found to their cost, when, fleeing before Deborah and Barak, the river Kishon swept them away. As the spring proceeds, the rivers shrink within their beds, the rains cease, and, as summer advances, the brooks dry up, the land becomes parched, and the latter rains are anxiously awaited. Should they be delayed, the ground gets harder and harder, until it seems like iron under foot, and many an anxious eye is cast upwards and watches for the disappearance of the yellowish haze which has given birth to the language of the curse, "Thy heaven that is over thy head shall be brass" (Deut. xxviii. 23), and for the appearance of the clouds from whence refreshing showers shall descend. One can imagine the condition of the country after three years drought, when every blade of grass was burned up from the parched and fissured earth, and only here and there a little vegetation was to be found in the neighbourhood of springs, or of rivers fed by the perennial snows of Hermon. From place to place, as pasture failed, the cattle would be driven, until at length the king himself and his chief officers were called upon personally to decide what should be done with the small remainder. Great would be the depression with which Ahab went forth to search the land. Great would the anger naturally be with which he cried to Elijah, "Art thou he that troubleth Israel?" But his anxiety for the future caused him to yield a ready acquiescence to the prophet's demands, almost insulting as they might seem to him (1 Kings xviii. 18).

A distress so great as to humble the proud king in this way, and to compel him to wander hither and thither in search of water, must have compelled many of the inhabitants to do as did Elijah, and to leave the country in search of subsistence. We have no record of the numbers who did this; we only know that Elijah himself had gone first to the Jordan valley, and afterwards to the Mediterranean coast, but we find that in former famines, such as that mentioned in the Book of Ruth, and that which led the Israelites to leave Canaan for Egypt, the same conditions had produced similar results. Want of food had caused migration. Nor are these isolated instances; other nations have been affected in like manner; and scarcity of food is the probable cause of the numerous migrations of peoples and tribes which have had such a mighty influence on the history of the world.

LECTURE IV.

NATURAL HISTORY.—PLANTS AND TREES—THEIR STRUCTURE AND GROWTH.

In moving from one country to another, nations have carried with them some of their animals, and seeds of some of their plants. Yet the productions of various countries, although thus to some extent assimilated, have not been rendered identical. Each country still retains more or less its own Fauna and its own Flora, adapted to the conditions of soil and climate which the country affords. On the terraces covering the long sides of the hills of Palestine we find the thriving olive, the fig-tree, the pomegranate, and the almond-tree; while in Egypt, on the rich clay mud by the riverside, we find the palm-tree, the cucumber, the onion, the melon, and the leek, and formerly the papyrus and the lotus flourished in the Nile water. On the plains of Sharon and Esdraelon, wheat grew in abundance, as it did in the delta of Egypt, but, though the two kinds resembled one another in appearance, and

ADAPTATION OF PLANTS TO COUNTRIES. 51

were both readily recognizable as wheat, they differed from each other, and no one could mistake the wheat of Egypt for that of Canaan. All through the world we

Fig. 1.—The lotus.

find the same thing prevailing, the same adaptation of the plants to the countries in which they grow, the same diversity of form and structure corresponding to diverse climes and soils, and these not only give a character of their own to the landscape, but affect the character, habits, and disposition of the natives. In Egypt, we get sharp contrasts of brilliant colour, the bright green grass, the darker green of the palms, and the brilliant yellow of the naked sandstone, rock, and sand, while in Palestine, the grey lichens which cover the rocks, and the ferns which grow in the crevices of the stone on the hill sides, give half tints which blend the bright blue of the sky with the dull green of the olive and the darker hue of the fig.

Unlike as are the plants and trees of different regions on the earth's surface to each other, is any kinship to be traced between them? Are any characteristics to be found to connect the melon of Egypt with the fig-tree of Palestine, or the stately palm-tree with the humble onion and leek? What link can we find to connect the cedar of Lebanon with the hyssop upon the wall? In talking of plants, how can we arrange them so as to have no disorderly medley, but a regular series in which each member is closely connected with those on each side of it?

We may adopt one of many plans of arrangement. We may class them according to their **leaves** and **stems,** which are the parts by which the life of each individual plant is carried on; or according to the **flowers** and **seeds,** which are the parts by which plants propagate their race.

THE LEAF—ITS VENATION.

Supposing that we were to take a **leaf** from the fig of the Syrian hills, and one from a melon in an Egyptian garden, and compare their structure, we would find that both are supported by a framework whose ribs branch out hither and thither along the back of the leaf, so as to form a complete network. Anxious to see if the same structure is to be observed in the palm, we pluck a leaf, and again compare it, but here we note that the ribs no longer form a meshwork, but run in parallel lines from one end of the leaf to the other. Taking a leek or an onion, we notice in it that the veins of the leaves run exactly as they do in the palm. Close by the onion, in a crevice of the wall, grows, perhaps a fern. On plucking this, and examining its leaves, we find neither the network of the melon nor the parallel veins of the palm and leek, but veins which split up, forming forks, which again subdivide and fork again until the margin of the leaf is reached. Close by, in a crevice between the stones, we see a bunch of moss, and, picking it up, we look at the leaves, but the most careful scrutiny can detect in them no veins at all. A stone at its side is covered with a grey lichen, and although, as we see it spreading day by day, we know that it is alive, we cannot class it either with the fig, the palm, the fern, or the moss. We thus see that from the leaves we can divide plants into at least five families,—those with netted veins, parallel veins, forked veins, no veins, and no leaves.

Fig. 2.—Netted-veined leaf.

Fig. 3.—Parallel-veined leaf.

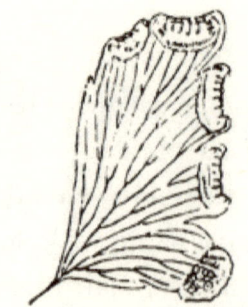

Fig. 4.—Forked-veined leaf of fern.

But these are also different in size. Is it not possible that, if we were to take them all when they were

ROOT-LEAVES OR COTYLEDONS.

young, and none much bigger than any of the others, they would be more alike? We plant, then, the fruit of an oak and of a palm, and we bury some of the old leaves of the fern and a bit of the moss under the ground, and we watch for the appearance of the first shoot. From the oak we see come up one small white

Fig. 5.—Germination of dicotyledon (mustard). 1. Seed. 2. Seed with the integument removed, showing embryo. 3. Rootlet pushing through the integument. 4. Cotyledons and radical or rootlet after throwing off the integument. 5. Young plant. All twice the real size.

shoot, bearing two tender green leaves opposite one another (Fig. 5), while from the date we find that only a single leaf appears (Fig. 6), and from the fern and moss we see no such leaf at all.

These root-leaves are called cotyledons, and thus again we get three great divisions of the plant kingdom; dicotyledons, monocotyledons, and acotyledons. The dicotyledons include all the netted-leaf plants, the monocotyledons all the parallel-leaf plants, and the

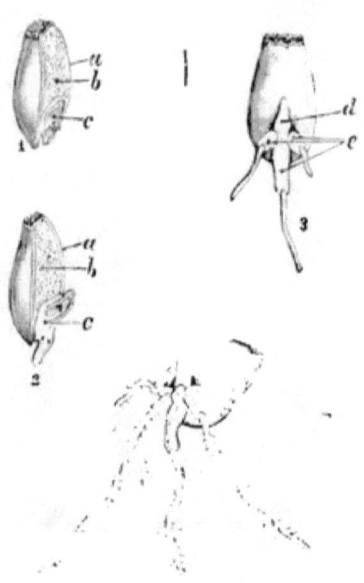

FIG. 6.—Germination of a monocotyledon (wheat). 1. Seed cut vertically, showing —*a*, the integument; *b*, the albumen; *c*, the embryo. 2. The same farther advanced. 3. Back view of grain with (*d*) plumule, and (*e*) sheathed rootlets. 4. The same, farther advanced. All twice the real size.

acotyledons all the plants with forked veins, with no veins, or without leaves,—the ferns, the mosses, and the lichens. To put this in a tabular form we have :—

    Dicotyledons   with   netted veined leaves.
    Monocotyledons   „   parallel   „   „
                               ⎧ forked   „   „
    Acotyledons   „   ⎨ no veins.
                               ⎩ no leaves.

We notice, too, that where there are no leaves, there is also no **stalk**, so that the leafless plants are also stalkless, and further, that the plants whose leaves have no veins have also soft stalks, while those in which we find a hard framework to the leaf have also a hard framework to the plant. Some have said that the leaf is to be regarded as a type of the plant, and have seen, in the arrangement of the veins in the leaf, a general resemblance to the form of the whole plant. We must not carry this resemblance too far, for, in the graceful maiden-hair, with its numerous rounded fronds, and in the stiff bracken, the veins are alike forked, but in the angular net-work of the oak-leaf we may trace a resemblance to the sturdy form of the oak tree, and in the arrangement of the veins of the willow leaf we may see a similar likeness to the graceful outlines of the willow.

Let us now examine the structure of the **stem**, in the oak, the palm, and the fern, and see if we can find any difference between them as we do between the forms and venation of the leaves. If we cut an oak twig in two, the first thing that strikes us is that, between the bark outside and the wood inside there is a sharp distinction. The outside of the bark is hard and dry, but almost immediately below the surface in the young twig we find that it is soft and succulent, and can be easily stripped off, leaving the surface underneath it moist and glutinous. The wood itself seems to some extent to repeat this character, for it is not of the same consistence throughout, but exhibits concentric rings, surrounding a soft centre of pith. Each of these rings represents a year's growth, and from the number of rings we find in the trunk we are able to estimate the age of the tree.

The oak grows thicker as it grows older. A new ring

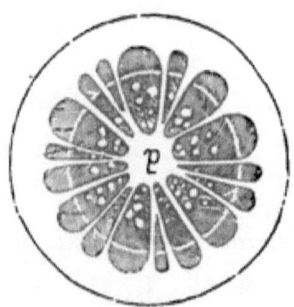

Fig. 7.—Diagram of a cross-section of the stem of a dicotyledon. *p*, the pith.

is added every year to the **outside** of the wood just underneath the bark, and trees which grow in this way are called **exogenous**, and we may sometimes guess at the age from a simple glance, even although we have no opportunity of counting the rings in the trunk. The outside of the trunk being composed of young wood is much softer than the old wood at the centre or heart of the oak. If, on the contrary, we look at the palm tree, we cannot tell from its thickness how old it is,

ENDOGENOUS AND EXOGENOUS STEMS.

and if we examine a section of the tree we can see the reason of this. Unlike the oak, the palm tree has no bark which we can separate, nor any concentric rings in its wood, which exhibits an even surface, dotted all over with minute dark points.

These points are most numerous, and the wood is hardest at the outside of the palm, instead of being hardest at the heart like the oak. It was supposed that the soft part in the centre was the newest, and

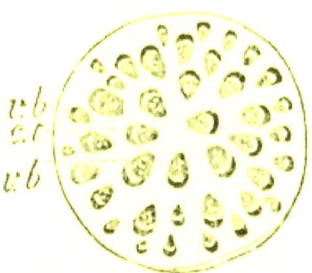

FIG. 8.—Diagram of a cross section of the stem of a monocotyledon. *v.b*, fibro-vascular bundle, *c.t*, cellular tissue.

that the palm and other plants having stems similar to it, grew from the **inside**. They were therefore called **endogenous**.

If we cut across the stem of a fern, we find an appearance differing from that of either the oak or the palm. We have no concentric lines, as in the oak, no bark which can be separated, but instead of the points we find dark lines, which, to the imagination of children, have seemed in the common bracken to present either the figure of an oak, or a rough resemblance to the letters J C. The growth occurs chiefly at the top, and the fern stem is called **acrogenous**.

In order to understand what these concentric dots and lines represent, we must examine into the **microscopic structure** of the various stems. On looking at the stem of the oak, we see that the part corresponding to the pith presents numbers of somewhat irregular circles, lying close to, or more or less intersecting each other. In the first ring we see other circles, but very much smaller, and thicker walled, with here and there larger rounded openings, and the same thing is repeated in each concentric ring until we come to the bark. Between this and the wood we see a row in which the circles are so flattened as nearly to approach an oval, and outside this again we find other rows in which the circles are more or less altered. Besides this, however, we find running out from the pith to the bark, and dividing the wood into wedge-shaped portions, rays, which look as if they were composed of minute paving-stones.

In order to understand what these appearances mean, let us now make a longitudinal section of the same piece of wood. On looking at this, the pith no longer presents a number of irregular circles, but a hexagonal appearance like a piece of honey-comb. Corresponding to the small circles in the concentric rings, we see elongated, spindle-shaped bodies, and, where the larger openings appeared in them, we observe long tubes with their walls variously marked. The ring of oval-shaped bodies between the bark and the wood still appears of an oval-shape, and if we happen to cut across one of the rays which stretch from the pith to the bark, and which have consequently been called medullary rays, we find that it still presents the paving-stone appearance.

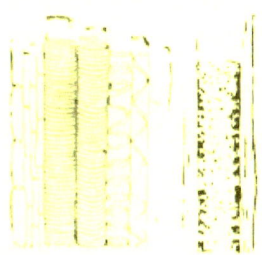

Fig. 9.—Longitudinal section of vegetable tissue, showing cells and vessels.

A comparison of these two sections shows us that the pith is composed of more or less hexagonally shaped bodies, the ends of which appear somewhat circular when cut across; that the wood in the concentric circles is composed of long spindle-shaped bodies, intermixed with long tubes; that between the bark and the wood there are a number of oval bodies, and that the rays running from the pith to the bark are built up of bodies like minute paving-stones.

These bodies hexagonal, spindle-shaped, oval, and quadrangular are all termed cells, the long tubes are called vessels, and of these two structures **cells** and **vessels**, all the tissues of plants are composed.

We see, from these sections, that the cells are everywhere, but that the vessels are only present in some parts of the plant, and if we were to examine moss or lichen, we should find that in them, as well as in seaweeds or fungi, no vessels whatever were present, the whole structure being composed of cells.

The cell, then, is the fundamental structure in all plants, and, as we shall see by and by, in all animals likewise. We must therefore devote a little time to the consideration of the cell.

In the pith of the oak we have seen that the cells aggregated together appear more or less like the cells of a honeycomb But have these cells ever been filled with honey? If so, where is the honey, and where are the bees which have made them? They may now be empty of everything but air, like the honeycomb which has been drained of its contents, but they were not always so. When the young twig first began to shoot, these cells were much softer than they are now, and each then contained a living occupant, who built it up. This living occupant was

THE CELL.

a little mass of soft gelatinous matter, to which the name of **protoplasm** has been given. This protoplasm, like all living beings, contained nitrogen, and had the power of taking to itself nutriment, and thereby moving or growing. If we had looked at it in its young state, while it was still actively engaged in building its cell, we should have seen lying in the centre of the protoplasmic mass (a, Fig. 10) a little body, to which the name of nucleus (b) has been

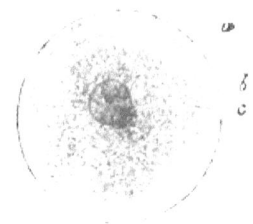

Fig. 10. Diagram of a cell. a, the protoplasm. b, the nucleus. c, the nucleolus.

given, and very probably within this a small dot, which has been called the nucleolus (c).

Usually then, though not always, the three parts of a complete cell are the nucleus, the protoplasm or cell contents, and the cell wall, which the protoplasm has built around itself. It was formerly thought that all these parts were essential to the cell, but it has now been found that the cell wall, though present in most cells, is absent from some, and that even the nucleus may be dispensed with.

The Protoplasm, then, is the most essential part of every cell, and as all vegetables are built up from cells, and, as we shall see afterwards, all animals too, protoplasm is inseparably connected with all living bodies, and therefore well deserves the name, which Huxley has given to it, of "the physical basis of life."

At present, however, we are talking of the young cells in the twig of the oak. At its end, where growth is going on, the young cells absorb nourishment and grow larger, but the simple growth of each individual cell will no more make the twig than the growth of a man and woman will make a family. In order that the twig may grow, the cells must multiply.

Now there are various ways in which cells multiply, just as there are various ways in which a household may increase. First, then, the cell may split into two, each half growing and forming a new cell, or only part of a cell may be thrown off, and this part may grow into a new cell, or inside one cell a number of others may grow up, and, finally, bursting the parent cell may mature each for itself, or, yet again, two neighbouring cells may unite and from their union new cells may arise. It is in the first way that growth takes place in the twig, and the latter modes of cell increase are reserved, not for growth, but for the reproduction of new organisms in various classes of plants.

MULTIPLICATION OF CELLS. 65

In growing, then, the simple cell which we have been considering in the oak twig, first begins to

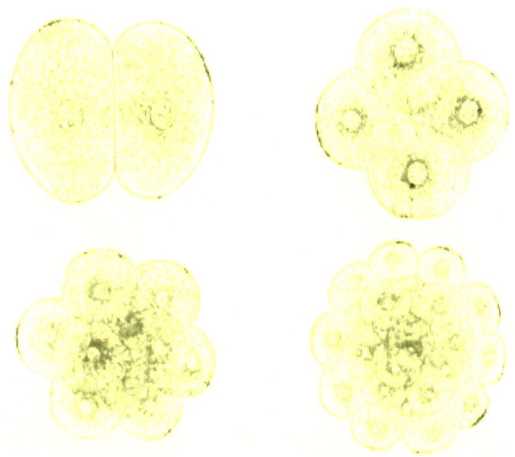

Fig. 11.—Multiplication of a cell by subdivision.

divide at the nucleus. This splits into two, and each half becomes rounded like the parent nucleus.

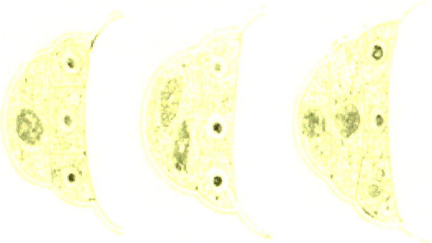

Fig. 12.—Growing point of a stem, showing the mode of growth by subdivision of cells.

Next the protoplasm begins to divide, and the cell wall sends in a little projection between the dividing

F

portions, which becomes larger and larger until it forms a complete partition, and thus we have two distinct cells. Each of these may go on dividing as before, and thus we get cellular tissue increasing both in length and in thickness.

We have already noticed, however, that the oak twig was not composed of cells alone, but that it contained many different bodies, some tubular, some spindle-shaped, and some oblong or hexagonal. These bodies were all originally cells but some of them have become much modified during the progress of growth and others have actually become converted into vessels. As the cells grow older they generally increase in thickness, and may also become modified in shape. In the hexagonal cells of the pith, the protoplasm, after building the cell wall, dies and disappears, leaving the cell filled either with water or with air. In some of them the protoplasm, instead of any longer completely filling the cell, begins to exhibit small spaces in its substance which are filled with fluid, and these increase until the protoplasm may appear reduced to a thin layer round the inside of the cell wall, either with or without branches ramifying through the bodies of the cell, and uniting the protoplasmic layers on the different sides. It may then finally disappear, leaving the cell filled either with fluid or with air. Before its death, however, it accomplishes very different work in the various cells of the vegetable tissues. In the pith it forms only a thin cell wall, which generally assumes by pressure a polygonal shape, but in the wood itself, it forms

Fig. 13.—Cell imperfectly filled by protoplasm.

long spindle-shaped cells in which the wall is very thick. These spindle-shaped cells are also known by the name of woody fibres, and constitute the chief part of the stem and branches of the tree. Side by

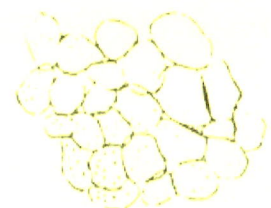

Fig. 14.—Cellular tissue of pith.

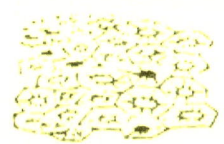

Fig. 15.—Cells with thickened walls from the stone of a stone fruit.

side with these spindle-shaped cells are others, which, instead of developing a thick cell wall all round, do so only at their sides, while the upper parts and ends of the wall at the point where it touches the cells

F 2

above and below it become thinner and thinner and disappear, so that the rows of cells, uniting together, form a tubular vessel.

The point at which this growth of new spindle-shaped woody cells, and of new vessels takes place in the oak and in other plants of the same class, is at the outside of the wood, just where the bark joins it, and therefore trees growing like the oak

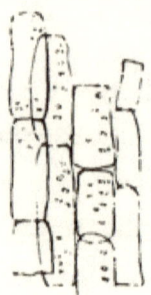

Fig. 16.—Elongated cells with their walls thinned here and there so as to form pits.

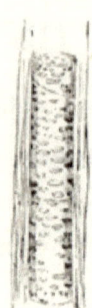

Fig. 17.—Pitted cells united to form a vessel. At each side are spindle-shaped woody cells or fibres.

from the outside are called exogens. Every spring, the return of warmth and moisture stimulates the growth of the cells, and if we then strip the bark off the twig, we find that it peels away readily from the wood, and that both the outer surface of the twig and the inner surface of the bark seem to be covered with a mucilaginous fluid, which is a mixture of protoplasm with cell fluid. During the heat and drought of summer the growth progresses more slowly, and is reduced to a minimum during the cold of winter. These changes we see marked in the concentric rings of the wood, the inner part of each ring being fuller of vessels, and less dense than the outer. We have said nothing as yet of the medullary rays composed of bricklike or muriform cells. These are simply unaltered portions of the original cellular tissue of the plant. These rays, when cut across, make the beautiful markings of oak, beech, and maple.

In exogens, then, the active, growing cells unite with one another so as to form a regular layer, called the **cambium** layer, on the outside of the wood, between it and the bark.

Such is not the case in **endogens,** which have received their name from its being supposed that they grow rather from the interior, the oldest wood being on the surface, and the youngest in the centre, exactly the converse of what is found in exogens. This is not exactly correct. What we find in cutting across the palm stem is a number of dots, more closely aggregated near the surface. These represent bundles of vessels, with active growing cells surrounded by woody cells. Between these rows of vessels lies unaltered cellular tissue. The growing cells or cambium, instead of forming a ring with hard woody tissue on its inside, and the softer tissue of the bark outside, here surround themselves with hard woody tissue, and thus in a short time check their own growth in all directions except upwards. Therefore it is that the palm, instead of growing .thicker with age, ceases to do so after a certain time, although it may still increase in height.

In ferns, the vessels are distributed in groups or bands, between which lie other bands of hard, thick-walled cells. But the chief increase takes place upwards, at the top of the plant, and not laterally, and ferns have, therefore, from their mode of growth, been termed **acrogens.**

In all these three classes, exogens, endogens, and acrogens, we have both cells and vessels; in mosses, lichens, algæ, and fungi, we have no vessels, but only cells, which by subdivision produce the leaves and stems of mosses, and the flat extensions of sea-weeds and lichens.

These plants, then, may be grouped together as cellular, in contradistinction to those containing vessels, which are designated vascular. In some of the most highly organised cellular plants, a differentiation may be observed between the cells composing them, those on the surface for example, becoming denser and harder than those inside, and thus tending to protect the plant from injury, but in others the whole structure is similar throughout.

RECAPITULATION CELLS AND VESSELS.

In all plants, then, the cell is the essential part. In some—the cellular plants—it is the only constituent of the tissue. In others—the vascular plants—it is associated with vessels, but even these vessels are developed from cells, and they may be looked upon as cells in another form. By the multiplication of cells the plant

FIG. 18.—Diagram representing a common arrangement of the tissues in a fibro-vascular bundle; *l*, the fibre; *c*, cambium layer; *w*, wood; *v*, wide vessel of the wood.

grows, whatever its position in nature may be—the oak as well as the lichen, but in the lichen the cells always remain cellular, whilst in the oak they become altered in form and structure, in order to be adapted to the more complex functions which they have to fulfil in the higher plant.

LECTURE V.

PLANTS AND TREES.—MODE OF CONTINUING THEIR RACE OR REPRODUCTION.

The essential part of every cell is the protoplasm it contains; so long as this is alive, the cell may grow, but when the protoplasm dies the cell can no more grow than a honeycomb in which all the bees have been destroyed. The simplest forms of plants consist of single cells, and they grow simply by multiplication, each cell giving birth to two or more, which separate and form perfect individuals. The plant grows in number, but does not increase in size.

Some fungi consist of rows of cells attached one to another by their ends, and by the cells which compose it subdividing, and each new cell formed in this manner again growing, without separating itself from its neighbours, the plant increases in size, but all parts of it still remain similar to each other.

In the higher algæ, and in mosses, the cells not only

multiply, but become to some extent differentiated, those on the surface, for example, becoming harder, and forming a skin which protects the softer structures inside.

In ferns and trees, the cells not only multiply and become differentiated, as in the smaller plants, but these higher members of the vegetable kingdom no longer present the simple external appearance of the

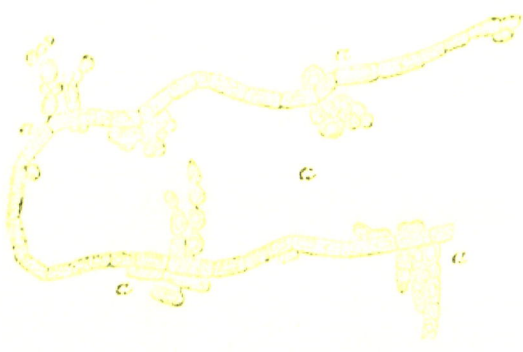

Fig. — Fungus, showing growth by subdivision of cells, which remain attached to one another.

lower orders. They have differentiated roots, stem, branches, and leaves, and, correspondingly, we find that the structure of the tissue becomes also more complicated, and that the cells, joining together in some parts, develop into vessels.

Everywhere the cell is the element of plant life. From its division we see structures of the most various sort arise, and at once the question suggests itself, Whence did the first cell come? So far as our present observation goes, we are only able to say that every cell has arisen from a pre-existing cell. *Omnis cellula e cellulâ.*

In the case of a growing bud, the cells divide, and the twig elongates. The power of growth is contained in the **bud** itself, and all that is requisite is that it should be supplied with sufficient nutriment. This is usually derived from the plant on which it grows, which draws up moisture from the soil; but if we cut it off from the parent plant, and embed it in the tissues of another plant of a similar nature to its own, it will again grow, the sap of its foster-parent supplying the place of its natural nutriment.

This process we call grafting, and in it we notice that, just as the oak and the apple-tree may draw nutriment from the same soil without becoming like each other, so the bud planted in the tissues of another tree still retains its own peculiar qualities, and does not become like the other branches. In the process of grafting, the sap is supplied to the new bud by the vessels of the plant or tree into which it is grafted.

But we often find that this process is unnecessary, and that the bud is able to draw from the earth itself all the nutriment that it requires. A simple slip cut from a rose-bush, and stuck into the earth will soon throw out new roots and grow into an independent rose-tree. Some plants, indeed, propagate themselves more or less in this way. The strawberry, for example, sends out branches which creep along the ground, and, here and there, instead of the buds developing into leaves, they develop into roots, which pass into the ground and form the bases of new plants, which, in their turn, repeat the process, until the ground is overspread for a considerable distance. In the case of the strawberry, the branches run along the ground; in those of the horse-radish and carices they run underground;

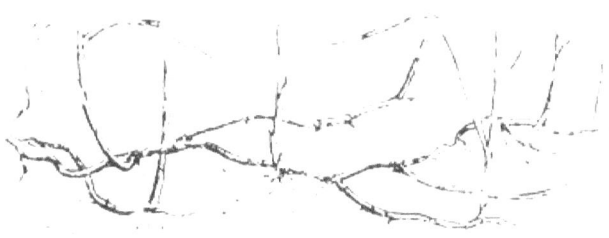

Fig. 30.—Creeping stems and roots of couch grass.

and in either case, when the branches are divided, the plants continue to grow independently of each other. In the banian, or Indian fig, rootlets drop down from the separate branches, and gradually extend themselves towards the ground until, reaching it, they form attachments and grow into new trees, so that, from a single individual may arise a complete grove, all whose members are united together.

In all these instances, the buds remain attached to

the parent unless separated by force; but in certain other plants the buds fall off spontaneously, as, for example, in the bulbiferous lily amongst endogens, and the aspidium bulbiferum amongst ferns, where, at a certain period of the plant's growth, the buds are cast off and grow independently.

Buds are formed likewise in cellular as well as in vascular plants. In mosses, any part when cut off, will grow into a new moss, and, at an early stage of the plant's growth, little buds, having a similar power are put forth. In liverworts, small bodies called gemmæ are formed in a little cup-shaped receptacle, and these likewise seem to be buds, which, on falling into a favourable soil, develop into new individuals. In the substance of lichens, also, are formed little bodies, termed gonidia, which apparently are buds like the gemmæ of liverworts. In some fungi we have cells simply thrown off from the jointed stalks which compose the plant. In others we have little bud-like processes sprouting from the end of the larger cell. In some of the algæ, such as the diatoms, the cells subdivide, and, after remaining attached to each other for a short period, the daughter cells break off and move away alone. In the lowest forms of vegetable life, the whole plant consists of a simple cell, the subdivision of which may be looked upon as the giving off of a bud.

We see, then, that all kinds of plants, from the

highest to the lowest, may multiply themselves by giving off living buds. In the lower classes this takes place frequently and spontaneously, but in the highest it occurs only exceptionally. Such a mode of propagation is convenient enough for the multiplication of the plant in the district immediately surrounding it. But buds, in their very nature, are soft, and easily injured, and therefore badly fitted for transportation to a distance.

In almost all plants, then, we have other means of propagation besides that by buds; and inasmuch as the essential feature in this process seems to be the union of two cells of different characters, which are regarded as male and female, it has been termed sexual propagation.

Sometimes we find two cells, apparently almost identical with each other, united together, and from their union results a spherical mass of protoplasm which is capable of growing into a new plant. This is seen in some of the algæ, such as those long, green, thread-like confervæ, existing in ponds and canals, with which most of us are familiar.

In the case just mentioned the spore is formed by the union of the contents of two cells which are apparently alike. In other algæ we see the spores formed by the union of dissimilar cells.

Special protuberances arise on the surface of the

plant, in one of which, called the antheridium, or male organ, a number of small bodies, which move rapidly by means of vibratile threads at their extremities, are developed; while in the other, called oogonium, appears a mass of protoplasm. Both of these now burst; the vibratile bodies, called spermatozoids, reach the protoplasm, mingle with its mass, and disappear. It also immediately changes. It assumes a sharp outline, which soon develops into a double cell-wall, and this now forms a spore, as it is termed. This spore cell swims away, and then finding a suitable spot attaches itself, divides, and subdivides until it forms a plant like its parent.

In some algæ the spores are not merely passive bodies, carried hither and thither at the mercy of the currents, but are furnished with mobile hairs, or cilia, by means of which they can swim about with considerable rapidity.

In a fungus such as the common mushroom the spore first forms a mycelium of branching threads, resembling in form some of the algæ, and from this grows the stalk and top with which we are familiar. On the top of this stalk are produced spores which grow from the gills.

In mosses the spore when it begins to germinate gives rise to branching filaments resembling some forms of algæ, and from this by lateral branching and by the differentiation of cells the stem and leaf arise. On this leafy plant the reproductive cells

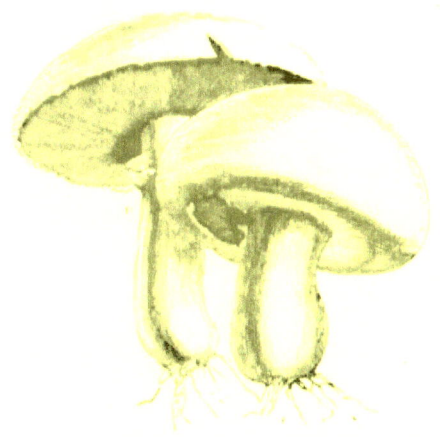

FIG. 21.—Mushroom, showing stalk or pileus, on the gills of which the spores grow.

with their different contents are formed, and from their union a spore again arises.

FIG. 22.—Hair moss. *a* The stalk, or seta, bearing a spore case or sporangium. *b* A sporangium covered by its hood or calyptra. *c* Head of antheridia bearing the male inflorescence.

In ferns a flat cellular alga-like expansion, or prothallium, grows from the spore, and on it are produced the antheridia and oogonia, from which the spore-bearing plant is produced.

In both mosses and ferns, then, we have an alternation of generations, the spore germinating into a plant

FIG. 23.—Fern (Aspidium Filix-mas).

which does not resemble the parent but resembles an alga, a plant lower in the scale. Here it may be well to say what we mean by the term lower and higher as regards plants.

By lower we mean that the plants are not so much

differentiated, every part being to a considerable extent like every other and able to perform the same functions. In higher plants the various parts are differentiated. They become unlike one another, each part ceases in great measure to perform the functions of the other parts, but confines itself to its own, and does that well.

Thus in algæ the plant consists of cells only, and these cells are all nearly alike; they are not differen-

FIG. 24.—Part of fern leaf, bearing clusters of spore cases.

tiated into cells of the root, of the stem, and of the leaves.

In mosses they are differentiated in this manner—roots, stem, and leaves being all different, but still they are composed only of cells.

In ferns we have some of the cells uniting so as to form vessels, but still we have no such differentiation of the reproductive apparatus as in the exogens and endogens.

In lycopods or club mosses, those trailing plants which we see so commonly on Highland moors, there is the same alternation of generations as in mosses and ferns, the spore produces a prothallium, but with this difference, that the prothallium remains within the spore and does not grow as a large cellular plant

Fig. 25.—Lycopod.

from it, as in mosses and ferns. It has, as it were, got a start of the mosses and ferns, for their spore has to develop into a cellular expansion, which has to grow on the ground for some time before it can produce

GYMNOSPERMS.

sexual organs from which a plant like the former is to come. But the spore of the lycopod develops its cellular expansion bearing reproductive organs within itself, so that when it falls on the ground the new plant is ready to grow up like its parent.

The lycopods also differ from the mosses and ferns in the formation of the spermatozoids, for these are

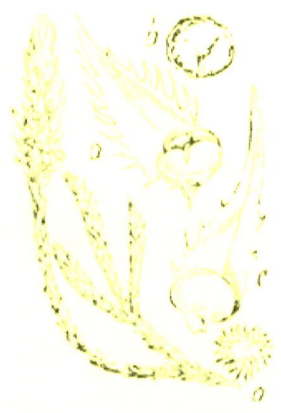

Fig. 26.—Lesser club moss (from Oliver). *a*, Scale with sporangium containing large or female spores (macrospores) *b*, Single macrospore. *c*, Scale with sporangium containing small or male spores (microspores). *d*, Single microspore, magnified.

developed within small spores which remind us of pollen grains.

From the lycopods we make a wide leap to the next class of plants, the gymnosperms, for here we have no longer to do with spores, which do not reproduce the parent plant, but one of a lower order, on which the true sexual organs which give birth to the next generation are situated. In the place of this, we have true **seeds** which give rise at once to a sexual plant resembling its parent. These seeds differ from spores in producing at once a plant like the parent, but they resemble spores in being themselves produced by the union of two cells of different kinds. We no longer, however, meet with the mobile spermatozoids resembling those of animals, their place being taken by thin-walled cells, the so-called pollen cells or grains, which form the male element in the reproduction of the higher plants, and instead of the oogonium or female element of the lower plants we have a highly-developed cellular structure, the **ovule**.

These bodies are generally placed at no great distance from each other in that part of the vegetable structure known as the **flower**. The flower usually consists of several parts, which are regarded as altered or modified leaves. These take various forms in different plants. In the pines, for example, they form hardened scales arranged around an axis; but in most plants they form, first a circlet of greenish leaves known as the calyx, the leaflets composing which are termed sepals, and inside this is a second circlet of coloured leaves termed the corolla, the leaflets com-

FIG. 27.—Female flower of yew.

posing it being called petals. It is in the axil or part where those modified leaves are given off from the axis or stem, that the reproductive organs are formed, just as new buds generally sprout from the axil of a branch.

Fig. 28.—Vertical section of flower of hypericum, showing sepals, petals, stamens, ovary and styles.

The formation of the male element begins as a little cellular projection. The cells composing this multiply, the mass grows larger, and then begins to show signs of differentiation. In its body larger cells appear, which form separate clusters, each surrounded by smaller cells, which form a distinct covering for it. Within these large cells the **pollen** is developed.

The **ovule**, or female element, likewise begins as a small cellular projection, the cells of which multiply until it becomes an ovoid mass, and then it also undergoes differentiation. In its interior, near its upper end, a cavity begins to form, and to this has been given the name of the embryo sac. Usually, also, the cells on the exterior are altered so as to form a double covering to the body or nucleus of the ovule, leaving, however, at the upper end a small opening

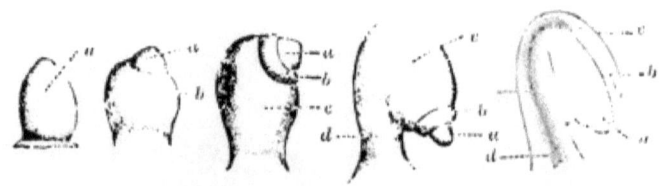

Fig. 29.—Growth of ovule of celandine. *a* Nucleus. *b.* First formed covering. *c* Second covering. *d.* Funicle, very greatly enlarged.

or foramen, the other end still remaining attached to the point from which it originally sprung, and through it the ovule continues to derive its nutriment from the parent plant. The pollen grains, as we

Fig. 30.—Single stamen of mallow with 1-celled anther.

Fig. 31.—Anther after dehiscence.

have said, are formed in the interior of the cellular mass, which gradually elongates until it forms a more or less club-shaped body, which is known as the stamen, the upper extremity of which is called the anther. When the pollen grains are ripe, the cells intervening between them and the surface of the anther gives way, and the pollen is thrown out in the form of fine dust.

In pines and cycads the ovules are naked, and are protected simply by the scale, at the foot of which they

Fig. 32.—Staminal scale of Scotch fir.

Fig. 33.—Scale of Scotch fir bearing ovules.

are produced, but in all other flowering plants the ovules are produced within a special structure, which we may compare to the womb of an animal, called the ovary.

All the higher plants, all those which are produced directly from seed, are divided into two classes; **gymnosperms**, in which the ovule is naked, and **angiosperms**, in which the ovule is formed within the ovary. The class of gymnosperms contains only the pines and cycads, and plants closely allied to them; all other flowering plants are angiosperms.

The seeds grow within the ovary until they have attained maturity, and then, by its bursting or destruction they are set free and scattered abroad. The ovary is generally a more or less egg-shaped or globular hollow vessel, attached at one end, and sending off at the other one or more prolongations called styles,

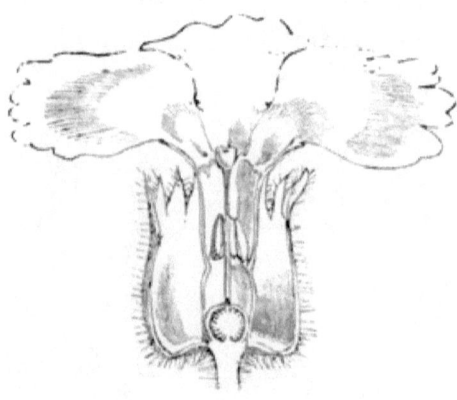

Fig. 34.—Vertical section of flower of China primrose, showing ovary with ovules.

each of which is terminated by a somewhat flat or club-shaped appendage covered with glutinous fluid, and called a stigma. The little mass of cellular tissue in the interior of the ovary from which the vessels spring is called the placenta, just like the nutritive structure to which the embryo is attached in the womb of an animal.

In the case of ovules growing within the ovary, it is impossible for the pollen to come directly in contact with them as it can with the naked ovules of gymnosperms. When extruded from the anthers it falls upon the glutinous sticky surface of the stigma, and at once the pollen tube begins to grow from the pollen grains, and penetrates through the

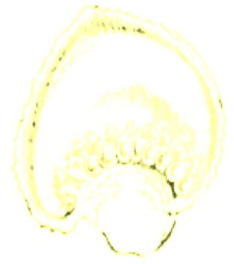

Fig. 35.—Scale of cypress with naked ovules.

Fig. 36.—Transverse section of ovary, enlarged, showing ovules attached to placenta.

Fig. 37.—Pollen grains of buttercup.

Fig. 38.—Diagram representing pollen grains on the stigma of a carpel of buttercup, which have developed their tubes reaching to the micropyle of the ovule. The tubes are so delicate it is almost impossible to trace them the whole way in the buttercup.

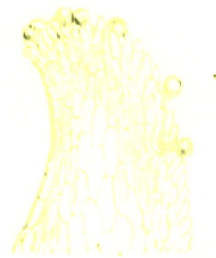

Fig. 39.—Pollen grains of buttercup on the stigma, with their tubes extending—both very much enlarged.

cellular tissue of the style until it comes in contact with the ovule, which it enters at the foramen, just as we have seen to be the case in gymnosperms. When it reaches the embryo sac, the latter divides and subdivides, forming numerous cells, which gradually arrange themselves so as to form the **embryo** or young plant which is contained in the **seed.**

This is now ripe for growth, and, whenever it is planted in a proper soil, with warmth and moisture,

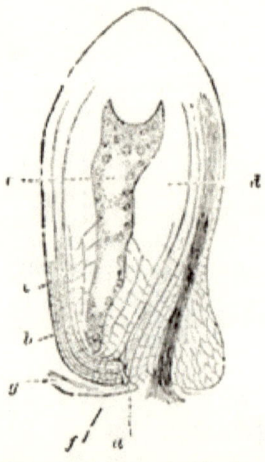

Fig. 40.—Longitudinal section of ovule of heartsease. *a.* Vascular bundle. *b.* Outer coat. *c.* Inner coat. *d.* Nucleus. *e.* Embryo sac, with the germinal vesicle at its small end. *f.* Micropyle. *g.* End of pollen tube—very much enlarged.

it begins to sprout, and produces a plant like its parent. Sometimes the seed contains the embryo or young plant alone, but usually it also contains a quantity of nutritive matter sufficient to supply the wants of the young plant until it has reached that point of growth at which it is capable of drawing nourishment from the soil.

IRRITABLE STAMENS.

In all cases, it is necessary that the pollen shall unite with the ovule, in order that it may develop into the seed containing the embryo or young plant. To secure this, numerous contrivances are provided by nature. We have, first of all, the sticky fluid on the surface of the stigma, which will prevent any pollen grain that has once touched it from falling off. The pollen grains, being light, may be carried by the wind, and this agent probably helps materially in bringing the pollen grains of pines in contact with the ovules. In many flowering plants the stamens are irritable, and, when the pollen grains are ripe, show distinct movements. Some of them gently approach the stigma. Others, as in the barbery, are irritable on their inner surface, and, when touched, move quickly towards the stigma. In the plant called stylidium the stamens and pistils are united into a jointed column, which is irritable, and when touched moves rapidly from one side of the flower to the other, so as to burst the anthers and shake out the pollen upon the stigma. In the nettle, the stamens are elastic, and are kept bound down within the flower until the pollen is ripe, when suddenly they are liberated, and, flying up, scatter the pollen forcibly. In the *cornus canadensis* the stamens are likewise elastic, and are bound down by the corolla, the segments of which have elastic joints at their bases, and long hairs at their apices. When the pollen is ripe, the least touch on one of these hairs causes the corolla to fly back, liberating the stamens, and

Fig. 41.—Male flower of nettle.

scattering the pollen. In other plants, again, the pollen is chiefly applied to the stigma by means of insects. At the base of the petals, in many flowers, are honey-glands, which attract bees. When gathering honey, these disturb the anthers, and scatter the pollen upon the stigma of the same flower, or, the pollen adhering to the insect's body, is carried by it to the stigma of another flower which it then fertilizes. In some species of aristolochia, the flower is shaped like an irregular funnel, ending below in a rounded dilatation, within which the stems and pistil are situated. Insects crawl down this funnel in order to reach the sweet secretion contained in it, but their return is prevented by a number of hairs, which are arranged like the wires in some kinds of rat-traps, allowing the insect to pass in easily, but effectually opposing its return. When thus imprisoned, it moves about actively, and, in its attempts to escape, scatters the pollen upon the stigma. When the flower is thus fertilized, the

Fig. 42.—Flower of spotted orchis.

corolla fades, and the insect escapes, after having effectually served the purpose of fertilizing the flower. In orchids, the anthers are peculiarly placed, being

Fig. 43.—Single pollen-mass of spotted orchis, with its caudicle and gland.

united with the pistil into a column, the anthers being placed at the upper part and the stigma at the lower. The pollen is also arranged in masses, and it would be difficult for these to become applied to the surface of the stigma without some external agency. Around the column honey is freely secreted, and, in gathering it, the insects touch the pollen, which adheres to them, and is thus conveyed to the stigma of the next flower to which they pass. It

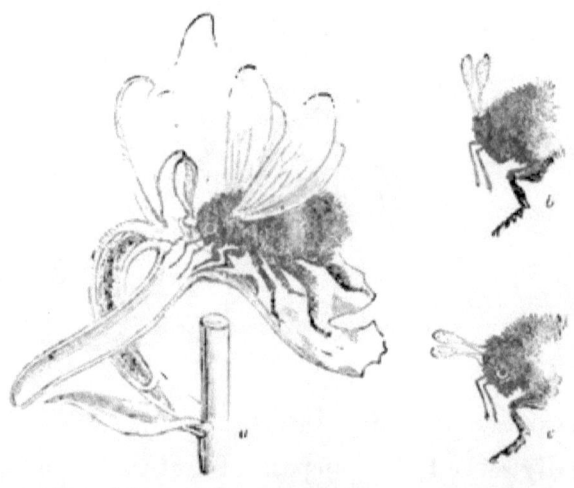

Fig. 44.—*a*. Section of a flower of orchis, showing a bee standing upon the lip, with its head touching the sticky gland, to which the pollen masses are attached. *b*. Bee's head, with the pollen masses erect, as removed. *c*. The same, with the pollen masses after they have moved forwards. All enlarged.

has been noticed that orchids assume very peculiar shapes, and very often bear a striking resemblance to the insects of the districts they inhabit. This resemblance has given rise to the names by which many of these flowers are known, such as bee-orchids, humming-bird orchids, and so on.

In the arrangement of the parts of the flower, just as in the arrangement of the veins in the leaf, we see the distinction between exogens and endogens. In exogens, the leaves are **netted** veined, and the parts of the flower occur in **fours** or **fives**, or multiples of these numbers. In endogens, the leaves are **parallel** veined, and the parts of the flower are arranged in **threes** or multiples of three. In both endogens and exogens, we find that the parts composing the flower are sometimes separate and sometimes united. Those in which they are separate are called **polypetalous**, while those in which they are united are designated **gamopetalous.** To the latter belong some of the orders of plants which are most susceptible of variation, and of thus becoming useful to man under cultivation, such as the pea tribe, and those plants nearly allied to the roses, such as almonds, apples, pears. quinces, plums, &c. All these, which are bitter or acid in their wild state, become delicious fruits under cultivation, and are amongst the most prized productions as well as the greatest ornaments of our orchards and gardens.

LECTURE VI.

PLANTS AND TREES.—NUTRITION AND GROWTH OF THE INDIVIDUAL.

LET us now return to the point from which we started in our survey of the vegetable kingdom. We have seen that the cedar of Lebanon and the fern, the lichen, and the palm, the onion, the melon, and the leeks of Egypt, and the oaks of Bashan, unlike as they are in their general appearance, are yet alike in this, that each and all of them are formed by the multiplication and growth of simple cells, simple masses of protoplasm inclosed within a wall of cellulose. They are all alike in this, that they may be propagated by the separation from them of a growing part or bud, which, when planted in a suitable soil, will grow into a plant resembling its parent. In the lower orders of plants, multiplication by means of buds, which separate spontaneously, is common, but this is exceptional amongst the higher plants, although even in them it occasionally occurs. But the bud, on account of its tenderness and softness, is unfitted for transport. It cannot live long after its separation, unless it falls into a convenient soil and begins to grow, and therefore we have in all plants, in addition to budding, a means of propagation by the union of two dissimilar cells, the male and female, or the sperm and the germ cells. In the lowest plants these are usually situated close together, and the male element in them consists of a moving filament with a rounded head like the spermatozoon of animals. As we ascend higher in the scale of plant life, these are replaced by pollen grains, consisting of granular matter, surrounded by an outer cell wall, which are much better adapted for conveyance to a distance than the spermatozoids, which consist of soft naked protoplasm. In all of them, the male element either spontaneously seeks, or is conveyed to the female element, which remains stationary until it is sufficiently developed to be ready for independent growth. We can easily see the reason of this; for the female cells, or collections of cells, are much larger than the male. The male simply gives to them the impulse which causes them to increase, develop, and differentiate, until they form a spore, or seed, while the female requires to supply the material which is to yield the spore or embryo,

H

and must be in a place where it can readily obtain supplies from without.

In all plants, the female element, like the male, is derived from one or more cells. In most of the lower classes of the vegetable kingdom it develops a spore from which a plant grows, which is unlike its parent, but resembles some other plant lower in the scale, and from this second source a plant resembling the original parent proceeds. As we move up we find that this intermediate plant never gets outside of the spore, but fructifies within it, as in the lycopods, so that we would at first imagine that the spore itself yielded a plant exactly like that which had produced it, although a more accurate observation shows that here also we have got an alternation of generations.

As we ascend still further, to the gymnosperms, such as the pine and the cedar of Lebanon, we find that we come to a naked ovule in which the contact of the pollen causes division of cells which at first arrange themselves in elongated rows, supposed by some to represent the prothallus of the lycopod, and which ultimately develop into the embryo within the seed.

Higher up still we have the angiosperms, in which the ovule is no longer naked, but is formed within an ovary, which serves the function of the womb.

In this class we have the endogens, such as the onion, the leek, and the palm, and the exogens, among which we find the creeping gourd and the stately oak. At first sight one would say that there was much more resemblance between the stately palm and the oak than between the palm and the leek, the oak and the gourd; but although those trees are so lofty and these plants so lowly, the palm resembles the leek more than the oak, and the oak the gourd rather than the palm, in the essentials of their being, viz., the mode in which they are nourished and grow, and the method by which they propagate themselves.

But how is each individual **cell nourished**, and how does it grow, for it is evident that if a cell were to divide and subdivide without the parts into which it splits up growing, they would soon become infinitesimal, and the plant would crumble into dust. Each cell, then, grows by absorbing water and salts through its envelope or wall, through which liquids and gases readily pass. But water and salts are insufficient for the whole growth of the plant, and yet we sometimes see plants growing without any other apparent nutriment. Yet the nutriment is there, though we do not see it. All air contains a certain proportion of carbonic acid, that gas which is formed whenever we burn a piece of wood or anything containing carbon.

Under the influence of light and heat, the plant cells absorb this gas and decompose it, retaining the carbon, with which they build up their own tissues, and giving out the other constituent of which the gas is composed, viz., oxygen. In this process, the energy supplied to plants by the sun in the form of light and heat is transformed by them into chemical energy, and when the plant is again burned, whether rapidly, as when thrown into a furnace, or slowly in the process of decay, for decay is a slow combustion; the tissues, uniting with the oxygen of the air, again form carbonic acid, and again give off the energy stored up within them as light or heat.

We now know that all forms of **energy** are convertible; heat into light, chemical energy, or mechanical power, or electricity, and mechanical power, also into heat, light, and electricity, and so on. When we throw a lump of coal into the fire, its chemical energy is transformed into heat, and by a proper apparatus, as in the steam-engine, we may again transform this heat into mechanical power, as in the steam-hammer or locomotive. If we apply the steam-engine to drive a wheel in front of a magnet, we convert its mechanical power into electricity, and, this again, may be used for lighting our houses or streets, or may be made to decompose metallic solutions,

TRANSFORMATION OF ENERGY.   101

and deposit the pure metal upon a surface or within a mould, as in electroplating or electrotyping.

In all these cases, the energy we use is really the light and heat of the sun, transformed long ages ago into chemical energy in the plants of the carboniferous era, stored up in their tissues during the long ages in which they lay buried as coal, and now again converted by us for our own use into heat, light, electricity, or mechanical power.

But energy is not merely **transformed qualitatively**; it is also transformed **quantitatively**, that is to say, a definite amount of heat is not transformed into an indefinite amount of mechanical work, or *vice versa*, but so much heat will only produce so much mechanical work, and no more, and so much mechanical work will only produce a certain quantity of heat. In order to get so much heat as would raise the temperature of a pound of water one degree, we must have as much mechanical energy as would be given by a pound weight falling 772·55 feet, and in a perfect machine, as much heat as would raise the temperature of a pound of water one degree would also suffice to raise it 772·55 feet in space. No machine, however, is perfect, and in every transference of energy a certain quantity of it is lost, and escapes as radiant heat.

Now we distinguish between two forms of **energy**,

potential and actual. A pound weight, suspended at 772·55 feet above the earth's surface, has potential energy sufficient to raise a pound of water one degree, that is to say, it has the power to do it if allowed to exercise such power. If the support be removed, and the weight fall, its potential will be transformed into actual energy, and, in a proper apparatus, the pound of water would be heated one degree. The difference between potential and actual energy will be understood by comparing the former to money in the pocket, and the latter to its expenditure. So long as the money is in the pocket, its possessor has the power to expend it in various ways, but, when once it is expended, its power is gone, he has converted the money into something else. In the words of the old proverb, "You cannot have your cake and eat it too." One penny will not buy as much as twopence; it will buy a pennyworth, and no more. Although very different returns may be obtained by expending the penny in different ways, yet the return is always a pennyworth, and not twopence worth. Just so it is with energy.

As energy is therefore definite in quantity, it is obvious that, if the plant were to move about, it would use up part of the heat and light which it derives from the sun in the form of the mechanical work involved in locomotion, and it would therefore have less to apply to chemical work in the form of building up its tissues. When we consider, further, how slowly many plants grow, even when rooted to the ground as they are, we can readily imagine that a removal from place to place would render the light and heat daily supplied to them by the sun not only insufficient to enable them to grow at all, but would hardly allow even of their motion.

In these respects, then, plants differ from animals. Plants, as a rule, do not move, and they use up the energy supplied to them as light and heat from without, in the simple act of growth, splitting up carbonic acid and water, and building up the carbon and hydrogen contained in them into complex structures. Animals, on the other hand, generally move about, and, the light and heat supplied to them from without being insufficient to maintain the mechanical energy which they expend in motion, they are forced to draw upon other stores of energy, and these they find in the tissues of plants or of other animals which they consume, again converting the potential energy stored up by the plants into actual energy. The plant, then, may be likened to a miser, who expends little or nothing, and amasses a quantity of money, while the animal which eats it may be compared to the spendthrift heir, who quickly squanders all that his predecessor has with so much labour gathered together. There are, however, some exceptions. At the time when plants are developing their reproductive organs, they use up energy and give off carbonic acid, and the consequence of this is seen in the fact that some of them die as soon as they have produced seed. Some of the very rapidly growing lower plants, such as the fungi, cannot obtain sufficient energy for their growth in the form of light and heat, and these also, like animals, are forced to obtain stores of energy by feeding upon and consuming highly organised materials. Usually, however, it is the light and heat derived from the sun which supply the plant with its power to grow, and the organs by which they are chiefly utilised are the **leaves**.

These originate in small cellular projections, which, like that already described as terminating the twig, grow and develop until the fully-formed leaf appears, with its stalk, its blade, and its veins. On the under side of the leaf are a number of little stomata, or mouths, through which the plant appears to breathe and to take in moisture from the air. Although at first all the cells in this cellular projection present exactly the same characteristics, they are not under exactly the same conditions, for some, being nearer to the surface than others, are more exposed to light and heat, while others, being nearer the centre from which the sap is supplied, more readily obtain nutriment. At some point or other these two conditions are so adjusted to each other as to produce certain

USES OF VESSELS.

changes in the cells, causing them to elongate, and their walls to thicken, so as to form woody cells or fibres such as have been already described. Other cells, again, join together to form tubes, on the walls of which cellulose is deposited more or less irregularly. Some of these tubes seem to contain air, and others juices. Thus, in the very interior of the twig or stem, we have a supply of air which either aids in the pro-

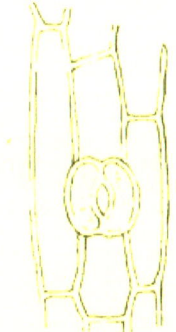

Fig. 45.—Fragment of epidermis with a stoma.

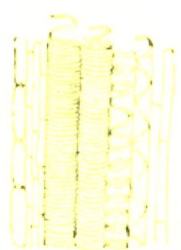

Fig. 46.—Spiral vessels with cellular tissue on each side, many times the real size.

duction of the chemical changes occurring in growth, or is the product of these changes. From every twig the cells and vessels thus produced seem to shoot downwards, aiding in the growth of the stem. In some instances, especially in monocotyledons, such as a species of palm, these bundles of vessels make their way actually out of the stem near the ground, and appear again as so-called adventitious roots. They may to some extent discharge the functions of roots, but the true root is a different thing.

The root begins in the same way as the bud, as a little cellular projection, which gradually develops woody fibres and vessels, pushing its way downwards into the ground in much the same way as the twigs push their way upwards into the air, but the cellular mass at the end of the root never develops into leaves,

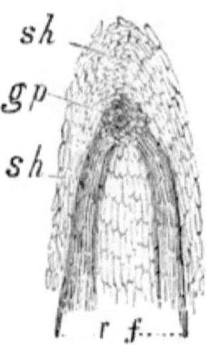

Fig. 47.—Longitudinal section through the extremity of a root-fibre of buttercup, magnified. *gp.* Growing point. *sh.* Sheath. *rf.* Root-fibre.

as it does in the bud, but always remains as a cellular cap, and if it be cut off, the growth of the root ceases. This is the reason why, in transplanting a tree, it is so important that the ends of the roots should remain intact, and why, if they be destroyed, the tree is so very apt to wither away instead of growing in the new situation.

Both roots and branches show an amount of adaptation to the circumstances in which they are placed that it almost looks as if they were endowed with reason. The sunflower, for example, rotates more or less around its axis, so as to follow the sun, and keep the disc of the flower always exposed to its light. Twining plants, when their tendrils have been torn away, will push out new tendrils until they find a proper spore by which to climb. When trees are planted in a dry soil, at a considerable distance from a spring of water, they will send out their roots in that direction until they reach the moist soil, and thus obtain the fluid requisite for growth. When planted on a sloping bank, they will throw their roots out in such a direction as to cling to the part where there is the greatest depth of earth, and thus prevent their overthrow.

The same adaptation is noticed in the flower. We have already spoken of the provision made for the transference of pollen from the stems to the stigma for the purpose of fertilization, but there are other contrivances to allow of the proper ripening of the pollen itself, and to prevent a premature bursting of the anther in which it is contained. Supposing that the anther became moist, the cells which cover the pollen might burst prematurely, and thus the pollen would be thrown out before it was properly ripe. The moisture might be caused either by dew or rain, but in either case the results would be alike disastrous. Now, in plants whose habitat is in a warm dry climate where rain rarely falls, we find that the anthers have little protection from the petals of the flower, but, on the other hand, in changeable, rainy climates, the petals sometimes form a tube, which acts as an umbrella-

Fig. 48.—Tea-plant with exposed stamens.

like cover to the anthers, and sometimes the petals close up at the approach of rain. This tendency to close at the approach of wet weather is so marked in the little pimpernel that it has received the name of "the farmer's weather-glass."

Other plants, such as the wood-sorrel, have a habit of going to sleep, as it is called, shutting up their flowers

SLEEP IN PLANTS.

as evening comes on, so that the anthers may be sheltered from the action of the dew or from the cold of the night. Regularly, as evening comes on, they close their flowers and droop their heads, and this is not due simply to the change of temperature or the absence of light during the night, for if kept constantly in the dark

Fig. 49.—Section of flower of periwinkle, with the stamens protected by the tube of the corolla. The stigma is figured to the left.

they will still go on opening and shutting their flowers, but no longer with their accustomed regularity. They would almost remind one of a sleeper anxious to awake, seeming to be constantly on the watch, and anticipating the times of rest and of awakening, so that in the course of six days they would gain as much as half a day, and therefore exchange night for day as their time of wakefulness.

The leaves of some plants are sensitive to touch, and show their sensibility much more quickly and distinctly than many animals. That little species of acacia known as the sensitive plant, in a warm room, and in bright sunlight, expands all its leaves, so that they stand out boldly fringed on either side with regular rows of oblong leaflets. At the least touch of one of these leaflets it droops, as if vexed or ashamed, and in a little while its adjoining neighbours follow its example, and if the touch has been at all rough, every leaflet on the branch will droop, and then the branch itself will fall down by the side of the stem. By and by the leaflets slowly begin to reopen, and the branch gradually rises until it regains its former position. When exposed to chloroform it behaves exactly like an animal. When the vapour is too strong, the plant droops just as if rudely struck, while an animal, under similar circumstances, would struggle violently. A long time elapses before the leaf again rises, and it seems, as it were, to remain in a state of stupor. If the vapour be gently administered, insensibility seems gradually to steal over the plant,—the leaflets remain expanded, and the leaf continues to retain its usual position, but when touched, it is no longer sensible, and even considerable irritation has no power to make the leaflets droop.

DIGESTION IN PLANTS.

The leaves of the sundew or Drosera are covered with little hairs, secreting a glutinous liquid, which evidently has also some sweetness or other property which renders it attractive to insects; but as soon as the fly settles upon the leaf, its little feet are stuck fast by the glutinous secretion, and, while it struggles, the

Fig. 56.—Sundew (*Drosera rotundifolia*).

remainder of the leaf seems to learn what is going on, and gradually folds over the unfortunate insect until its escape is absolutely impossible. The poor creature is thus inclosed, as it were, in a stomach, and here it is gradually digested, just as it would be in the stomach of an animal, for this liquid, secreted by the leaves of the drosera, has very much the same properties as the gastric juice of the human stomach. In another plant of the same order, the Dionea, or Venus fly-trap, we do not find a glutinous secretion, but this plant catches flies with equal or greater readiness than its congener the sundew. The leaves of the Dionea have a joint in

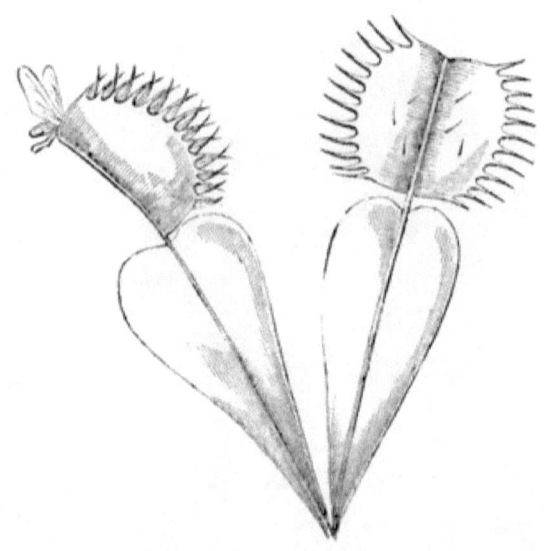

FIG. 51.—Dionea, or Venus fly-trap. The leaflet to the right hand is open ready to catch a fly; the leaflet to the left has caught and closed upon one, which it is now digesting.

the centre, so that the two halves of the blade fall together. The edges of each are fringed with hairs, which interlock, and in the centre of each half are three isolated hairs, reminding one of the bait in a rat-trap. As soon as an insect touches one of them, the two halves of the leaf close together, the hairs on their edges interlock, and the insect is securely imprisoned. In this position the leaf remains until the insect dies and is digested, when it slowly unfolds, and is ready for a fresh prey. In the Sarracenia the leaves have a peculiar shape, the leaf-stalk being developed into a sort of pitcher, at the top of which the true leaf lies like a kind of lid. Inside this pitcher is a sweet liquid, and insects, attracted by it, crawl down the pitcher's side. Having become intoxicated by the nectar they have sucked, their return is further hindered by a number of hairs, and they fall down to the bottom of the pitcher, where they, too, are digested.

In these instances we see arrangements for the nutrition of the plant by feeding on flies, but one may be inclined to ask, What good can a few flies do to the plant? From recent investigations it seems probable that some of these arrangements are not merely of benefit by aiding its nutrition, but also by preventing the insects from harming the plant. In the orchids we have seen the remarkable resemblance of the flowers to insects, and the strange position of the reproductive parts of the flowers so admirably adapted for ensuring fertilization by means of insects. But there are other plants in which there are contrivances equally wonderful for ensuring that insects which will not benefit the flower shall not gain entrance to it, and that those insects which can assist its fertilization shall only gain

I

access in the proper way to ensure their serving this purpose. I mentioned that in exogenous plants the parts of the flower are usually five. In pentstemon the petals are five, but there are only four stamens with a rudimentary fifth. This is often regarded as simply a useless remnant of one that had previously existed in the flower, but it now seems that its use is to ensure insects fertilizing the flower. The corolla forms a large bell, at the mouth of which the anthers are placed. At the closed end of the bell are glands containing nectar; and the fifth stamen, which has no anther, is placed across the bell in such a position as to ensure insects rubbing against the anthers and thus scattering the pollen.

In the Parnassia palustris, too, there are staminodes which form a trellis-work across the flower and force the bees to settle upon it in the proper manner.

In some flowers the nectar might be sucked by little insects which had crawled up the stem and which were too small to fertilize the plant, but these are prevented by *hairs* on the stem and by a perfectly *waxy* surface. Kerner, to whom we owe these observations, thinks the secretion of Pinguicula serves to prevent insects doing harm, and so also Drosera.

LECTURE VII.

PLANTS AND ANIMALS.

The highest plants and the highest animals are utterly unlike one another, and there is no chance of our calling a lion a plant, or a palm-tree an animal. The most notable difference between them is that the **plant is fixed**, while the **animal moves** from place to place. The plant has no **muscles** by which locomotion can be effected, no **nervous system** to put them in action, no separate **digestive canal** by which to assimilate its food. The **food** itself is of a different nature, the animal living upon plants or animals, while the plant lives upon water, air, and inorganic salts. The products of the **chemical changes** going on within them are different. The animal burns up the food it takes, and gives out carbonic acid and water, while the plant takes up carbonic acid and water, and stores up within itself cellulose and starch. The **tissues** of which they are formed are different. Those of the animal contain much nitrogen, and are generally allied in composition to the albumen or white of an egg, and are therefore called albuminous, while those of the plant contain little nitrogen, the chief of them being cellulose and starch, which are composed of carbon, hydrogen, and oxygen.

But when we get down to the lowest forms of plant and animal life the distinction between them is exceedingly difficult, and in some cases almost impossible. Diatoms shoot about in the water very much as we might expect an animal to do, and the spores of some algæ are furnished with vibratile hairs or cilia, and move about like some of the lower animals, while some animals, like the corals, are fixed to a spot from which they grow like vegetables.

Fungi, as we have already seen, do not take up carbonic acid and give out oxygen like plants, but, on the contrary, take in oxygen and give out carbonic acid like animals.

All plants in which there is protoplasm contain more or less nitrogen, and as the proportion of protoplasm within them increases, so does the proportion of nitrogen, until we come down to those simple cellular structures in which the proportion of nitrogen may be almost as great as in animals. Cellulose is the most abundant and distinctive of all vegetable products, yet it does not appertain exclusively to the vegetable kingdom, for it has been found in some animals, Ascidians or Tunicata, a class of beings to which, as we shall see afterwards, a special interest attaches.

It is thus impossible to draw a sharp line of distinction between the animal and vegetable kingdoms, for the characteristics which, when fully marked, seem distinctive of one, may be found to a greater or less extent in the other. In many cases it is only by knowing the life history of the plant that we are able to decide its position. The ciliated embryo of the algæ might perfectly well be an animal, and would be reckoned as such were it not that we know it to proceed from an undoubted plant, and to grow into a plant again. If we pass downwards still lower in the scale of life than the algæ, we come to forms which can hardly be reckoned either as animal or vegetable. All we can say regarding them is that they are alive, and we distinguish them from dead matter, *first* by their power of reacting to an external stimulus, a power which we term **irritability**; *secondly* by their power of taking into themselves nutriment from without, and assimilating it to their own substance, that is the power of **nutrition**; and *thirdly* by the power of producing other beings like themselves, or the power of **reproduction**.

These three properties are characteristics of all living beings, both animals and plants.

In plants, it is true, we see the powers of nutrition and reproduction more marked than that of irritability, but it may be recognised in them even when there are no marked movements, such as those of the sensitive plant, to betray it. When we lop off a branch of an oak, the tissues around will grow up to scar over the wound, and although the tree may not seem to feel the woodman's axe, yet the twig shows, by the excrescence or gall which it forms, its sensibility to the sting of an insect. In animals the irritability is generally much more marked, and it may present all phases of development, from the simple contraction which a touch produces in the jelly-like mass of a sea-anemone, to its highest development in the complex movements of the highest animals.

Throughout all classes of the animal kingdom we find these three properties—**irritability, nutrition,** and **reproduction**—irritability, which enables the animal to defend itself and to obtain nourishment; the power of nutrition, by the exercise of which it can assimilate its food, and thus sustain or increase the strength and health of the individual; and that of reproduction, by which it is enabled to continue the race. To those three simple qualities the German poet and philosopher, Goethe, has reduced the complicated actions and history of mankind. "Warum treibt das Volk so und schreit? Es will sich ernähren, Kinder zeugen, und sie ernähren wie es vermag." "Why are people so busy, and why do they make such a noise? They want to feed themselves, beget children, and feed them as best they can."

But in the lowest classes of the animal kingdom the property of **irritability** shows itself simply as the power of contraction when touched. In them we find no trace of the complicated structures which we observe in such beings as the lion and the elephant. They consist only of a mass of structureless jelly. There is not even a nucleus or a cell wall; nothing but mere simple protoplasm, which stretches out long arms from any part of its surface, and draws them in again, enveloping any body sufficiently small to be absorbed, and of such a constitution as renders it fit to serve as nutriment.

To this structureless, protoplasmic mass the name of **monera** has been given by Haeckel. It is impossible to say whether it belongs to the animal or the vegetable kingdom, and so this naturalist has placed it provisionally in what he terms the kingdom of PROTISTA, which is neither animal nor vegetable. But the monera is distinctly a living being, and possesses all the powers just mentioned. When irritated, it contracts. It moves freely from place to place. It feeds itself in the simplest possible manner, by actually getting outside of the substance it is going to eat, the structureless protoplasm seeming, as it were, to flow over it. As soon as it is digested the protoplasm opens out, and the residue is ejected; or rather, the protoplasm simply moves away, leaving its refuse behind. It reproduces itself by simple division, each of the divided parts again growing anew.

Moving upwards a step to the lowest division of the

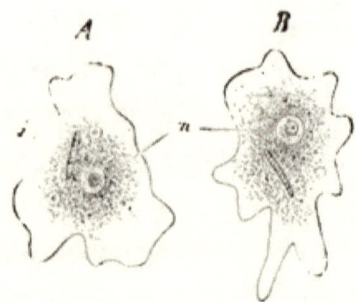

Fig. 52.—An amœba figured at two different moments during movement. *n.* Nucleus. *i.* Ingested food. Some vacuoles may also be noticed.

ANIMAL KINGDOM, or **Rhizopoda**, we find that in a typical specimen such as the amœba, the protoplasm, instead of being structureless, presents a nucleus, and a little vacuole, as it is termed. This appears to be a cavity in the interior of the protoplasm, filled with fluid, which alternately contracts and dilates, so that the fluid must be more or less driven through the protoplasmic mass. But there is still no cell-wall. The protoplasm moves freely about, elongating itself in one direction and contracting in another, so that the form of the animal is never the same for two minutes together. From the power of throwing out protoplasmic arms or feet, called pseudopodia, possessed by the amœba and its congeners, the order to which it belongs is named **Rhizopoda**. The amœba nourishes itself in the same way as the monera, and reproduces itself by fission, the nucleus first dividing, and the protoplasm following suit.

Simple as this creature is, it contains the germs of the complicated functions of **circulation** and **respiration**, by which the power of movement is sustained in the higher animals. Like the monera, the amœba contracts when touched. It is sensitive to heat and cold. Cold renders it torpid, and heat, up to a certain degree, quickens its movements, but beyond that degree heat causes it to pass into a state of so-called tetanus, in which the protoplasm is contracted to its very utmost in every direction, and the animal thus assumes a perfectly spherical form. If the heat be not carried too far, the creature will again commence to move when the temperature is reduced, but if the temperature be raised too high the tetanic contraction passes into the stiffness of death. This little animal, too, is sensitive to the effects of poisons; a minute portion of strychnia will accelerate its movements, but a larger quantity will kill the animal, and thus completely arrest them.

This leads us to consider how these movements are carried on and why they cease.

We know that all movement implies energy, and that the movements of the protoplasmic arms or pseudopodia of the amœba imply the conversion of potential into actual energy. This energy is derived from the substances on which it feeds, and which it renders available by the process of **digestion**. In digestion its solid nutriment is dissolved, and is either converted directly into the protoplasmic mass of the amœba, or is distributed throughout it in a fluid form. For the conversion of the potential energy contained in the food or the protoplasm of the creature's body into the actual energy shown in the movements of the pseudopodia, chemical changes are required, and these consist in the absorption of oxygen and the giving out of carbonic acid or **respiration**.

The process of the conversion of potential into actual energy in the amœba, and in every member of the animal kingdom, is ultimately the same as that in the locomotive engine. In both, the fuel combines with oxygen, and is thus burned, giving out carbonic acid in the process. In both a supply of oxygen is required. In the locomotive this is yielded by a draught of air streaming into the furnace door. In the amœba it is obtained from the air which is held in solution by the water in which the creature swims. If the amœba is to continue its movement, or the locomotive its course, the fuel and the oxygen must be brought into contact. If the ingress of air to the locomotive's furnace be completely stopped the fire will go out, and the wheels will stand still. If the air be completely removed from the water in which the amœba is living, its movements will also cease, and the animal will die. In the monera, all parts of the simple, undifferentiated protoplasm of the body may come successively in contact with the surrounding water, or the nutriment they enclose, and oxygen and fuel being thus brought into contact, the movements of the creature are sustained. But in the amœba we have a trace of differentiation. The nucleus never comes to the surface of the body. It always remains in or about the centre, and thus it would be placed at a disadvantage unless there were some means of conveying nutriment and oxygen to it, and this we find in the pulsatile vacuole. As the protoplasm surrounding this cavity contracts, the fluid it contains is driven through the animal's body, and as it again dilates the fluid returns, and, permeating the entire substance of the little creature, it will take up all the soluble nutriment which the food has yielded. In its passage to and fro, too, it will take up any carbonic acid which has been formed in the centre of the body, and give it off to the water at the surface, taking in exchange oxygen, which it will bring back with it to the centre.

The **circulation** thus caused by the contractile vacuole removes the disadvantage at which the central part of the animal would have been placed with regard to nutriment and oxygen, as compared with the surface, and equalises nutrition and oxidation throughout the body.

But it is easy to imagine that a contractile vesicle might not always be able to do this, and that under certain conditions the outside of the animal would acquire a different structure from its interior, and this we actually see. In one little creature, composed, like the amœba, of a single cell, we find that the surface of the body has become tough excepting at one point, and that instead of throwing out pseudopods at any part of the surface, it can only do so at this particular point. Here it is obliged to take in all its nutriment and throw out all the undigested refuse, and at this point only is it capable of moving. In another we find the same thing, with the exception that instead of the surface merely becoming hardened and tough; it is covered with particles of sand, which the animal seems to have the power of gluing on to itself. In others the surface is either covered with isolated spicules of silica, or with a flinty coating consisting of these more or less united, leaving holes between them through which pseudopodia can be protruded. In others, again, the case is composed of chalk, which the animal seems to have the power of secreting. From the holes or foramina in the case such rhizopods are called **Foraminifera**. Some of these amœba-like creatures, instead of separating from each other completely, as the two

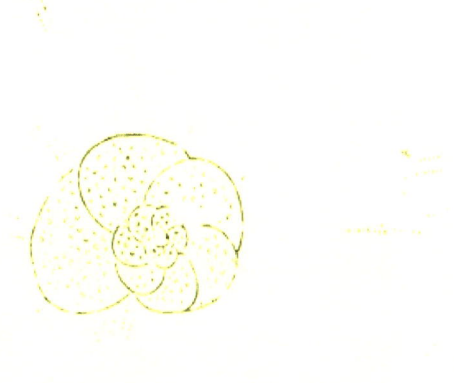

Fig. 23.—A foraminifer with extended pseudopodia which pass through the pores of the multilocular shell.

halves of a dividing amœba would do, remain partially attached, and thus form a multiple animal. Each member of this community, as we may term it, surrounds itself with a shell, often of a most beautiful structure, and, small though the creatures themselves may be, they swarm in the seas in such immense multitudes that their accumulated shells have built up the pyramids of Egypt and the chalky cliffs of England's coast.

The next order, that of the **Infusoria**, is considerably higher in the scale than the amœba order, or rhizopoda, which we have already considered, but it

Fig. 51.—Transverse section of a foraminifer, showing the arrangement of the separate chambers in the shell. After W. Carpenter.

must nevertheless be ranked with them, inasmuch as the infusoria consist of single masses of protoplasm, and not of a number of distinct cells. In them, however, we have a very distinct differentiation of the protoplasm. They have no longer the power of throwing out pseudopods, nor can they take in food at any

RUDIMENT OF DIGESTIVE CAVITY.

part of the body indifferently. The pseudopods are replaced by cilia, and there is always at one part of the body an indentation which serves as a distinct mouth

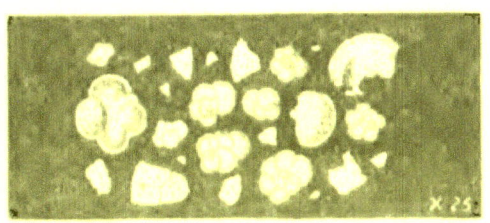

Fig. 55.—Grains from a piece of chalk, showing the cases of foraminifera. Magnified.

and rudimentary digestive cavity. This indentation is often lined internally with cilia, and thus the proto-

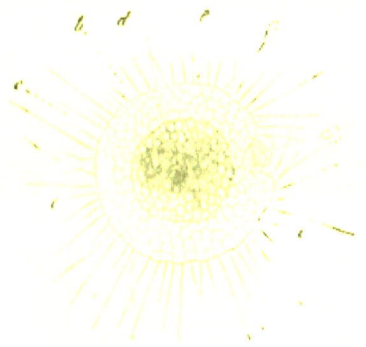

Fig. 56.—Actinosphærium, a rhizopod. *a*. A morsel which has been taken in as food, and just pushed into the soft cortical layer. *b*, by the animal. *c*. Central parenchyma of the body. *d*. Some balls of food in it. *e*. Pseudopodia of the cortical layer.

plasm forming its wall is shown to be somewhat differentiated, but it resembles the ordinary soft protoplasm of the amœba's body in so far that when a particle of

128 NUTRITION AND REPRODUCTION IN INFUSORIA.

food gets into the cavity it simply passes into, and becomes embedded in, the protoplasm of the animal's body. As one particle of food after another sinks into the body, they may seem to stud every part of the animal, so that the microscopist Ehrenberg, who studied the infusoria, believed that each food-particle was contained in a separate stomach, and gave to the

FIG. 57—Diagram of the digestive cavity of one of the Infusoria (paramœcium). *a.* Body space filled with soft protoplasm, into which the food is taken. *b.* Mouth. *c.* Anus. *d.* contractile vesicles. After Lachmann.

order the name of Polygastrica. Like the amœbæ, the infusoria each contain a nucleus and a contractile vesicle. They reproduce themselves either by subdivision or sexually. In the former case the whole body divides into two, the division beginning at the nucleus, and each half grows into a new individual. In the latter case two infusoria become joined together, generally at the mouth. The nucleus of the one seems to pass into that of the other, and from their union a number of new individuals proceed.

All these amœba-like forms, floating freely in water, may readily meet with food, and can easily obtain oxygen. But, supposing that they were accumulated in larger communities, this might no longer be the case, and then, they being unable to move to the food and the oxygen, a special arrangement would be necessary in order that the food and oxygen might be brought to them. This we find in the case of the **Sponges.** In its native state, the tough, porous framework with which every one is so familiar in the household sponge, is clothed throughout with numbers of these amœba-like forms. It is obvious that those in the interior of the sponge would have little chance of obtaining food, and that the water in its pores would soon be deprived of all its oxygen and charged with carbonic acid given off by the protoplasm, were it not that some of the amœbæ have developed on their surface a number of small vibratile hairs, or cilia, by means of which a constant current is kept up in the water. It is drawn in at one opening of the sponge, carrying with it food and oxygen to the living beings within, and, after it has served its purpose, it is thrown out at another opening, carrying with it all the refuse of the animals' digestion, and all the carbonic acid and other products of waste which have been formed within them.

K

130   NUTRITION IN SPONGES.

"The whole sponge," as Huxley remarks, "represents a kind of sub-aqueous city, where the people are

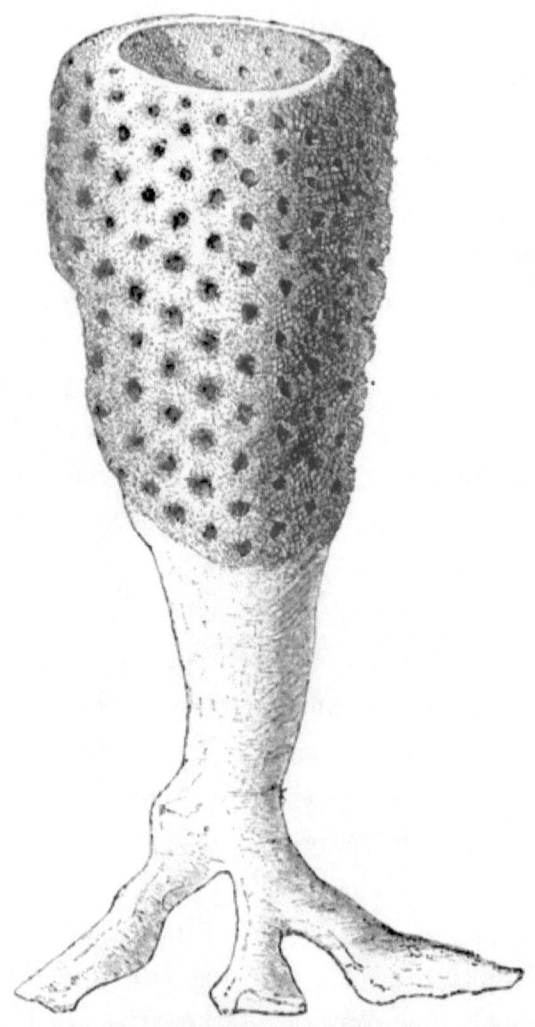

Fig. 58.—A sponge (*Ventriculites simplex*). Toulmin Smith. Once and a half the natural size.

ranged about the streets and roads in such a manner that each can easily appropriate his food from the water as it passes along," and we might also say, casts into it all his refuse.

The sponge reproduces itself both by buds and by sexual generation. The buds appear at the approach of winter in the sponge, which becomes filled with rounded bodies, with gemmules or buds. These consist of a leathery coat, covered with protoplasm, in which are embedded a number of flinty spicules. At one point is an opening into the interior, which is filled with a number of cells. These burst out at the approach of spring, through the opening, and develop into new sponges.

The second mode of reproduction is that one amœba-like body develops within itself spermatozoa, and another develops ova. The ova become fertilized by the spermatozoa, and develop into embryos, which swim about by means of numerous cilia until they find a place suited for them, where they fix themselves and develop into full-grown sponges.

We have seen that the constituent parts of a sponge resemble so many amœbæ, but then there is this very important point to be noted about them, that they have begun to undergo differentiation. Some of them are provided with cilia, which are used not only for their own benefit, but for that of their neighbours. Some of the protoplasmic masses or cells, as we may term them, are devoted to aiding the nutrition of the whole community, others to its reproduction. Each member of the community no longer does the same as any other; division of labour has commenced, and in this respect the sponges stand midway between the protozoa, whose

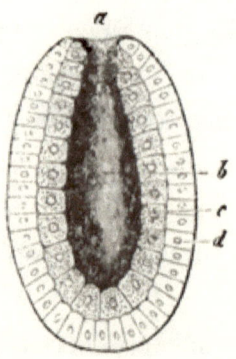

FIG. 59.—Diagram to represent the first differentiation of the organism into ectoderm and endoderm and the formation of a digestive cavity. *a*, mouth. *b*, enteric cavity. *c*, endoderm. *d*, ectoderm. (In transverse section.)

bodies consist of only **one cell**, and the higher animals, in which the body consists of **many cells**.

In the reproduction of sponges too, there are some things which require particular notice. The fertilized ovum divides into two, and then into several cells, and these arrange themselves so as to form a simple hollow bag which is composed of two layers, an inner and an outer, differing in the nature of the cells composing them. The inner is made up of small cubical cells without cilia, the outer of elongated cells with cilia, on their external surface, so that the whole animal is ciliated externally. (Compare Fig. 59.)

This bag in many respects resembles the permanent form of the next division of the animal kingdom—the **Hydrozoa**.

All the animals hitherto mentioned consist of **single** cells, or of protoplasmic masses united together, but undifferentiated, and are included in the great sub-kingdom of the Protozoa. On the other hand, all the animals contained in the sub-kingdom which we have yet to consider consist of **many** cells, variously differentiated.

The animals included in the next sub-kingdom to the Protozoa, the **Hydrozoa**, differ then from those belonging to the Protozoa in being composed of several cells; and they are distinguished from the rest of the animal kingdom by their having no intestinal canal separate from the body cavity.

The type of this class is the little hydra, which may often be found adhering to the duck-weed on a pond. It consists simply of an elongated cup or tube, closed at one end and open at the other. By the closed end it attaches itself to any convenient piece of weed, and the open end is its mouth. Around the mouth are several tentacles, by which it is able to seize any food within its reach and convey it to its mouth. The external surface of this living tube is a little harder than the internal, and the former is thus adapted for protection, while the latter is better fitted for digestion. The difference, however, is so slight, that when the animal is turned inside out, what was formerly the stomach serves for the skin, and *vice versâ*. If it be cut into two also, it is not thereby destroyed; on the contrary, it is multiplied, for the mouth end develops an attachment, and the attached end develops a mouth, so that instead of one hydra we have two. The hydra itself multiplies in two ways, by budding, and sexually. Sometimes a little projection appears at the side of the hydra, which grows and develops a mouth and tentacles, and then, separating from its parent, swims away, and starts life on its own account. But, besides this, other little projections are to be noticed in the wall of the tube. One of these develops spermatozoa, the other germ cells or ova. At the proper time these spermatozoa break loose, they reach the germ-cells and fertilize them, and from the cells proceed embryos covered with cilia, like infusoria, which swim about until, meeting with a suitable place for settlement, they attach themselves, the cilia drop off, a mouth and tentacles develop, and a new hydra is the result. Here, then, in the hydra, which we regard as an animal, we find that the embryo swims about by means of cilia, just like that of the alga, which we class among the plants, and we notice, too, that the embryo hydra resembles a member of the class below it,—the Protozoa, just as the embryo fern resembles an alga, a plant which is below it in the scale.

The buds of the hydra, as we have said, are thrown off, and assume an independent existence, but in other animals of the same class this is not the case. In them the buds remain attached to the parent body, and thus, instead of a simple tube, we get a branched tube. Some of these surround themselves with a calcareous shell, just as we find the protozoa do, but this shell is not pierced like that of the foraminifera, as these hydræ, which consist of cells, can no longer throw out pseudopodia, like the protozoa, which consist of simple protoplasm. In some of them this chalky covering only surrounds the branches of the tube, but in other cases it forms a little cup at the end of each branch, into which the whole of the little hydra-like creature or polyp can contract itself, tentacles and all. In these orders of hydrozoa, as they are called, owing to their resemblance to the hydra, the reproductive organs form special buds. We might almost imagine, indeed, that the part of the body in which they would appear in the hydra, having been covered by a chalky shell, they are obliged to grow upwards until they can find an opening for themselves. At first, indeed, they are nothing more than little buds with thick walls, but after this has attained a certain size, the body of the wall around them grows like a cup, until at last the original bud, instead of projecting, lies in a hollow, as the clapper lies in a bell. The original body-cavity of the animal does not extend equally throughout the bell. It only sends into it four canals, and these are all joined together at their extremities by a circular canal extending around

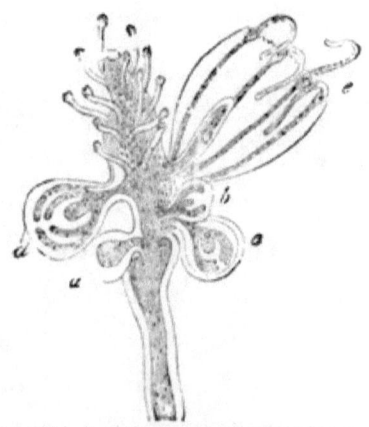

Fig. 60.—Syncoryne, with a number of budding medusæ on it at different stages (*a—c*) of development. After Desor.

the mouth of the bell. On the clapper, or manubrium, as it is called, sperm cells and ova are produced, and the ova, when fertilized, develop an embryo, just as in the hydra. But in some genera the process does not stop at the formation of a bell. The bell-shaped body detaches itself from the parent and swims about. It develops a mouth at the extremity of the manubrium, becomes thus an independent animal, and rapidly grows, sometimes attaining an enormous size, and forming the well-known jellyfish of our coasts.

Fig. 61.—A portion of a colony of hydroid polyps with budding medusae. *p p*, nutritive polyps. *a b c d e f*, different stages of budding medusae. *m m'*, free medusae in different positions.

Closely allied to the hydra tribe is the sea-anemone or actinia, and its allies **Actinozoa**. They resemble the hydra in the body cavity being also the digestive canal, but they differ from it in there being a partial division between them, for a rudimentary

138   SEA-ANEMONE.

gullet passes down a certain distance from the mouth, and then opens into the general body-cavity. From the end of this tube little septa pass to the body wall, and hold it in position. Around the mouth are a number of contractile tentacles, which, as well as the body of the animal, are often brightly coloured,

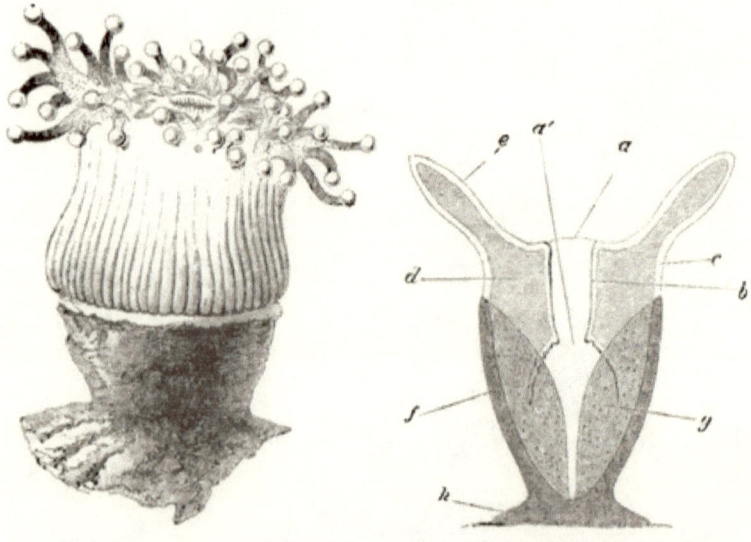

Fig. 62.—Sea-anemone or actinia.

Fig. 63.—Section of sea-anemone or actinia. *a*, the mouth. *a'*, the gullet.

and when fully expanded they resemble the petals of a flower, as in the case of the ordinary well-known sea-anemone. This animal, like the hydra, consists of a single organism, with a soft body, but some of its allies secrete a chalky substance, either within the body or around it. Minute as these animals are,

their chalky skeletons form the well-known coral
reefs and coral islands. These little creatures cannot
live much below the surface of the sea, nor can they
exist much above its level, for in the first case they
could not obtain food, and in the second they would
dry up and be destroyed. They therefore swarm
around the margin of a continent or island, round the
shores of which they build a chalky ridge. When
this lies close to the land, it is known as a fringing
reef. But sometimes it forms an outer belt or wall
around an island or along a continent at a distance of
several miles from the shore. In other cases, again,
coral islands are found rising up from the deep water
of mid-ocean without any other land whatever being
near them. These coral islands, or atolls, are all nearly
circular, and have a salt-water lake, or lagoon, in their
centre. The formation of these reefs and islands was
long a mystery, as it seemed inexplicable that these
structures should apparently arise sheer up out of
deep water as if they had been built up from the
bottom of the sea, when the little polyps which erected
them were unable to live much below the surface of
the water. Mr. Darwin, however, cleared up the
difficulty by showing that both the barrier reefs and
coral islands were simply another form of the fringing
reef. The little polyps first began their operations
along the surface of the land, in the shallow water

which suited them. The land on which they built gradually subsided, as we know many districts of the

FIG. 64.—Diagrammatic section of an island surrounded by a fringing reef. A, the island. B, the reef.

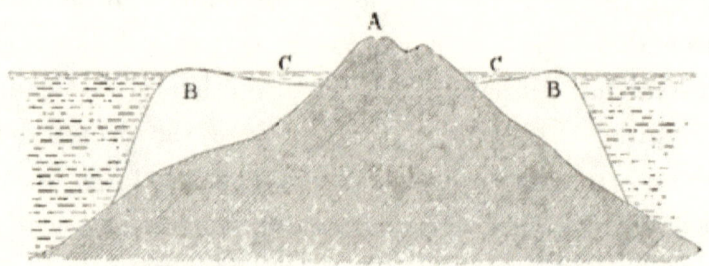

FIG. 65.—Diagrammatic section of an island surrounded by a barrier reef, with intervening lagoon. C, the water between the reef and the island.

FIG. 66.—Diagrammatic section of a coral island, or atoll, with central lagoon, C.

earth's surface are doing at the present moment. As the subsidence went on, the polyps died as the water deepened around them, but those at the surface still went on building, and thus the reef rose like a wall, separated by a considerable breadth of water from the land which it had originally touched. When the land

FIG. 67. Coral island with central lagoon.

had sunk until it had completely disappeared, the fringing reefs became circular rings of coral, simply inclosing a salt-water lake or lagoon. As the sea dashed against the outer surface of the reef or island, its spray kept the corals moist at a greater height above the water level on the outside than on the inside of the reef, and consequently the coral wall was higher towards the sea. On these walls of coral sea-birds appeared, leaving their excrement, which, with the decaying seaweeds, formed the basis of a soil. Upon this the seeds, which had been swallowed by birds and left in their evacuations, or carried thither by ocean currents from neighbouring continents or islands, took root, and thus the coral island became filled with vegetable life.

Some of the other actinozoa, unlike the coral polyps, are not fixed in one position, but float about freely in the water by means of cilia. Their body-wall is much thicker than that of the actinozoa, and instead of the body-cavity presenting the form of a simple bag, it is divided up into several canals, which radiate through the body, as, for example, in the cydippe (Fig. 68). All

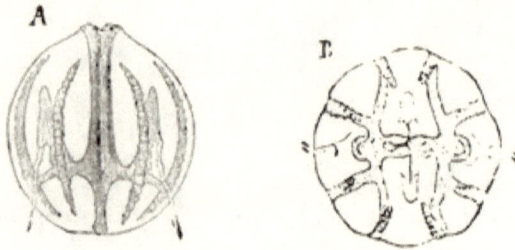

Fig. 68.—The gastrovascular system of a cydippe. A, lateral view—the mouth turned upwards. B, seen from the central pole.

these are furnished with cilia, which serve to keep up a constant current of fresh water, thus bringing up new supplies of oxygen to all parts of the body. This vascular arrangement reminds us of the vacuoles of the amœba, or of the currents kept up by the cilia of the sponge, and connects the circulation in them with the water-vascular system of the next sub-kingdom.

LECTURE VIII.

GENERAL SKETCH OF THE ANIMAL KINGDOM — INVERTEBRATA.

In the next sub-kingdom, the **Annuloida**, we have a distinct advance on the Hydrozoa, inasmuch as the animals contained in it have a digestive canal shut off from the body-cavity. This separation prevents the sea-water and the oxygen it contains from circulating freely through the body, and thus necessitates a separate provision for the supply of oxygen and removal of carbonic acid, or, in other words, for respiration. This is effected in the annuloida by the so-called water-vascular system, a system which reminds us of the vacuoles in the amœba, although much more complicated — a set of canals communicating with the exterior of the body, and in which fluid is kept circulating. In some members of this sub-kingdom, such as the sea-urchins and star-fishes, this water-vascular system is much developed, and sustains the progression of the animal. In the echinus, little rows of tentacles project from the surface of the body in several bands. These are connected with the water-vascular system, and can be filled

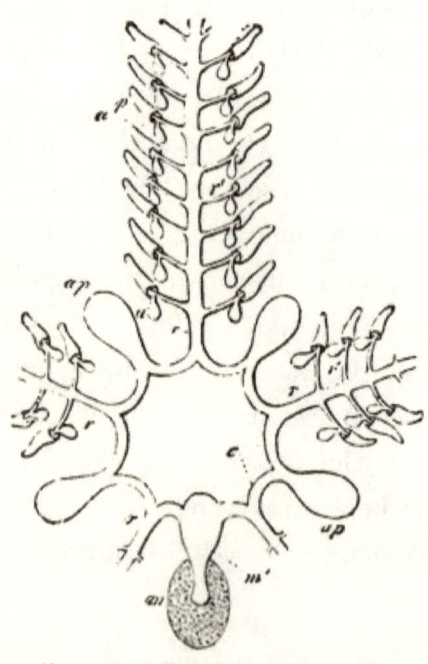

FIG. 69.—Diagrammatic representation of the water-vascular system of a star-fish. *c*, circular canal. *a p*, Polian vesicles. *m*, madreporic plate. *m'*, stone canal. *r*, radically arranged principal trunks (ambulacral canals). *r'*, lateral branches. *p*, suckers. *o*, their ampullæ. Part only of their ambulacral canals and their appendages are figured.

with water or emptied at the pleasure of the animal. When full they project far enough to touch the ground, and by means of them the animals crawl along. In the star-fish the same sort of tentacles are found

ANNULOIDA—ECHINODERMATA. 145

running along the surface of the arms. In some of the allies of the star-fish the arms, instead of being short and thick, are long and thin, but the animal,

Fig. 70.—A Starfish, *Archaster bifrons* (Wyville Thomson). Oral aspect. Three-fourths the natural size.

like the star-fish itself, can move about freely and is not attached. In others, again, we have similar organisms with long arms, not floating about, but fixed to the end of a long, jointed calcareous stalk.

L.

Fig. 71.—Stone-lily or crinoid. *Pentacrinus wyville-thomsoni* (Jeffreys). Natural size.

Some of these are fixed in this way during the whole of their lives, but others only during the earlier portion of it. After they have attained a certain age they loosen themselves from the stalk and float away. The long arms of the stalked species give the animals somewhat the semblance of a flower, and in ages long

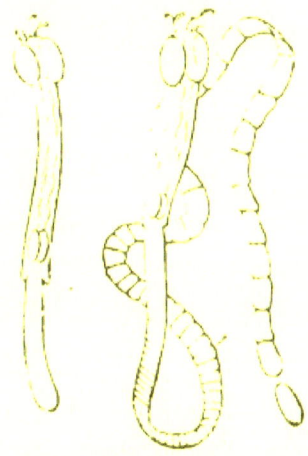

Fig. 72.—1, tape-worm; a sexual form (Nurse). 2, the same in the joint-forming stage, in which the last joints are breaking off one by one.

gone by they formed a considerable portion of the living inhabitants of our globe, and their fossil remains are now known by the name of stone-lilies. The star-fishes and sea-urchins more or less suggest the spokes of a wheel springing from its nave, and thus they used to be called radiata, but they are now known as **Echinodermata**.

In other members of the same sub-kingdom of annuloida no trace of radiate structure is to be observed, but they agree with the echinodermata in possessing a water-vascular system. A great number of them are parasitic upon various animals, living in the intestine, or in the substance of some solid organ, such as the liver. They make use of the juices of their host, and thus do not require any digestive system, and so in some of them, such as the tape-worm, we find no intestinal canal whatever. Some of them show little or no trace of division into joints, but in others again this tendency can be clearly seen. (Fig. 72).

In the next sub-kingdom, the **Annulosa**, we see everywhere a distinct segmentation of the body. The alimentary canal is completely shut off from the general body-cavity, and there is always a distinct nervous system present. Sometimes also we have a true vascular system containing blood. The nervous system consists, in its typical form, of two cords running along the whole length of the belly, and having a nervous swelling or ganglion in each segment. The first pair of ganglia is situated above the gullet, so that the nervous cords, descending to join the second pair, encircle the gullet with a ring or collar. The presence or absence of limbs furnishes a distinction by which the annulosa are divided into two branches—**anarthropoda**, where limbs are absent, and **arthropoda** or **articulata**, in which limbs are present. To the former belong leeches, earthworms, and the lobworm of our coasts, while the latter consist of crabs, spiders, centipedes, and insects.

The lobsters and crabs are all adapted for life in the water, and they breathe by means of gills.

Here we have a much more complicated arrangement for the conveyance of oxygen to the tissues of the body than in any of the classes yet described.

Fig. 73.—Nervous system of insects. B, of a beetle. C, of a fly.

In the simple protista, such as the monera, all parts of the creature's body could obtain oxygen from the surrounding medium; in the protozoa, such as the amœba, we had a provision for driving the nutritive juices of the animal throughout its protoplasmic substance by means of a vacuole; in the hydra and sea-anemone it was supplied by the sea-water which bathed both the external surface of the animal and the interior of its body cavity; in the annuloida it was carried by the water vascular system which communicated with the water in which the animal swims; but in the annulosa we have something quite new. In them we find true blood, a fluid which carries oxygen to the tissues in order to keep up combustion and maintain functional activity, and at the same time conveys to them nutriment, to supply the waste which occurs in the process. The muscles in the claw of a lobster, for example, are shut out by its hard shell from the water, and the oxygen contained in it cannot penetrate through the hard covering. Nor is there any provision for carrying water holding oxygen in solution into the interior of the claw by means of vessels.

But we now find a fluid, **blood,** which will take up a much greater quantity of oxygen than ordinary water can, which can convey it to the muscles of the claw as well as to all other parts of the body, and there give it off, taking up in return the carbonic acid formed by combustion in the muscle during its activity, and any other products of waste. But this action of the blood would soon be exhausted, and it would become so loaded with carbonic acid as to be unfit for its purpose, were there no means of

EXTERNAL RESPIRATION—GILLS AND LUNGS. 151

renewing the oxygen and removing the acid. This is effected by means of **branchiæ** or **gills** in aquatic animals, and by **air-tubes** or **lungs** in land animals. In the branchiæ the blood circulates freely, with only a thin layer of tissue between it and the water. Through this tissue oxygen comes from the water, and carbonic acid is given out to it. The same is the case in the lungs, except that instead of water

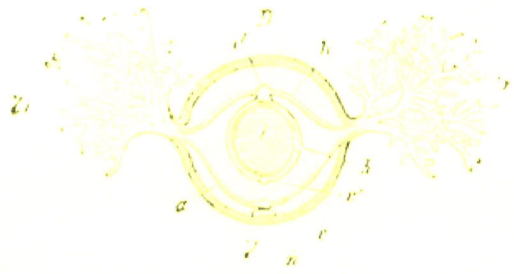

FIG. 74.—Diagrammatic transverse section through the hinder half of the body of a sandworm, to show the arrangement of the vessels, and their connection with the branchiæ or gills. *D*, dorsal. *v*, ventral side. *n*, ventral medulla. *i*, enteric cavity. *b, b*, branchiæ. *r*, ventral vascular trunk. *v b*, branchial vessels. *d*, dorsal vascular trunk. *h*, branch surrounding the enteric canal. *v*, visceral ventral vessel.

on the one side of the membrane we have air. This exchange of gases between the blood and the water or air external to the animal's body is termed **external** respiration. The blood thus purified passes to the interior of the body, and has there to undergo the changes already described in maintaining the nutrition of the tissues. The interchange of gases which there takes place between it and the tissues,

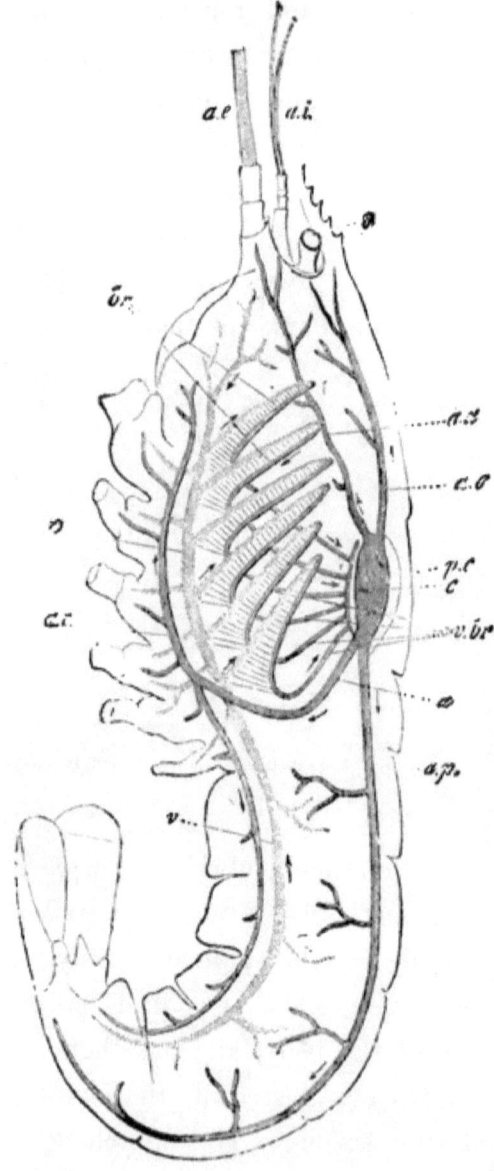

FIG. 75.—Diagram of the circulatory system of a lobster. *o*, eye. *ae*, lateral antennæ. *ai*, mesial antennæ. *br*, branchiæ. *c*, heart. *pc*, pericardium. *ca*, median anterior aorta. *ad*, hepatic artery. *ap*, posterior artery of the body. *a*, trunk of the ventral artery. *ai*, anterior ventral artery. *v*, ventral venous sinus. *v.br*, branchial veins. (The arrows indicate the direction of the current of the blood.)

the giving off of oxygen and the taking up of carbonic acid, is termed **internal** respiration.

This would soon come to an end if the circulation were to stop, and some apparatus is necessary to keep the blood moving. This is provided in the shape of a heart, which in the annulosa is always placed at the back. Crabs and lobsters are all provided with a case of greater or less hardness, and are adapted for existence in the water. Some of their allies appear at a very early period in the history of our globe, and, from the circumstance of their bodies being divided more or less into three lobes, they were called "Trilobites." Closely connected with the lobster tribe, or **Crustacea**, are the spiders and scorpions, or **Arachnida**, but these are adapted only for existence on land, and consequently, instead of branchiæ, they have either little bags or tubes, into which the air comes, and around which the blood flows.

The next class, or **Insecta**, have derived their name from their peculiar formation, all the members of this tribe being divided into three segments, the head, the thorax, and the abdomen. The latter two are sometimes connected by a mere thread, so that it would almost appear that the insect had been cut in two. The metamorphoses of insects, the egg developing not into an insect but into a caterpillar or larva, this becoming dormant and apparently lifeless during the chrysalis or pupa stage, and this developing into a perfect insect or imago are too well known to require to be more than merely mentioned at present. The marvellous development of instinct, if not of reason too in such insects as the ants is most astonishing. The subdivision of labour amongst them, some being workers and others warriors, their flocks of aphides which they take the trouble to feed regularly in order to enjoy their milk, and their means of communicating intelligence to one another, reminds one

Fig. 76.—Insect showing the three segments.

more of the actions of human beings than of those of the lower animals.

Highly organised and intelligent as some of the higher members of the group of insecta are, we can see no link connecting them with the vertebrata on the one hand, or the mollusca on the other. The wise ant is utterly unlike the subtle fox, and no resemblance to the cuttle fish can be traced in either. We have hitherto been able to trace, very rudely it is true, a general connection between the various groups of the animal kingdom, which we have already considered, but we have now come to the end of the chain, and must go back to a lower link, the sub-kingdom of **Molluscoida**.

Some of these are well known to visitors at the sea-side, under the name of white sea-weed. In appearance, this sea-weed either presents a flat, somewhat horny expanse, studded with minute, dot-like cavities, or of little jointed calcareous filaments which are the horny or chalky covering of minute polyps, only to be seen with the aid of a magnifying glass, and which so much resemble little hydræ that they were long classed with them.

They completely differ from the hydræ in their structure, however, for they possess a very distinct alimentary canal, furnished both with a mouth and a vent, and they have also a distinct nervous system, consisting of a single ganglion.

In the hydra, too, the reproductive organs are situated externally, on the body wall, whereas in the molluscoida they are contained in the body cavity. Both, however, have the power of forming buds and in both the buds may remain attached one to another so that instead of a single individual we get a regular colony, and from this property these white sea-weeds, or, as they are sometimes called, sea-mosses and sea-mats, have received the name of **Polyzoa**.

Another order of molluscoida is the **Brachiopoda** so-called from their long fringed arms or feet. They look like ordinary shell-fish, and might at first sight be supposed to be very closely related to the common mussels, but they have not the same developed internal structure. The valves of their shell are placed laterally and not on the front and back of the creature. The two valves of the shell are more or less unlike, but the two sides of each valve are like one another, whereas in the mussel, the two valves are like one another but the two sides of each valve are unlike.

The Brachiopoda are of comparatively slight importance now, but at an early period of the world's history they swarmed in the seas, and one of them, the Lingula, has come down from a very early period until now without undergoing almost any change.

In the next class, the **Tunicata**, or **Ascidian molluscs**, the individuals sometimes remain separate, and are sometimes united, but, whether separate or not, they all have a heart, and thus differ from the Polyzoa. The outer covering of the animal is leathery and elastic, and from it they have got their name of Tunicata. It contains a quantity of cellulose, which, as we have already mentioned, was formerly regarded as a characteristically vegetable product. From their external resemblance to a wine-skin, or two-necked leather bottle, they have been called Ascidians (Fig. 77).

The two necks of the bottle are connected with the two ends of the alimentary canal, the mouth and the vent. The wider mouth opens into a large cavity, called the respiratory sac, from the lower end of which passes the gullet, which widens into the stomach and again contracts into an intestine. This bending

Fig. 77.—Diagram of an Ascidian. *a*, mouth; *b*, respiratory sac; *c*, ventral groove; *n*, ganglion; *d*, digestive canal; *cl*, cloaca; *g*, generative gland.

on itself, empties into a cavity which is connected with the second or smaller mouth of the bottle, and which is known as the cloaca. These two sacs, the respiratory sac and the cloaca, occupy a great part of the animal. At the points where their walls come in contact, a number of perforations occur, through which water can pass from the one to the other. They are fringed with cilia, which are in constant action, and drive the water from the respiratory sac into the cloaca, thus keeping up a continual circulation of water in and between these sacs. The body cavity of the animal is filled with a fluid containing numerous solid particles or corpuscles, and this fluid serves the purpose of blood. It is driven first in one direction and then in another by a contractile chamber placed near the lower part of the animal, and serving the function of a heart. As the fluid thus oscillates in the body cavity, fresh portions of it are brought successively into contact with the wall of the respiratory sac, and thus an exchange of oxygen and carbonic acid is maintained between the blood and the water contained in the sac. Between the two necks of the bottle the body wall of the animal is somewhat thick, and in it is placed a single ganglion (n, Fig. 77). The position of this ganglion will be seen further on to be of great importance, and must therefore be clearly borne in mind, as it is in the tunicata or ascidians that we find the nearest connecting link between the mollusca and the vertebrata.

In the next section of molluscous animals, the **Mollusca** proper, we find the nervous system more developed, so that instead of the single ganglion we have three, and instead of the heart with a single chamber, we have a heart with at least two and sometimes more chambers.

Two subdivisions of the Mollusca, the Lamellibranchiata and Gasteropoda are important on account of their numbers. They constitute the so-called shellfish, one class of which, like the oyster, has two valves to its shell, and another, like the whelk or periwinkle, only one.

The **oyster** and shell-fish like it, have no head. They breathe by means of two large thin folds of tissue, containing numerous blood-vessels and which are bathed on their outside by the sea-water when the animal opens its shell. On account of this mode of breathing they are called **Lamellibranchiata**.

The **periwinkles** or whelks have a distinct head, and a fleshy organ, or foot, which they protrude from their shell, and by means of which they are able to move about. Whelks and periwinkles are adapted for living in water, and they breathe by means of gills, lying in a chamber within the body, but to which however, water has access.

Snails resemble periwinkles in most other respects, but they are fitted for existence on land instead of water. They breathe by means of lungs, little bags like those of the periwinkle, but into which air passes instead of water. In all of these the foot protrudes from the under-surface of the body, or belly, and they are called **Gasteropoda**. The foot of the periwinkle, as we all know, consists of a rounded disc. In the snail and slug it is rounded or oblong, and its margins are quite smooth.

In the next subdivision of the Mollusca the Cephalopoda, the foot attains an enormous development, being split up so as to form long tentacles or arms which are furnished with numerous suckers, so that they can lay hold of objects and cling to them with the utmost tenacity. These arms surround the mouth, which is furnished with a parrot-like beak, and below the arms are two huge staring eyes. As the arms here apparently proceed from the head, the creatures are called **Cephalopoda**. The body looks like a large leathery bag, within which is a sac, containing the branchiae or gills. To this sac, water is admitted, and, by forcibly contracting its walls, the water can be violently driven out through a sort of funnel, and the animals propelled rapidly backward like a rocket. Some of these creatures attain an immense size, such as the octopi or cuttle-fishes which are said to exist in the West Indian seas with tentacles ten feet long. The cuttle-fish has two gills, and a leathery body without any external shell.

Other cephalopods have four gills, and a shell which is divided into chambers. To this class belongs the paper nautilus, and in the paelozoic, or ancient period, of our earth's history, cuttle-fishes of this sort were very common, and some of them were of immense size. Some of these had straight shells such

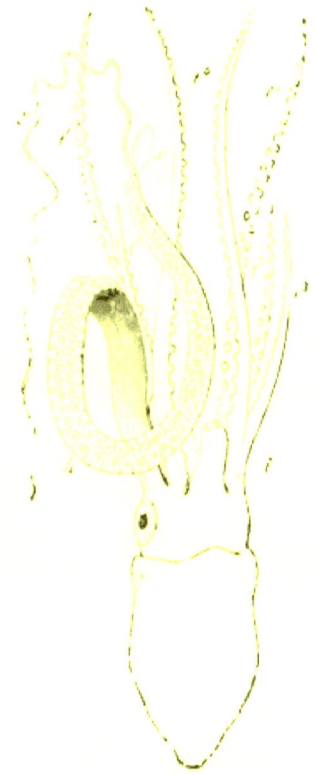

FIG. 78.—Cephalopod. *t*, *t*, arms furnished with suckers; *i*, funnel by which the water is expelled.

as the Orthocerata, and others, like the Ammonites, formed beautiful spirals. Some of the Orthocerata had shells six or seven feet long, and as thick as a man's body. Unlike the Orthocerata, the Ammonites do not belong to the paleozoic but to the secondary period.

The octopus and its allies are highly developed. They have in their heads a large nervous ganglion, which might be compared to a brain, eyes which externally look almost like those of a vertebrate, and powerful locomotive and prehensile organs, which they are able to wield with great facility. They stand distinctly at the head of the class of Mollusca, but it is impossible to see any sort of likeness between them and the class to which we next come, that of the Vertebrata.

Just as in the case of the mollusca itself we were unable to find any connecting link with the highest members of the Annulosa, and were obliged to go far down in the chain before we could meet with any resemblance, so must we do in the case of the Vertebrata also. We can find no relationship between the higher members of the Mollusca and Vertebrata, the cuttlefish and the monkey, but there is a tolerably close relation between the low molluscous Ascidian and the Amphioxus, which is the lowest form of vertebrate animals.

LECTURE IX.

GENERAL SKETCH OF THE ANIMAL KINGDOM—VERTEBRATA.

THE **Vertebrata** are distinguished from all other animals by the possession of a bony, jointed internal

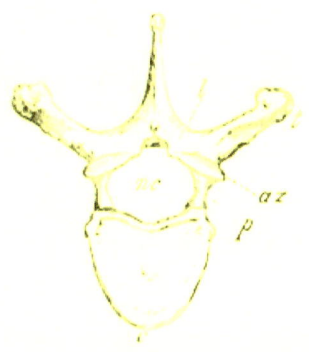

Fig. 79.—Single Vertebra seen from above; *n*, neural canal; *c*, body of the vertebra; *a z*, one of the condyles or joints by which it is connected with the vertebra in front of it (or above it in man).

skeleton, the most important part of which is the backbone or spine, consisting of a **Vertebral column** composed of a number of small bones, or vertebræ, jointed together. From each of those bones, projections

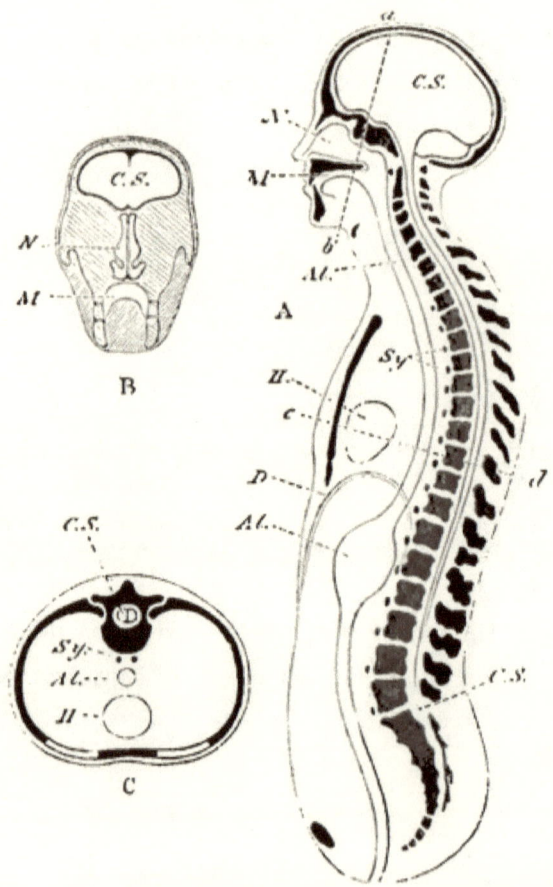

FIG. 80.—A, a diagrammatic view of the human body cut in half lengthways. *C.S.* the neural canal consisting of the cavity of the brain and spinal cord. The hæmal canal consists of several cavities, *N*, that of the nose; *M*, that of the mouth; *Al. Al*, the alimentary canal represented as a simple straight tube; *H*, the heart; *D*, the diaphragm.
B, a tranverse vertical section of the head taken along the line *a b*; letters as before.
C, a tranverse section taken along the line *c d*; letters as before.
The black parts of the diagram represent bone. The thick black parts in front of the neural canal *C.S.*, correspond to the bodies of the vertebræ (*c*, Fig 79) seen in profile.

or processes, as they are termed, proceed. Two of these go upwards or backwards towards the back of the animal, and unite, so as to form a bony bridge, and the bridges of adjoining vertebræ lying close to each other form a jointed bony canal, in which a cord of nervous matter, the spinal cord, lies safely enclosed. This canal is therefore called the **neural**, or nervous canal.

Other processes project side-ways and a little forwards, and being prolonged by the bent bones termed ribs, which are jointed on to them, together form a second, but less perfect canal, in which the vascular system is contained, and which is consequently termed the **hæmal** canal.

The vertebrates thus consist of a **double canal**, the **neural** and the **hæmal**, whereas all the other classes have but the simple canal in which the nervous and vascular systems are contained in common.

At the anterior end of the spine, the vertebræ undergo a strange alteration, their parts being so expanded and modified as to form a bony case, **the skull**, which protects that collection of nervous matter which is known as the brain, and also to form organs for the seizure and mastication of food.

In addition to this we have two bony girdles, partially encircling the body at two points. The first is called the **shoulder-girdle**, and its position is implied in its name. The second is called the **pelvic girdle**, and is situated at the loins of the animal.

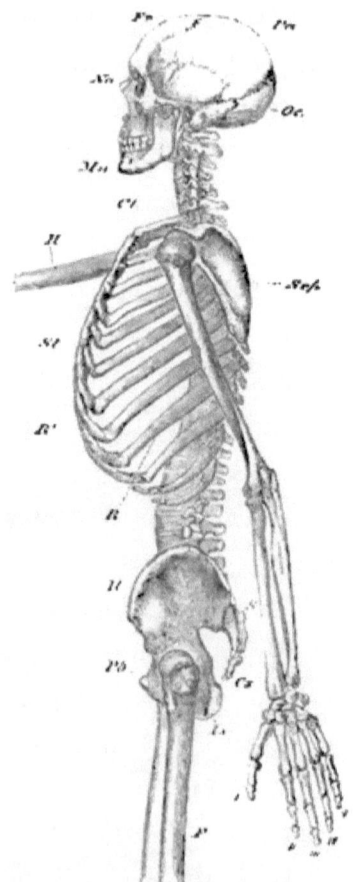

FIG. 81.—*Mn*, the mandible or lower jaw; *Cl*, the cavicle, or collar bone; *H*, the humerus; *Scp*, the scapula, or shoulder blade; *St*, the sternum; *R'* the cartilages of the ribs; *R*, the ribs; *Il*, the ilium or hip-bone; *F*, the femur.

Each of these girdles consists of several bones, which form the limbs of the animal, and unite them

SCAPULA AND ILIUM.

to the trunk. We have in each girdle two large flat bones, which serve as an attachment for the muscles which move the limbs. These in the shoulder-

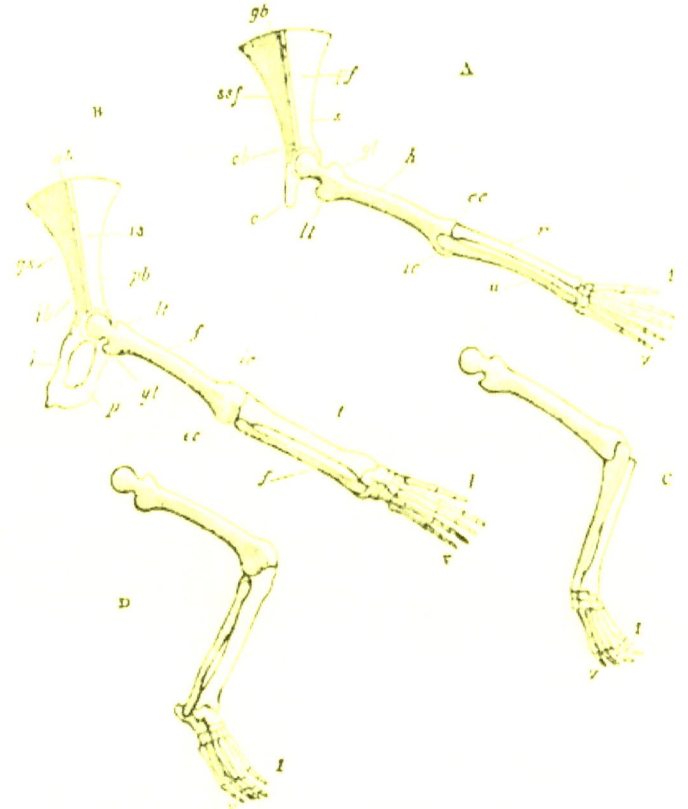

Fig. 82.—Diagrammatic representation of the limbs in mammalia. The anterior side is light, and the posterior is shaded. A and C are fore-limbs or arms, B and D are hind limbs. s, scapula; ix, ilium; h, humerus; f, femur; r, radius; t, tibia; u, ulna; f, fibula; 1, pollex in fore and hallux in hind limb; v, fifth digit.

girdle are called scapulae, or blade-bones, and in the pelvic girdle, ilia, or hip-bones.

To each of these is jointed a single long strong bone,

which in the anterior extremity is called humerus or arm-bone, and in the posterior, femur, or thigh-bone.

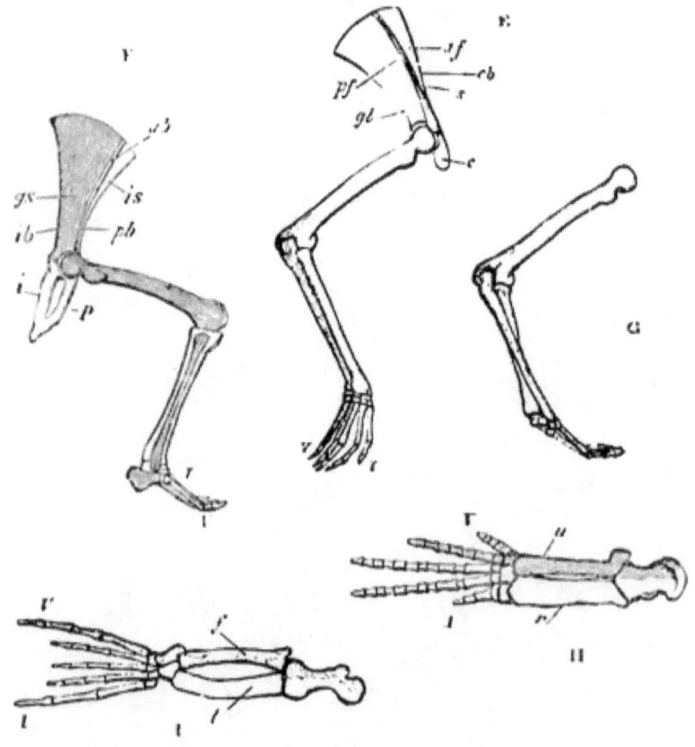

Fig. 83.—Diagrammatic representation of the limbs in mammalia. F and G are fore limbs; F, a hind limb; H, fore-limb of a cetacean; I, hind limb of a seal. The letters indicate the same parts as in Fig. 82.

Next come two bones which run side by side from the lower end of the humerus and femur. Those in the fore-leg, supporting the arm, are termed radius and ulna, those in the hind leg are called tibia and fibula. The ulna is jointed to the humerus closely, so as to give firmness to the forearm, while the radius is less firmly attached to the humerus. The bones of the hand or fore-foot are attached to the radius, and thus acquire a much greater mobility than they

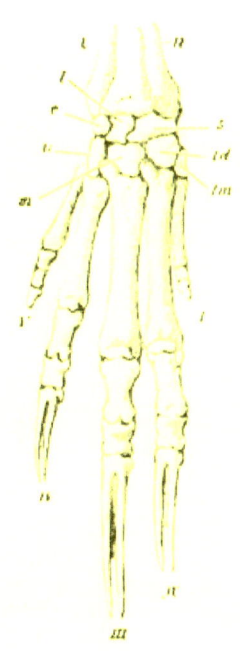

Fig. 84.—Diagram of the fore limb of an amphibian. The dotted lines indicate the rays to which the different parts belong. H, humerus; R, radius; U, ulna; r, radial bone of carpus; u, ulnar bone; i, intermediate bone; c, double central bone.

Fig. 85.—Manus of a marsupial. R, radius; U, ulna; s, scaphoid; l, lunar; c, cuneiform; td, trapezoid; tm, trapezium; m, magnum; u, uncinate.

would have if the radius were more firmly fixed to the humerus, at the same time the radius is supported in position by the ulna; and thus the steadiness is given to it which is necessary for precision of movement in the hand.

170   MANUS AND CARPUS.

The chief bones of the wrist, or carpus, are three: one attached to the radius, another to the ulna,

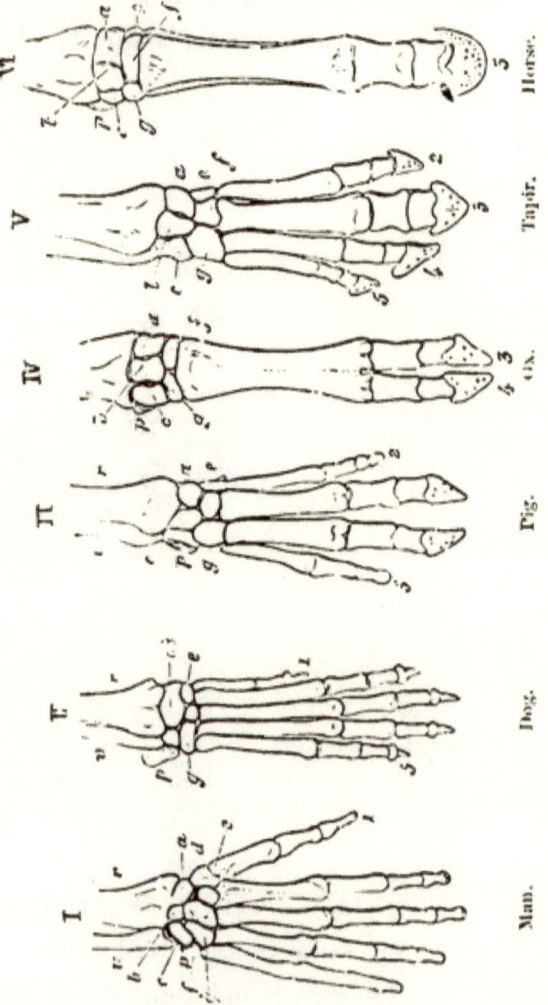

Fig. 86.—Skeleton of the manus or hand of various mammals. I. man; II. dog; III. pig; IV. ox; V. tapir; VI. horse. *r*, radius; *u*, ulna; *a*, scaphoid bone; *b*, lunar; *c*, cuneiform; *d*, tapezium; *e*, trapezoid; *f*, magnum; *g*, uncinate; *p* pisiform.

HAND AND FOOT.

and the third lying between them. Attached to this intermediate bone is another one or two, the central bone or bones of the wrist (Fig. 84), and then, arranged

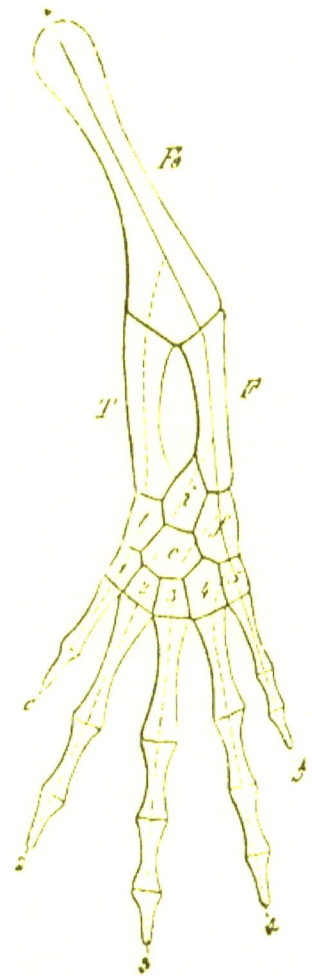

Fig. 87.—Hinder extremity of a larva of salamander. The dotted lines are drawn through the rays to which the different pieces belong. *Fe*, femur; *T*, tibia; *F*, fibula; *t*, tibial; *f*, fibular bone of tarsus; *i*, intermediate bone; *c*, central bone.

like an arch beyond these are five other small bones, from which proceed the five digits, each of which contains four bones, or phalanges, except the first, which contains only three. This may be looked upon as the typical wrist, but it is almost always much modified in various animals by the fusion together of one or more of these bones in various ways.

A similar arrangement may be looked upon as typical in the foot also, but here the arrangement is even more disturbed than in the hand or fore-foot (Fig. 87).

In most animals the hind legs are merely wanted for steady progression and support, and the flat bones, or ilia, of the pelvic girdle are usually firmly and closely united to the vertebral column.

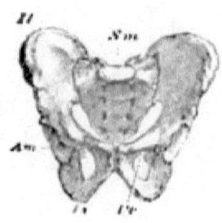

Fig. 88.—A front view of the pelvis. *Sm*, the sacrum; *Am*, the acetabulum *Il*, the ilium; *Pb*, the pubis; *Is*, the ischium.

But greater freedom of motion is required in the fore-legs to enable them to overcome any obstacles in the way of locomotion, or to adapt them for the seizure of prey. In them, therefore, we find that the blade-bones, or scapulae, are not so closely united to the spine, but stand away from it at some little distance, and may, indeed, have no bony connection with it whatever, being attached to it simply by muscles, as in the horse and sheep. In many animals, however, they are attached, though only indirectly, by means of thin bones, the clavicles, or collar-bones. At one end these are jointed to the scapulae, but the other ends do not go directly to the spine. They go to the sternum, or breast-bone, a long flat bone which we have not yet mentioned, which runs down the centre of the hæmal arch for some distance, and to which the anterior extremities of some of the upper ribs are attached.

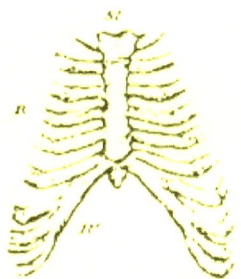

Fig. 80.—A front view of the sternum, *St*, with the cartilages of the ribs, *C*, and parts of the ribs themselves, *R*.

The various pieces of this bony skeleton are moved upon one another by means of **muscles**. These muscles, known to us commonly under the name of flesh, consist of bundles of contractile threads, or fibrils, which have the power of shortening, on the application of certain stimuli. This may be noticed by anyone in the muscles of the ball of the thumb. On striking them sharply with the back of a table knife they may be seen slightly to contract, and the thumb to move. This is much more evident if a current of electricity be passed through them, but the usual way in which they are made to contract is by a stimulus which they receive from their nerves.

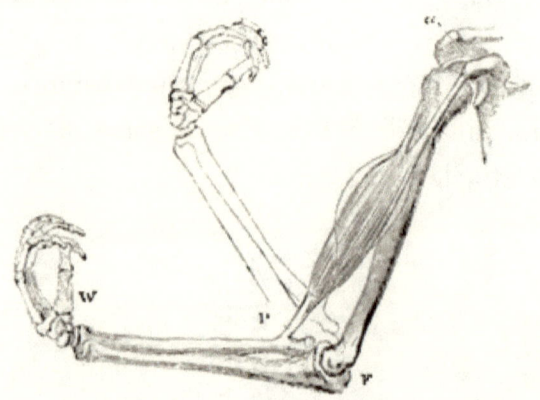

Fig. 90.—The Bones of the Upper Extremity with the Biceps Muscle.

The two tendons by which this muscle is attached to the scapula, or shoulder-blade, are seen at *a*. *p* indicates the attachment of the muscle to the radius, and hence the point of action of the power; *r*, the fulcrum, the lower end of the humerus on which the upper end of the radius (together with the ulna) moves; *w*, the weight (of the hand).

To each muscle, one or more **motor nerves** pass down from the spinal cord, and by them the muscle is set in action. One of the commonest occasions of the action of muscle is the stimulation of a **sensory nerve,** and yet sensory nerves have no direct connection with muscles, nor any power to make them contract.

The sensory nerves are, however, indirectly connected with muscles through the **spinal cord**. From all parts of the spinal cord motor nerves pass to the muscles, and to all parts of the spinal cord, sensory nerves pass from the skin. When one of these sensory nerves is stimulated, the impression passes up to the corresponding part of the spinal cord, and is thence transmitted, or reflected, as it is termed, down a motor nerve, causing the muscle to act.

This is called **reflex action**, and one of the simplest examples of it is given in tickling the palm of the hand, the sole of the foot, or by touching the eyeball. When the foot and hand are tickled, they are involuntarily drawn quickly back, and when the eyeball is touched, the eyelids close without any wish on the part of their owner, or even against his will.

The reflex movements, effected by the spinal cord alone, are simple in their character; while those effected by the nervous masses, or ganglia, into which the spinal cord enlarges at the head of the animal, are more complex. These ganglia are contained within the skull, and together are known as the encephalon or popularly as the **brain**. The encephalon consists of the cerebrum or brain proper, the cerebellum, the basal ganglia and the medulla oblongata. It is through them that the movements of respiration, and those necessary for prehension of food, are maintained, their complexity increasing with the development of the brain.

To carry nourishment to the bones, muscles, and nervous system, we have a system of **vessels**, containing **blood**, which is propelled through them by means of the heart. This blood always contains, swimming in it, a number of little round or oval bodies, called corpuscles. These have a red colour, and possess to a very great extent the power of taking up oxygen, and giving it off again, with great readiness. This oxygen is obtained by the blood from the air or water in which the animal lives, by means either of gills, or lungs, through which the blood circulates.

To supply the animal with nutriment to repair the waste of the tissues we have a **digestive canal**, consisting of mouth, stomach, and intestines, with various glands attached, which furnish secretions necessary for digestion. The mouth is generally provided with teeth, which serve both to seize the food and to break it up, so that it may be more readily dissolved by the digestive juices. The first of these is the saliva, which is poured out in the mouth; the second, the gastric juice secreted by the stomach; the third is the bile, poured out by the liver; the fourth is the secretion of the pancreas, and the fifth that of the intestine. By means of these the food is dissolved, and it is then absorbed by a number of small vessels, called lacteals, which carry it into the general circula-

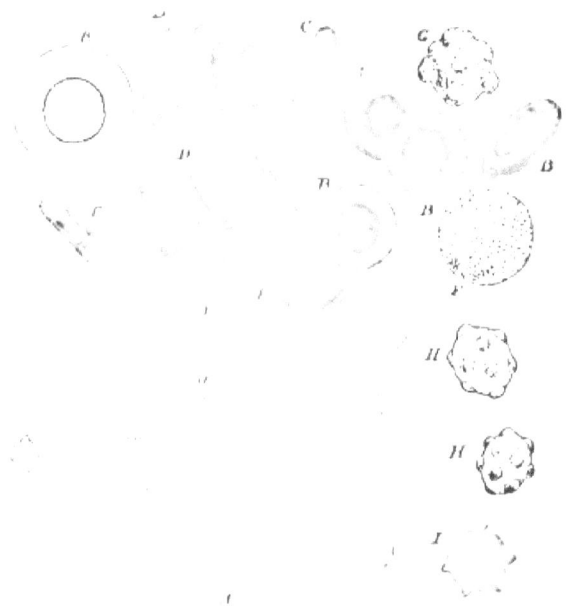

Fig. 91.—Red and White Corpuscles of the Blood magnified.

moderately magnified. The red corpuscles are seen lying in rows like rolls of coins; at *a* and *a* are seen two white corpuscles.
B, red corpuscles much more highly magnified, seen in face; C, ditto, seen in profile; D, ditto, in rows, rather more highly magnified; E, a red corpuscle swollen into a sphere by imbibition of water.
F, a white corpuscle magnified same as B; G, ditto, throwing out some blunt processes; K, ditto, treated with acetic acid, and showing nucleus, magnified same as D.
H, red corpuscles puckered or crenate all over.
I, ditto, at the edge only.

tion, where it mixes with the blood, and goes to nourish the tissues.

But the tissues, in their functional activity, yield other products than simple carbonic acid, which can escape by the gills or lungs like the smoke from the chimney of a furnace. Besides it, there is nitrogenous waste, which may be compared to the ashes of a furnace, and which requires to be carried off, as otherwise it would choke the tissues, and stop their action. To carry off this waste, we have special organs, the kidneys.

The vertebrata never reproduce themselves by budding. Reproduction is always sexual. Spermatozoa and germ cells unite to produce ova, which grow into the perfect individual. These ova are sometimes extruded in the form of eggs, which are hatched either by the heat of the sun or that of the parent animal. When this is the case, the animals are called **oviparous**. Others are retained until hatched within the body of the parent animal, and the young are then brought forth alive. Such animals are called **ovoviviparous**. In the higher animals the eggs or germ cells are so small as to require the aid of a microscope to see them, and do not contain sufficient material for the development of the young individual, which must therefore receive a special supply of nutriment from the parent. In such cases the ova being insignificant, and the animals being brought forth alive, the animals are called **viviparous**.

LECTURE X.

GENERAL SKETCH OF THE ANIMAL KINGDOM—VERTE-
BRATA—COLD-BLOODED ANIMALS—FISHES—AMPHIBIA
—REPTILES.

THE vertebrata have been divided by Professor Huxley into three great orders—**Ichthyopsida**, or fish-like animals; **Sauropsida**, or lizard-like animals; and **Mammalia**, which have breasts, and suckle their young. The **Ichthyopsida** are distinguished by the possession of gills, either during the whole or a part of their lives, which the sauropsida never have. The **Sauropsida** are distinguished again from the **mammalia** by the fact that they never suckle their young. But besides this there are other characteristics. The blood corpuscles in the two first divisions have a nucleus, which those of the mammals never have. The skeleton of the sauropsida, too, differs from that of the mammals in certain points, so that it is possible from one or two bones to ascertain to which class the animal belongs. In the sauropsida the skull is jointed to the vertebral column by one articulating surface, or condyle, while in the mammals there are two condyles. In the sauropsida the lower jaw is composed of several pieces, and is united to the skull by means of a special bone called the os quadratum, or quadrate bone, while in the mammals the lower jaw is composed of only two pieces, and the quadrate bone is wanting.

Each of the first two divisions has been further subdivided into two, the former into **Fishes** and **Amphibia**, and the latter into **Reptiles** and **Birds**.

Fishes are entirely adapted for a watery life. They breathe by means of gills, and their extremities are modified into fins. The lowest member of the group is one of very great interest, inasmuch as it supplies the link connecting the vertebrata with the mollusca. This little fish differs from all other members of the vertebral kingdom in having no distinct head, and it is called the **amphioxus** from the two ends being more or less alike. It is about one-and-a-half inches to two inches long, and from its lance-like shape has also been termed lancelet. It burrows in the sands, more especially about the Mediterranean shores. It has no vertebral column, and so one might think at first that it ought not to be reckoned as a vertebrate at all; but although there is no bony spine, there is a spinal cord, and below

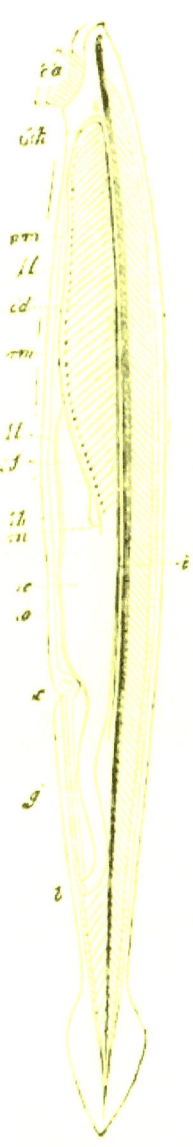

Fig. 92.—Amphioxus Lanceolatus. *a*, mouth surrounded by cirri; *b*, anus; *c*, abdominal pore; *d*, branchial sac; *e*, gastric portion of the enteron; *f*, cæcum; *g*, hind gut; *h*, colon; *i*, notochord, below which is the aorta, which accompanies it for nearly the whole length; *k*, aortic arches; *l*, aortic arch; *m*, enlargement of the branchial arteries; *n*, heart of the vena cava; *o*, heart of the portal vein (after Quatrefages).

it, where the spine ought to be, there is a rod of gristle. As this same gristly rod or notochord is found in all other vertebrates before the spinal column appears, and as it is from this rod that the spinal column is developed, we are fully warranted in classing the amphioxus amongst the vertebrates. It has no proper extremities or fins, but it moves by means of a membranous fin-like expansion running along the middle of the whole of its back and part of its belly. Near its anterior end is a longitudinal slit-like mouth which has no teeth, but some gristly projections, and is surrounded by several vascular filaments. It opens into a wide gullet in which there are a number of slit-like openings. From this gullet, an intestine proceeds, which opens externally by a distinct anus. There is no heart, but the blood vessels have pulsatile dilatations upon them, and the blood itself is colourless. The water, which is taken through the mouth into the dilated pharyngeal or branchial sac, passes through the clefts into the abdomen of the animal, and is again ejected by a small opening placed in front of the anus.

A little while ago I mentioned that the **ascidians** were interesting as affording a **connecting link** between the mollusca and the **vertebrata**.

It will be remembered that between the two necks of the bottle there was a somewhat thicker layer of tissue than in other parts of the body, and that in this layer of tissue a ganglion was situated. But this is not all. In the young ascidian, underneath the ganglion, is situated a small cartilaginous rod, in the same position as the vertebral column in vertebrata, or the notochord in the amphioxus. If you imagine this part of the ascidian greatly lengthened out until it forms

Fig. 93.—Diagram of an Ascidian. *o*, mouth; *b*, respiratory sac; *c*, ventral groove; *n*, ganglion; *d*, digestive canal; *d*, cloaca; *g*, generative gland.

the whole of the back of the animal, you will see that the ascidian type approaches very nearly to that of the amphioxus. The single ganglion, thus elongated, will form a spinal cord, and the little rod of cartilaginous matter will form a notochord. In both animals there is a mouth, opening into a large sac, perforated in the ascidian with holes, and in the amphioxus with slits.

Through this the water pours into another sac, and makes its exit through an aperture situated at or near the anal aperture of the animal.

Allied to the amphioxus, but a good deal higher in the scale than it, are the **Myxinoids** or **hag-fishes** and lampreys. These have worm-like bodies, and are without limbs. In them also the notochord persists during life, and there is no proper vertebral column, but, unlike the amphioxus, they have a head and a skull, the skull being simply cartilaginous and not bony. They also differ from the amphioxus in possessing a distinct heart, consisting of two parts, an auricle, into which the blood is received from the veins, and a ventricle, through which it is propelled into the arteries. Their pharynx is not wide and chamber-like, as in the amphioxus, but narrow, and in either side of it there are seven holes, which open into sacs, in which the gills are contained, and which have also an external opening by which water can enter them from without. These gills consist simply of folds of the mucous membrane lining the sac. In them the branchial vessels ramify, and the blood is thus exposed to the action of the air dissolved in the water circulating in the sacs. The mouth in these fishes is not a simple opening, like that of the amphioxus, the inner side being provided with jaws, like the mouths of the higher fishes. It takes the form of a disc, or cap, like a boy's sucker, or like the

sucker of a leech. By means of this the fish is able to
fix itself to any object, but after doing so the water
could not enter the mouth as it does in other fishes, and
the current is therefore not maintained from the mouth
through the branchial apertures, but the water entering
instead at an opening in one side of the neck,
passes through both branchial sacs and out at the
other side. In hag-fishes, also, the nose is peculiar, the
nostrils being situated at the top of the head, behind
the mouth, and opening into two nasal sacs, which
communicate by a canal with the throat, as they do in
the higher vertebrates. In other fishes this is not so,
as in them the nose consists simply of close sacs, which
do not communicate with the pharynx. In this respect,
then, the hag-fishes, although so low in the scale of
vertebrates, resemble the higher members of this sub-
kingdom, more than fishes, which are really much more
highly organised than they.

Next come the **Selachii** or **Shark** tribe. In
them there is a vertebral column, which is very often
simply cartilaginous, although sometimes bony. They
have a distinct skull, and a lower jaw, but the skull
is simply cartilaginous, and not composed of bones.
The gills resemble those of the hag-fishes in forming
a series of folds lining the inside of several pouches
which communicate internally with the pharynx, and
open externally by means of slits. Unlike the hag-

fish, the shark has distinct limbs, both fore and hind, which appear in the shape of two pairs of fins. The skin is covered with hard scales, in the form of tubercles, or plates, from which they have received the name of placoid, or plate-like. The tail is of a somewhat peculiar shape, the vertebral column being prolonged into the upper part of it, while the lower part simply consists of a membranous expansion. The two sides of the tail are therefore unequal, and tails of this sort are called heterocercal, or unsymmetrical.

The next order is that of the **Ganoids**, which have also an imperfect, generally cartilaginous skeleton, but their skulls differ from those of the sharks in being composed of distinct bones. They have also two pairs of fins, representing two pairs of limbs. These fins are supported by a cartilaginous framework, and the tail, like that of the shark, is heterocercal. Unlike the shark, the gills are not arranged in separate chambers, but are supported on a framework at the side of the pharynx, and they are all covered by a single large plate called the gill-cover, exactly as we see it in ordinary fish. Their bodies, externally, are covered with large bony plates, forming a complete armour, as we see in the sturgeons.

The next order, the **Teleostei**,—so-called from their skeleton being no longer cartilaginous, but completely bony,—contains all the ordinary fishes. The vertebral column is completely ossified, but the body of each vertebra is hollow before and behind, so that a somewhat globular cavity remains between them, and this is filled with the cartilaginous or gelatinous remains of the notochord. The vertebræ are thus united by a sort of ball and socket joint, which gives great flexibility to the whole column, and adapts the fish for rapid and easy motion through the water. They have generally, although not always, fins, which correspond both to the anterior and posterior limbs. These are supported by a bony framework; those corresponding to the fore-limbs being termed pectoral fins, and those corresponding to the hind-legs being called ventral fins. The tail differs from that of the shark and sturgeon in being symmetrical, both lobes being equal, and it is therefore called homocercal. The gills, like those of the ganoids, are comb-like, and situate in the cavity at each side of the pharynx, communicating with it by means of several slits, and opening externally by a gill slit covered by a single bony and membranous plate termed the gill-cover. The heart consists of two cavities, an auricle and a ventricle, and the skin is covered externally by more or less rounded scales, generally with smooth, but sometimes with fringed edges.

In all fishes, excepting the amphioxus and the

hag-fish tribe, there is what is usually called a swimming bladder, which contains air. In some fish this is completely closed, but in others it communicates with the pharynx, and some kinds of fish actually come up to the surface of the water and take air into it. This **swimming bladder** in the fish is the representative of **the lungs** in the higher animals.

We have already seen that when we wished to get a connecting link between two sub-kingdoms, we were obliged to go low down in the scale in order to find it, there being an inseparable barrier between the higher members of each kingdom; and so it is in the case of the fishes regarded in connection with the next class of vertebrate animals, viz., the **Amphibia**, for here we find the connecting link in the mud-fish, or **lepidosiren**. It is in appearance somewhat like an eel, but it has no proper spinal column like the higher fishes, the notochord being persistent, although the skull is more highly developed, and consists of distinct bones. It has two anterior and two posterior limbs, but these do not take the form of fins, having rather the appearance of smooth thongs. It has gills, contained in the branchial chamber, opening externally by a single slit, but in addition to these it has true lungs, the swimming bladder or air bladder being double, and communicating with the pharynx by means of a regular tube or wind-pipe. Occasionally it has yet another breathing apparatus, consisting of small, rudimentary external gills outside the neck.

It differs from all other fishes except the myxinoids in having, like them, nasal chambers, which are not closed, but communicate with the pharynx. In this particular it resembles the myxinoids, which are amongst the lowest fishes, and in this it resembles also the higher vertebrata.

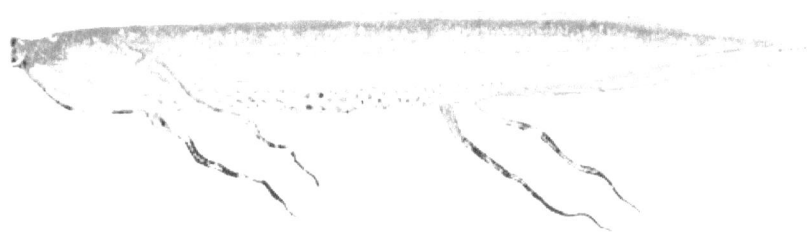

Fig. 94.—Lepidosiren Annectens.

It resembles the amphibia in having a heart consisting of three chambers, instead of two like the fishes, viz., a ventricle and two auricles.

Its structure is well adapted to its mode of life, for it inhabits rivers which during the dry season shrink greatly within their banks, and again swell up during the rains. The mud-fish appears to burrow in the mud, and remain there in a dormant condition during the time that it is dried by the sun, again coming out when the river, swollen by the rains, fills its channel afresh.

The animals composing the class of **Amphibia** resemble the fishes in always having gills at one period of their lives, but differ from them in always acquiring true lungs at a later period. In some of them the gills are retained during the whole of life, but in others they are cast aside when the lungs become developed. They all undergo a metamorphosis after leaving the egg. In their young state they are always more fish-like, and this resemblance becomes less as they grow older. Their limbs are never developed into fins, as in fishes, and their gills are generally external, placed outside the neck, instead of being situated in a cavity, as in the fishes.

We have already mentioned, however, that in the mud-fish we have both kinds of gills present, and the same is the case in the early condition of frogs and toads, both of which have external and internal gills, and the external disappear first.

The nasal sacs always open into the mouth, and there is a common cloaca, into which the intestine, kidneys, and reproductive organs all empty themselves. During the early part of the life of an amphibian, its circulation resembles that of a fish, there being only two chambers to the heart, but, as the animal develops, a third chamber appears, and then the condition

PROTEUS AND AXOLOTL. 191

Fig. 25.—Axolotl of Mexico. This is the tadpole of a kind of newt (*Amblystoma*), but is very remarkable from the fact that it goes on reproducing itself for several generations without ever assuming its perfect condition. It was long considered to be a perfectly developed animal and only very rarely does an individual Axolotl develop into an Amblyostoma.

Fig. 26.—The Proteus.

192   METAMORPHOSES OF AMPHIBIA.

is like that which we find permanently in the order next above the amphibia, viz., the reptiles.

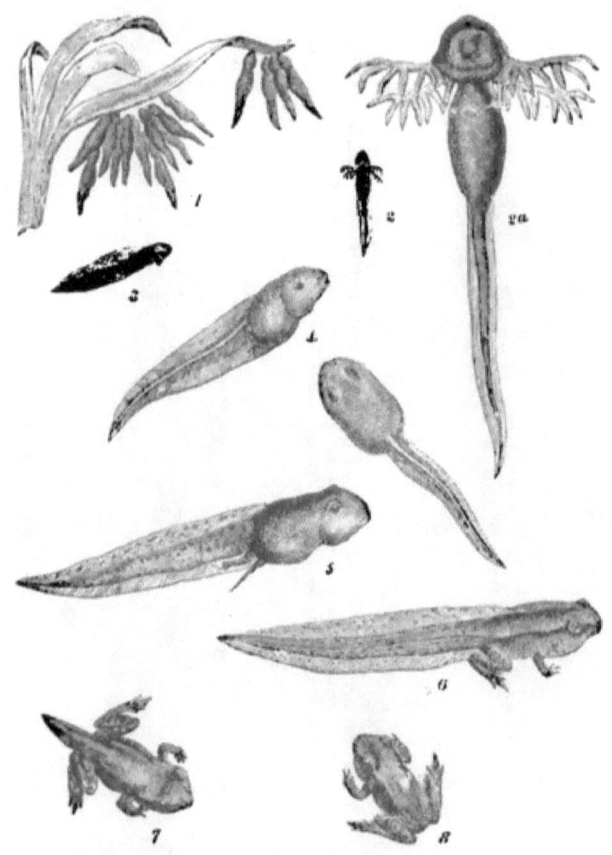

Fig. 97.—Tadpoles in different stages of development, from those just hatched (1) till the adult form is attained (8). 2a is a magnified representation of 2.

One of the lowest amphibians is a curious animal called the proteus, which is found in the caves of Adelsberg, near Trieste. In appearance and size it is not unlike a very clear, semitransparent earthworm, but at each side of the neck are two gills of a fringe-like character, and of a bright scarlet colour, and it has four very small and weak legs, the fore-feet having three toes each, and the hind feet only two.

In the proteus the gills remain during the whole life of the animal, but in the ordinary water-newt, which we see swimming about our ponds, the gills are cast off as the animal grows, and the lungs develop. The tail, however, always remains throughout life.

In frogs, on the contrary, both gills and tail disappear in the adult animal. When the egg of the frog is hatched, there proceeds from it at first a little tadpole, which is fish-like, breathing both by internal and external fins, and having a long, fish-like tail. It might now be said to correspond to a low form of fish. Next, small hind-legs appear, and then fore-legs, but the tail and gills still remain. It is now on a level with the proteus. Then the external gills disappear, and the lungs are developed, but the tail remains, and the tadpole is now on a level with the newt. Ultimately the tail also vanishes, and we have a fully formed frog.

In the next class, that of **Reptilia**, we find a very marked advance in the respiratory structures, for in them no gills ever appear at any period of their existence. In reptiles and all higher animals, respiration is effected entirely by lungs.

Some amphibians, such as the salamander, are very much like lizards, which are true reptiles, in appearance. But salamanders always have gills at one period of their lives, while lizards never have them at all.

There is, however, a sort of intermediate link in the land salamander, for its young sometimes lose their gills before their birth.

The reptiles also differ from amphibia and vertebrata, and agree with birds, which form the other class in the great division of the sauropsida, in having a skull united to the vertebral column by a single joint, or condyle, as it is termed, while in amphibia and vertebrata there are two condyles.

The jaw in reptiles is composed of several pieces, and united to the skull by a special bone called the quadrate bone—an arrangement which gives them power to open their jaws to an enormous width. There are generally four extremities, although sometimes, as in snakes, these may be absent, and the skin is covered with scales or bony plates. The heart generally contains three chambers, two auricles and one ventricle.

In the first order, that of the lizards, or **Lacertilia**, there are generally two pairs of distinct limbs, and even when these limbs are not developed, as in the common blindworm, which looks like a snake, there is always a scapular arch present, and they have always eyelids. They never have teeth with distinct sockets. In the next order, that of the **Crocodilia**, the teeth are

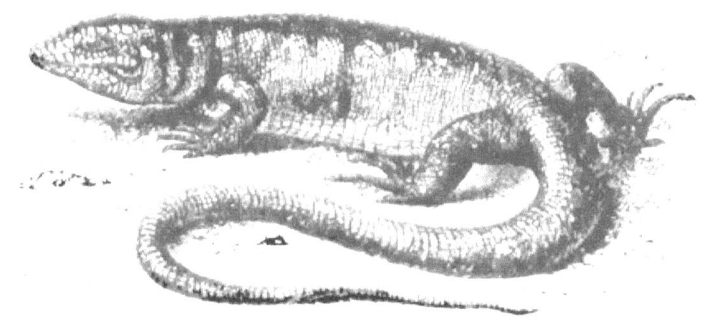

Fig. 98.—Lizard.

always planted in distinct, separate sockets, and the skin is partly covered by horny scales and partly by large bony plates.

Fig. 99.—Crocodile.

In the next order, the snakes, or **Ophidia**, the body is always long and cylindrical. There are no limbs, nor is there even the rudiment of a scapular arch.

They have no eyelids, the skin of the head being continuous right over the eye, although it becomes transparent so as to allow the animal to see. It is owing to this peculiarity that snakes have such an unwinking, extraordinary stare. The way in which they crawl along is very peculiar. The body is covered with scales, which on the back are small and roughly triangular, but on the belly have the form of transverse bands. The snake has a very great number of ribs, and each end of these horny bands is attached to a rib. Upon these bands the snake walks, in a way which we can readily understand if we think how a centipede would walk were a horny plate stretched from side to side between each pair of feet.

The next order is that of the tortoises, or **Chelonia**, in which the ribs and vertebræ are united so as to form a complete bony mass, which is covered with horn, composing a box within which the animal can entirely hide itself. One great peculiarity of this animal is, that the ribs being quite outside the body, the scapular and pelvic arches which support the limbs are within the ribs instead of outside them.

Besides these orders of reptilia, representatives of which exist at the present day, there have been others, all the members of which have long ago become extinct, although at one period of the earth's history they were really the lords of creation. These were gigantic lizards, of tremendous power, some of which were furnished with immense jaws and pointed teeth. Some of them lived upon land, others were furnished with paddle-like fins, and lived in the waters, while yet others, the pterodactyls, had wings like bats, with

Fig. 100.—A Mud-tortoise (*Trionyx*), showing the dorsal plates.

which they could fly through the air. Some of these latter were small, but others were of stupendous proportions, one of them measuring, as has been calculated, no less than twenty-seven feet across the wings from tip to tip.

In these flying lizards, the wings were probably somewhat like those of the bats of the present day,

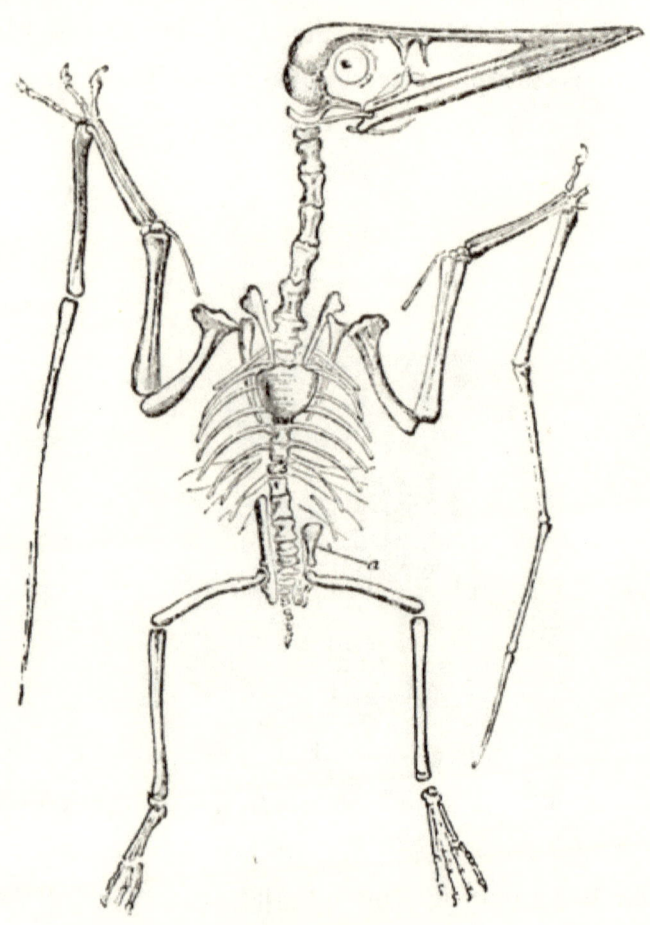

Fig. 101.—Skeleton of Pterodactyl.

—leathery, membranous expansions, stretching from the fore-legs to the hind-legs, and to the sides of the body. These lizards had five fingers, one of which, the outer one of the fore-paw, was enormously long, and served to support the wing. Their heads were large, and their jaws well furnished with teeth, but their bones were hollow and very light, being filled with air, and on the breast-bone there was a large keel-like projection, serving for the attachment of the great muscles which moved the wings.

LECTURE XI.

GENERAL SKETCH OF THE ANIMAL KINGDOM—WARM-BLOODED ANIMALS—BIRDS.

The lizards, now extinct, mentioned in last lecture, remind us in some points of the **Birds**, which belong to the next division of the sauropsidæ, or lizard-like animals. But the pterodactyl had no feathers, and its skeleton was in most points that of a lizard rather than that of a bird.

Birds, like reptiles, have the skull united to the vertebral column by a single joint or condyle, and have a lower jaw composed, at least in the young state, of several pieces, and joined to the skull by a special bone, the quadrate bone. But while birds are provided with a covering of feathers, reptiles never have this, their integument consisting only of horny scales and plates, and never of feathers.

SAUROPSIDA—BIRDS.

The bodies of the vertebræ are also shaped differently; the sternum or breast-bone, has a prolongation in rep-

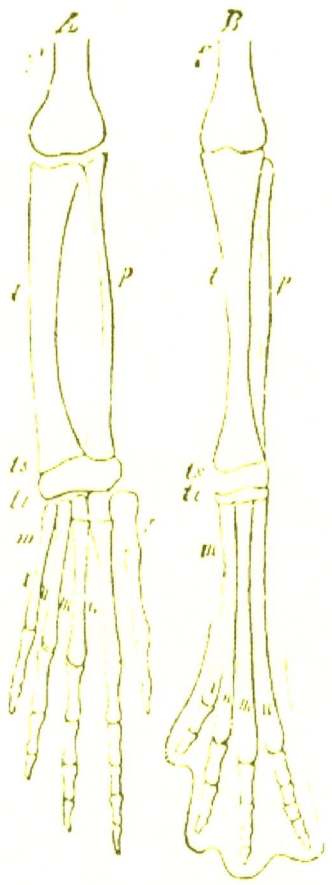

Fig. 102.—Skeleton of the foot of a reptile (lizard) (A) and a bird (B). The latter is in its embryonic state, in which the resemblance to the reptile is much greater than in the adult state (cf. Fig. 103). *f*, femur; *t*, tibia; *p*, fibula; *ts*, upper, *ti*, lower piece of the tarsus; *m*, metatarsus; i.e., metatarsalia of the toes.

tiles which it never has in birds; the hip-bones, or ilia, project further back in reptiles than in birds.

202 DIFFERENCES BETWEEN REPTILES AND BIRDS.

There are more bones in the foot of the reptile, and they are not fused together in the same way as in the bird. All these arrangements of the skeleton adapt birds better for flight.

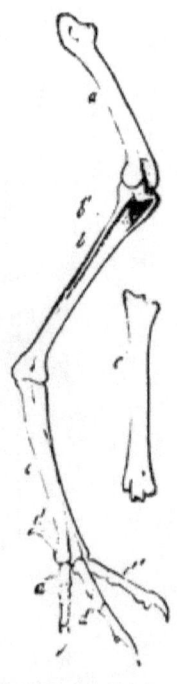

Fig. 103.—Hinder extremity of bird (*Buteo vulgaris*). *a*, femur; *b*, tibia; *b'*, fibula; *c*, tarso-metatarsus; *c'*, the same piece isolated and seen from in front; *d d' d" d'''*, four toes.

The heads of birds, too, although this cannot be looked upon as of importance, are much smaller than those of reptiles, and in none of the existing birds are there teeth in the jaws, both of them being covered with horn instead, which forms the beak.

Another great distinction between reptiles and birds is that the former, like the amphibia and fishes, have the temperature very little above that of the medium of the air or water in which they live, and they are consequently called **cold-blooded** animals. Birds, on the other hand, have, like the mammalia, a temperature very much higher than that of the media in which they live, a temperature which is kept up by constant oxidation or combustion in the body of the animal, and which remains nearly constant, whether the external temperature be high or low. They are therefore called **warm-blooded** animals.

We have said that oxygen is carried from the lungs to the tissues by means of the corpuscles of the blood. Although birds are warm-blooded and reptiles cold-blooded, yet the corpuscles in both have much the same characteristics, being oval in shape, and provided with a nucleus, but the arrangements for the circulation are quite different.

In reptiles, where less oxidation is necessary, the blood which circulates to the tissues is imperfectly oxygenated, and consists really of a mixture of venous blood returning from the tissues, and arterial blood returning from the lungs. These are mixed together in the heart, which consists of two auricles and one ventricle, and the mixture thence passes to all parts of the body. In the crocodile, where the circulatory apparatus is more perfectly developed than in other reptiles, there are four chambers to the heart; two auricles and two ventricles, but even there a provision is made for the intermixture of the two sorts of blood by a communicating branch, joining the two large vessels which spring from the heart.

In birds there are two auricles and two ventricles; the venous blood returning from the tissues, passes into the right auricle, thence into the right ventricle, which drives it through the lungs; it then returns, free from carbonic acid, and laden with oxygen, to the left auricle, whence it passes to the left ventricle, which drives it to every part of the body.

The lungs of birds consist of large sacs, into which the air is drawn by the movements of respiration; these sacs extend along the greater part of the animal's body, and from them prolongations pass to the bones of the skeleton, which are hollow, and filled with air, so as to render the bird as light as possible.

In trying to find a connecting link between birds and reptiles, we must not only go back to a low form of bird, but to one which is now extinct. The pterodactyl could fly, and had bones filled with air, like the bird, but its skin was that of a lizard. In the geological formations called the Trias and Jura, were reptiles which resembled birds in having a beak, but, after all, were reptiles and not birds. In the Jura

LINKS CONNECTING REPTILES AND BIRDS. 205

formation, however, there occurs another creature, the archeopteryx, which was like a reptile in having a long tail, but resembled a bird in having this tail fringed

Fig. 104.—Hesperornis regalis. Found by Professor Marsh in the cretaceous rocks in America.

with feathers. In the next formation, that of the chalk, a bird has been found in America called Hesperornis regalis, the skeleton of which resembles that

206 CONNECTING LINKS—THE ICHTHYO

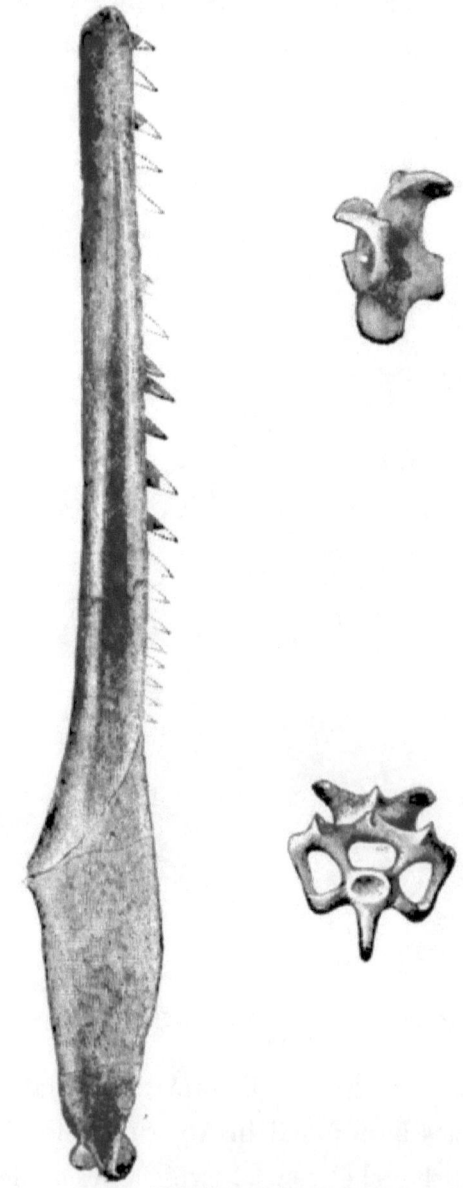

FIG. 105.—Jaw and vertebra of ichthyornis.

of a bird in every respect with the exception of the jaws, which are furnished with rows of teeth. Another bird, the Ichthyornis, has been found in the same rocks as the hesperornis, and has teeth situated in distinct sockets, while those of the hesperornis are only in grooves. In this respect the ichthyornis is still nearer the reptiles than the hesperornis.

Fig. 106.—Compsognathus longipes, a reptile resembling a bird in its long neck, small head, and partially-erect posture.

The skeletons of existing birds differ considerably from that of reptiles, but in the skeletons of certain extinct lizards, the Dinosaurs, we find intermediate forms.

On passing from the skeleton of the crocodile to that of the dinosaur, and thence to the skeleton of

208 CONNECTING LINKS—THE DINOSAURS.

the bird, we find the haunch-bone becoming longer,

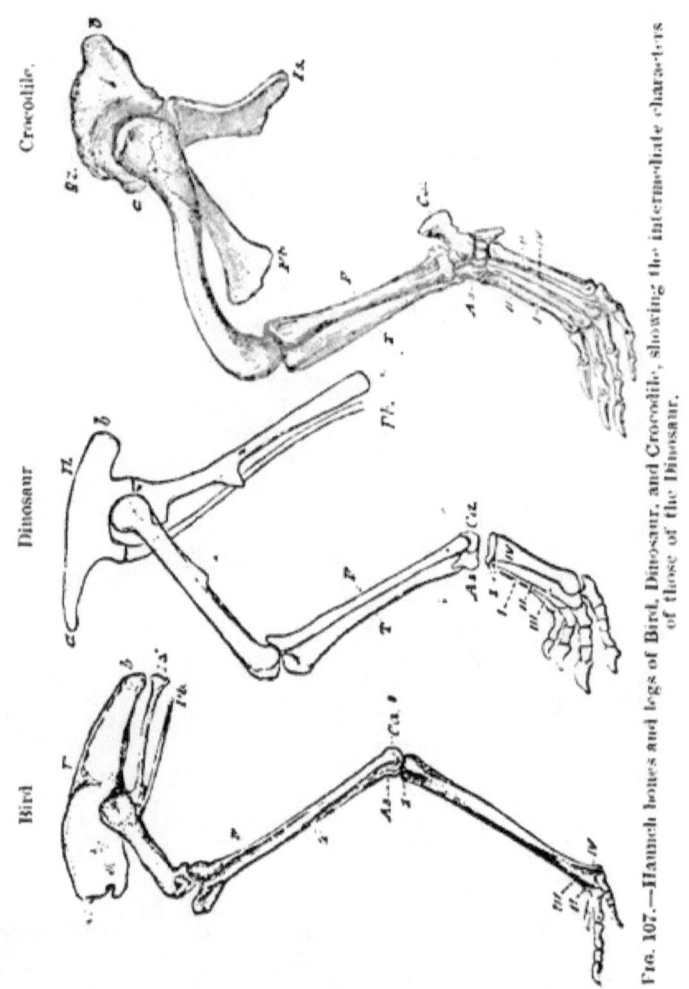

Fig. 107.—Haunch bones and legs of Bird, Dinosaur, and Crocodile, showing the intermediate characters of those of the Dinosaur.

the thigh-bone shorter, and the bones of the leg and foot more and more fused together.

CLASSIFICATION OF BIRDS—GRALLATORES. 209

The compsognathus presents another intermediate form. The neck is long, the head small, and it must have walked about on its hind legs like a bird. We do not know whether it had scales or feathers, and yet the nature of its skin would probably determine whether it should be called a lizard or a bird.

Fig. 108.—Woodpecker (Houtou).

The birds now living are divided into several orders according to their modes of life, and the adaptation of their forms to them. First, the wading-birds, or **Grallatores**, which have very long, naked legs, and long, straight toes, adapted for walking about in shallow water, such as herons and storks. Next we have the swimming-birds, or **Natatores,** such as ducks and geese, which have toes connected by means of a membrane, and very short legs placed very far back, so that the bird is very awkward on land, but well adapted for rapid swimming. The next order are the scratching birds, or **Rasores,** fowls, pigeons, pheasants, &c., which have strong feet with blunt

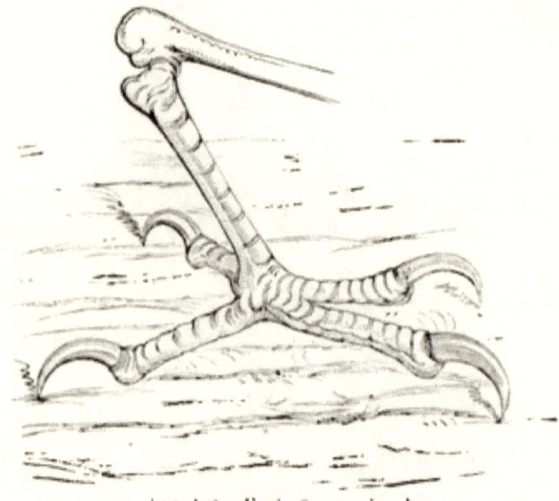

Fig. 109.— Foot of a woodpecker.

claws, suitable for scratching the ground in search of food.

Next, we have the **Scansores,** or climbing-birds, like parrots and woodpeckers, which have two toes turned backwards and two forwards, so as to fit the bird for laying hold of and clinging to the bark of a tree-stem. Then come the perching-birds, or **Insessores,** such as the linnet and nightingale, having

INSESSORES—RAPTORES. 211

three toes in front, and one behind, adapting the foot for perching on a branch. The next order, **Raptores**, or birds of prey, such as the eagle and vulture

Fig. 116.—Catching bird.

have strong legs, with three toes in front, and one behind, armed with sharp crooked claws. Their beak is also sharp and curved, so as to be fitted for killing and tearing up the small animals which serve them for food. The last order is that of the running-birds, or **Cursores**, such as the ostrich, in which the wings are no longer fitted for the purpose of flight. The legs, on the contrary, are large, strong, and well-developed, so as to fit the animal for running.

FIG. 111.—Vulture.

The other parts of the skeleton also become modified. The bones, unlike those of other birds, have few air-cells; and the wings, being no longer required for flight, do not need powerful muscles to move them. Consequently, the projecting ridge or keel, so well marked on the sternum of other birds, and which serves in them as a point of attachment for the wing

PECULIARITIES OF CURSORES.

muscles, is absent in the Cursores. In the rhea or American ostrich there are three toes, but in the African ostrich they are reduced to two on each foot. The feathers, too, are different from those of other birds. Instead of presenting that well-known remark-

Fig. 112.—Ostriches.

able structure, which gives the feathers of other birds such lightness, elasticity, and strength, and adapts them for the purposes of flight, the feathers of the Cursores are loose and somewhat hair-like, the barbs being unconnected by barbules.

LECTURE XII.

GENERAL SKETCH OF THE ANIMAL KINGDOM—WARM-BLOODED ANIMALS—MAMMALS.

We now come to the last division of the Vertebrata, viz., the **Mammalia**, or animals which suckle their young. It is this particular property of suckling their young with milk secreted by a special gland in the mother's body, which serves to distinguish the mammalia from all other animals.

The skin is always more or less covered with hair. The skull is joined to the spine by two condyles, as in the frog and other amphibia, and not by a single one as in reptiles and birds. The lower jaw is also jointed directly with the skull, without the intervention of a quadrate bone, and it consists of only two pieces united in front. In the kind of joint between the skull and the spine, the mammals remind us of amphibia.

In the circulation, however, they differ entirely from fishes, amphibia, and reptiles, but agree with birds.

The heart consists, in both mammals and birds, of four chambers, two auricles, and two ventricles; but mammals differ from birds in having blood-corpuscles destitute of nuclei, and in the nature of their respiratory apparatus.

The lungs in mammals no longer extend, as in birds, through both chest and belly, nor do they communicate with air cavities in the bones or other parts of the body. They are confined entirely to the chest, and this cavity is separated from the belly by a muscular partition called the diaphragm or midriff.

The members of the lowest order of mammals resemble birds in the possession of a cloaca, or common sac, into which the intestine and the ducts leading from the kidneys and generative organs all open. These animals also have no teeth, but one of them, the ornithorhynchus, has a kind of beak like that of the duck, and its feet are webbed so as to allow it to swim with ease. From the fact that the intestinal and all other ducts all open by one common aperture instead of several, the animals have received the name of **Monotremata**.

In the next order, that of the **Marsupials** or pouched animals, to which the kangaroos and opossums belong, the young are brought forth in an exceedingly imperfect condition, and they are placed by the mother in a pouch, or marsupium, upon the belly, within which her mammæ are situated. These have a distinct nipple, but the young do not obtain the milk by the exercise of sucking, which is spared to them by the milk being forced out of the

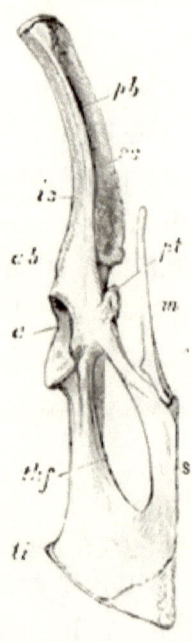

Fig. 113. Ventral surface of innominate bone of kangaroo (*Macropus major*). *si*, supra-iliac border; *sa*, sacral surface; *is*, iliac surface; *ab*, acetabular border; *pb*, pubic border of ilium; *pt*, pectineal tubercle; *a*, acetabulum; *thf*, thyroid foramen; *ti*, tuberosity of ischium; *s*, symphysis; *m*, "marsupial" bone.

nipples into their mouths by a muscle which covers the mammæ. In front of the belly are two bones, which project upwards, and are supposed to be partly intended to support the marsupium, or pouch, though this can hardly be the only reason for their presence, as they are present also in the monotremata, which have no pouch.

Neither the monotremata nor marsupials have any provision for the prolonged nutriment and growth of the young within the womb of the mother, and consequently they are brought forth in an imperfect condition. In all the remaining orders of mammalia, on the contrary, a provision of this sort is made in the presence of a structure called the placenta, by which the young are attached to the mother's womb, and draw from her the nutriment necessary for their growth and development. The higher orders of mammalia are therefore called **Placental**, while from the absence of this structure in the monotremata and marsupials, they are classed together as **Aplacental**.

The two divisions of mammalia into aplacental and placental have been further subdivided into fourteen orders, which are here given in a tabular form:—

Division A.—Aplacentalia.
 Order 1.—*Monotremata*.
  ,, 2.—*Marsupialia*.

Division B.—Placentalia.
 Order 3.—*Edentata*.
  ,, 4.—*Ungulata*.

MAMMALIA—EDENTATA.

Order 5.—*Hyracordia.*
„ 6.—*Proboscidea.*
„ 7.—*Sirenia.*
„ 8.—*Cetacea.*
„ 9.—*Carnivora.*
„ 10.—*Rodentia.*
„ 11.—*Cheiroptera.*
„ 12.—*Insectivora.*
„ 13.—*Quadrumana.*
„ 14.—*Bimana.*

The first order of the placental mammals is that of the ant-eaters, armadillos, and sloths. In these the teeth are imperfect, having no hard covering of enamel, and no proper roots. They also have only one set of teeth, and not two, as the other orders have. In most of them, too, the incisors, or cutting teeth, are absent, and the order has received the name of **Edentata** or **Bruta**.

The **Teeth** in mammals are important not merely on account of their utility to the animal, but to the naturalist, as a means of distinguishing between different orders and families. They are really developed from the skin, and consist of a root or fangs which enter into the jaw and fix the teeth in position, and of a crown which is used for cutting or grinding the food. The crown is composed of a peculiar substance called dentine, covered by a very hard enamel. There are generally two sets of teeth, one succeeding the other, the first being called the milk or deciduous teeth, because they fall out after the animal has attained a certain age, and the second set, called the permanent teeth because, having replaced the others, they remain during the animal's life. There are three

Fig. 44.—Great anteater.

kinds of teeth, one for cutting, called the incisors, one for tearing, called the canines, and the third for grinding, called premolars and molars. The premolars are situated near the front of the mouth, and also appear at an earlier age than the molars. The incisors are wedge-shaped, and are situated in the front of the mouth. They vary much in number. At either side of them is situated a single canine tooth, two in either jaw. These are sometimes called eyeteeth. They are conical in shape, longer than the others, and form most powerful weapons of offence and defence in those animals who have them highly developed, as the dog, from which they take their name. Behind these come the premolars and molars, or back teeth, which also vary considerably in number. In animals which live upon flesh, the grinding surfaces of the molars are more or less divided into sharp prominences or cusps, which cut the flesh up, whereas in herbivora the grinding surfaces of the molars are more or less flattened or covered with elongated ridges suitable for grinding vegetable food.

The next order, that of the **Ungulata**, or hoofed animals, is a very large one, and one of the most important of all, for it comprises most of the animals which are useful to man. They are distinguished by having the extremities of all their four limbs covered by a horny casing.

In some, as in the horses, there is only one horny toe; in tapirs and rhinoceroses there are three, and these animals are classed together as **Perissodactyla**, or odd-toed ungulates.

In the pig, hippopotamus, ox, camel, &c., the toes are either two or four, and these form the order of **Artiodactyla**, or even-toed ungulates.

DIVISIONS OF UNGULATA.

As this order is so large it may be well to put its subdivisions in a tabular form:—

ORDER—UNGULATA.

SECTION A.—PERISSODACTYLA.

    Group 1.—*Tapirs.*
        „ 2.—*Rhinoceroses.*
        „ 3.—*Horses.*

SECTION B.—ARTIODACTYLA.

    Group 4.—*Swine.*
        „ 5.—*Hippopotami.*
        „ 6.—*Ruminants* $\begin{cases} Oxen. \\ Deer. \end{cases}$

The tapirs may be looked upon as the connecting link between the two sections of **Perissodactyla** and **Artiodactyla**, for they have four toes on each of the fore-feet, and only three on the hind-feet. In external appearance they remind one of a large pig, but they have a long, flexible snout, which they use in stripping off the foliage of trees, or in picking up grass and herbs. They are natives of warm countries, and, like the hippopotamus, spend a great part of their time in the water. In the rhinoceros, each foot is furnished with three toes, and the large and heavy body is cased in a skin of great thickness and hardness, which is sometimes thrown into deep folds on the animal's shoulders and loins. The upper lip is shorter than in the tapir, but is still

Fig. 115.—African black rhinoceros.

long and flexible, and is also used for gathering leaves or grass.

In the horse there is only one toe, although on each fore-leg the traces of two others may be observed in the form of horny excrescences upon the skin. Its external form, unlike that of the rhinoceros or tapir, is exceedingly elegant, and the upper lip is not elongated, although very flexible and capable of great protrusion. The horse may be looked upon as more highly developed or specialized than the rhinoceros and tapir, and, consequently, in passing from this group to other groups of the order, we must follow the same course that we have taken in passing from one great subdivision of the animal kingdom to another, and look for the connecting link in their lower forms.

In external appearance the horse is quite unlike the hippopotamus, but the latter is not so unlike the tapir. Both of them are covered with thick skin, they resemble one another somewhat in the form of the body, and both pass a great deal of their time in the water. The hippopotamus, however, has a large, broad head, with a very slightly movable upper lip, while that of the tapir ends in a snout, and is provided with an elongated movable upper lip.

In the number of toes also the horse is unlike the hippopotamus, the horse having only one, while the hippopotamus has four toes on each foot. Between the horse and hippopotamus, however, we find intermediate forms in the tapirs and swine. The tapir has four toes on the fore-foot and three on the hind-foot. Amongst swine we find generally four toes on both hind and fore feet, but only two of them are used in walking, and two are small, and placed too high up the leg to be of much practical use; and in the swine, as in the tapir, we sometimes find the number of toes on the hind-foot reduced to three.

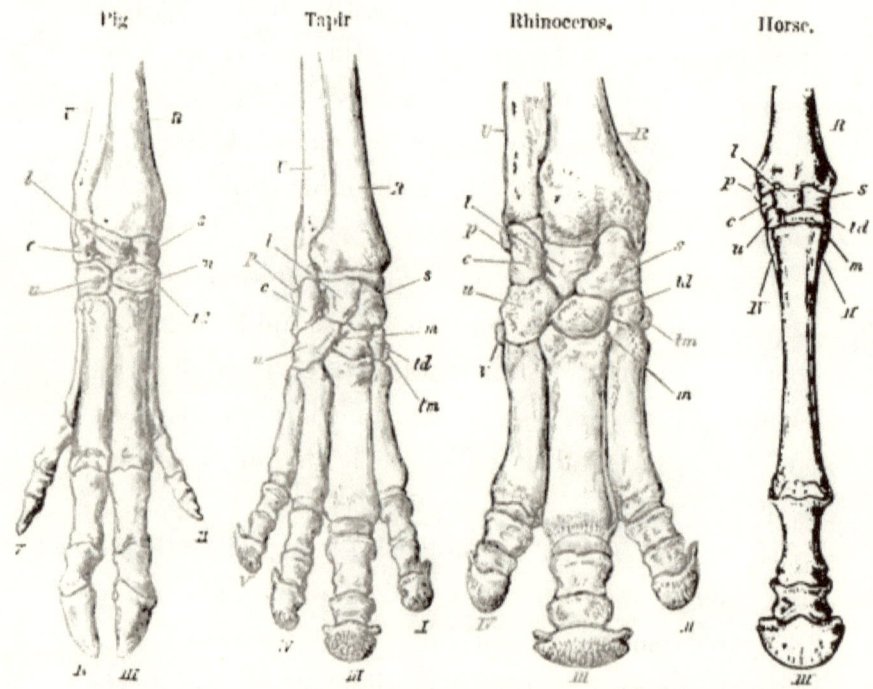

Fig. 116.—Bones of the manus of pig, tapir, rhinoceros, and of horse. The letter in all are the same as in fig. 85, page 169. U, ulna; R. radius; s, scaphoid; td, trapezoid; tm, trapezium; m, magnum; u, uncinate; c, cuneiform; p, pisiform; l, lunar. I, II, III, IV, V, indicate the digits.

In the next group of the even-toed ungulates, namely, **Ruminants**, comprising oxen, deer, &c., there are two large toes on each foot, which look as if they had been originally one, and had become divided or cloven, but generally there are also, as in the swine, two smaller toes at the back part of the foot, and above the others. The group to which the oxen belong, although it resembles pigs in the appearance of the foot, differs

Fig. 117. - Foot of deer.

from them in the digestive apparatus—a distinction which was used by Moses to mark out the pigs as unclean and not to be eaten, but the oxen as clean and valuable for food. In the pig there is only one simple stomach, while in the ox there are no less than four. The first of these is a large bag termed the paunch or

Q

rumen, into which the grass and other food of the animal first passes without being chewed. After a sufficient quantity has been collected the animal stops feeding and lies down quietly, and then proceeds to bring up the grass again from the paunch in small quantities at a time. To enable the animal to do this, the grass

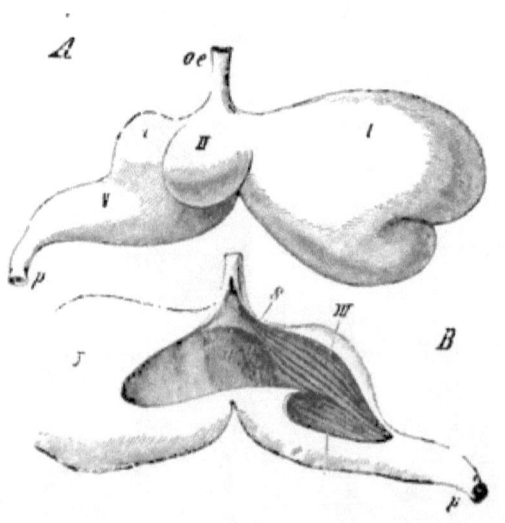

Fig. 118.—Stomach of an antelope. *A*, from in front; *B*, opened from behind; *oe*, œsophagus; *I*, paunch or rumen; *II*, reticulum; *III*, fiber or psalterium; *IV*, abomasum; *p*, pylorus; *s*, œsophageal groove.

or food is not thrown up directly from the paunch but is passed into a second small stomach, the reticulum, so called from the net-like folds of its mucous membrane. In this stomach the food is made up into small pellets, and then forced upwards into the mouth; there it is thoroughly chewed and swallowed a second

HORNS OF RUMINANTS. 227

time. It now passes neither into the paunch nor reticulum, but into the third stomach, liber (psalterium) or manyplies, so called from the numerous folds, rudely resembling the leaves of a book, into which the mucous membrane lining its interior is thrown. Then it passes into the fourth or true stomach, where

Fig. 119.—Section of cow's horn.

it is finally digested. This process is termed rumination, or chewing the cud. Most ruminants have horns. In some of them, as oxen, sheep, goats, and antelopes, they consist of a bony core, covered by a hollow horny sheath. In deer the horns are entirely bony, and generally branched. They usually fall off, and are reproduced every year. In the giraffes the horns are very short and are entirely covered with a hairy skin. In camels the horns are entirely absent, and the feet have no horny sheaths, but only two toes with very imperfect hoofs.

The **Hyracoidea** is a small order containing the coney mentioned by Solomon. This interesting animal is about the size of a rabbit, and its teeth resemble on the one hand those of the rhinoceros, and on the other those of the rodents, such as the rat and the rabbit.

In the next order, that of the **Proboscidea**, the feet are large and flat, and the five toes are only indicated by the number of nails which are arranged around the foot. The skin is thick, the body heavy, and the nose much more elongated, flexible, and strong than in the tapir, forming a cylindrical tube or trunk, at the end of which the nostrils are placed. They have no canine teeth, and very few molars, but these are exceedingly large. There are no lower incisors, but the two upper incisors are very thick and long, and form the well-known tusks of the elephant.

Elephants and rhinoceroses enjoy living in water. Tapirs and hippopotami live more in water than upon land.

The next order, the **Sirenia**, is comprised of animals which are adapted entirely for a watery existence, and unfit for life upon land at all. The order embraces dugongs and manatees, often known as sea-cows. In external appearance they have an elongated fish-like form, but their skin is not covered with scales. The anterior limbs are converted into paddles; the hind limbs are completely absent, and the hinder end of the body is converted into a bifurcated tail, in shape resembling that of a fish, but placed horizontally, and not vertically. In these particulars they resemble the whales, but their nostrils are placed a little further forward instead of being at the crown of the head, and the mouth is furnished with large molar teeth with flat crowns, adapted for grinding vegetable food. They frequent the mouths of large rivers, such as the Amazon, and feed upon the grass and water-plants growing in the water near their banks.

The animals of the next order, the **Cetacea**, resemble the Sirenia in appearance but are more fish-like. Among them are whales, dolphins, and porpoises. The back is sometimes furnished with a dorsal fin. The nostrils are placed in the very top of the head, which is closely joined to the body, and extremely large, and no distinct neck can be seen. They feed upon animal food; some of them, such as the dolphin and sperm whale, have conical teeth, but the Greenland whale has no teeth at all in an adult condition, although when young it has teeth, which, however, never appear through the gums. Instead of them it has plates of a substance called whalebone, which form a sort of fringe to the mouth. This large animal feeds chiefly upon jelly-fishes, which are caught and retained in the mouth by the whalebone, as in a net.

Fig. 120.—Fore-limb of young dolphin, showing how the bones are modified to form the so-called fin. *s*, scapula; *h*, humerus; *r*, radius; *u*, ulna; *c*, carpus; *m*, meta-carpus; *p*, phalanges.

The next order is that of the **Carnivora**, or beasts of prey, which live almost entirely upon other animals. Their teeth are suited for the purpose of killing and tearing up their victims. They have generally six incisors in each jaw, the canines are always four in number, two in each jaw, and they are very long and strong. The molars have generally sharp edges for cutting up the flesh on which they feed, their feet are also provided with claws, which are usually sharp and

SUBDIVISIONS OF THE CARNIVORA.

enable the animal readily to lay hold of its prey. The order is divided into three groups; the first is that of the Digitigrade animals, such as cats and dogs, so called because they walk upon their toes. Weasels and otters do so likewise, but they also put a part of the sole of

Fig. 121.—Polecat.

the foot to the ground, and thus form an intermediate link between the Digitigrade and the next group, the Plantigrade, such as bears which apply the whole of the sole to the ground in walking. The third group, or the Pinnigrade, contains those carnivora, such as seals and walruses, which live in the water, and are fitted by their external form for their mode of life, their hind feet being placed far back, and nearly in a line with the body, so that they serve the same purpose as the tail-fin of a fish.

We now come to the next order, the **Rodentia**. In all the orders yet considered, the placenta forms a band around the uterus, but in those we have now to consider it forms simply a disc.

In both vegetable and animal kingdoms, when we

want to find out the affinities of different groups, we must take them in their early or embryonic, and not in

Fig. 122.—Rat.

their fully-developed states. Thus, in classifying plants we pay much less attention to the size of the plant or the shape of its leaves than to the arrangement of the parts in the flower; and some of the most important characters in classification are the nature of the ovary and the position of the embryo in the ovule.

In classifying animals similar importance is given to embryonic characters, so that, as we have already seen, animals are divided into two great groups according to the presence or absence of the placenta; and, from its shape in the rodents, the rabbit is classed as nearer to monkeys than the dog.

The rodentia, or gnawing animals, derive their name from their habits, for which they are well adapted by the shape of their teeth. They never have any canine teeth, but the incisors are of a peculiar structure. They are not equally hard throughout, the front being formed of hard enamel, while the back part is of much softer dentine. They spring from a soft pulp in the jaw of the animal, and grow continuously during the whole of its life. In the act of gnawing, the friction of the hard wood or other substance wears down the soft dentine more than it does the hard enamel, and thus a sharp, cutting edge is always maintained in front, and the more the animal gnaws, the sharper does this ridge grow.

The next order, **Cheiroptera**, or bats, are distinguished by the enormous elongation of four of their fingers; these support a leathery membrane, which is always attached to the hind-legs and the sides of the animal's body, and by means of which they are able to fly about with ease.

The next order, the **Insectivora,** comprises moles and hedgehogs. They resemble the rodents in many respects, but differ from them in the nature of their teeth, canines being present, and the incisors not

FIG. 123.—Hedgehogs.

presenting the peculiarity which we have noted in the rodents. One would think that no difficulty should be experienced in saying whether an animal belonged to the tribe of the hedgehog, of the bat, or of the monkey, and yet there is one, called the flying lemur, regarding which naturalists have had much discussion, some classing it as allied to one, and some to another of these animals. It has a membrane stretching from the neck to the arms, legs, and tail, and this is not sufficient to allow it to fly, but only enables it to make very long leaps from branch to branch.

The next order is that of the **Quadrumana**, or four-handed animals, containing lemurs, baboons, monkeys, and apes. They are distinguished by the power of opposing, as it is termed, the thumb and great toe to the rest of the fingers or toes, so as to take a firm grasp of any object. The meaning of this term is most readily understood by laying one's hand upon the table or floor, and resting upon it. The thumb will then be seen to lie side by side with the fingers, like the toes in the paw of an animal; but if we now lay hold of any object, the thumb will be seen not merely to move away from the other fingers, but to be drawn backwards and inwards towards the palm of the hand, so that it comes to be opposed to the other fingers instead of being alongside of them. This power is markedly possessed by the thumb in man, but it is almost lost in the great toe, at least in civilised nations. The Hindoos, however, are said to be able to take up small objects from the ground with their feet, and certain acrobats are believed to be able to grasp a tight rope with the foot almost as well as with the hand. In children, the power of opposing the toe is very much more marked than in the adult, as may be noticed when a child's feet are being warmed before the fire. The toes are then spread out in a fan-like manner, and the great toe will be seen to perform the movement of opposition much more perfectly than in the adult.

Fig. 124.—Monkey.

The quadrumana are divided into three sections, distinguished by the position of the nostrils. The first section, or **Strepsirhina**, containing lemurs and lories, have the nostrils twisted, and placed at the end of the nose. The next section, or **Platyrhina**, have simple nostrils placed widely apart. The thumbs are generally wanting, or, if present, have not the power of opposition, and the tail is generally prehensile, so as almost to serve the purpose of another hand. In the third section, **Catarhina,** the nostrils are close together, and both thumbs and great toes have the power of opposition. The tail is never prehensile, and is sometimes absent altogether. There are several families in this section, the first being that of the macaques, so well known to us from being carried about our streets by organ-grinders. The next is that of the baboons, in which there is no tail, or only a very short one; but the head is very large and elongated, and the fore-feet are used more as paws for running upon than in the other families. The next family is that of the anthropoid apes, so called from their resemblance to man; this tribe contains the gibbons, chimpanzees, ourang-outangs, and gorillas.

LECTURE XIII.

GENERAL SKETCH OF THE ANIMAL KINGDOM—MAN.

THE first difference that strikes one between man and the anthropoid apes is, that man walks upright and securely, while the apes walk in a bent posture, and insecurely upon their hind-legs. The difference in skeleton corresponds to this. In man the pelvic bones are much more spread out than in the ape, so that he gets a much firmer basis of support. The bones of the leg are also more developed, the joints of the knee are much firmer, and the feet are placed so that the sole comes more or less flatly upon the ground, while those of apes' have the soles turned inwards, so that they are obliged to walk more or less upon the outside of the feet. This position of the foot in apes is advantageous for prehension, but unsuited for walking. It may be noted, however, that even in man this peculiarity is present to a greater or less extent. Many people wear away the outside of the heel and sole of the boot more than the inner part, and in infants this position of the foot, like the power of opposing the great toe, is much more marked than in the adult. For in the child warming its feet before the fire, the soles may be seen to be almost opposed to one another, as they are in apes.

Another marked difference is the size and form of the skull. The upper part of it, which contains the brain, is much smaller in apes than in man, whereas the jaws are enormously large and powerful as compared with his, the lower part of the face projects much, and the bony ridges for the attachment of the muscles of the jaw are very prominent. The canine teeth, too, in some of them, as in the gorilla, are very large and strong, forming a powerful weapon of offence.

It is not in his bodily form, however, but in his mental characteristics, that the difference between man and the ape is most striking. As the brain is the organ of the mind, we would naturally expect that the brain of man would differ very much from the brain of the ape; this is not the case, however, to anything like the extent we should imagine. The cerebral lobes are no doubt larger in man, and the furrows which mark them externally are deeper and more complicated, but still the general arrangement of these furrows is much the same in man and apes. It varies also in man; the furrows, or sulci, as they are called, and the intervening

240   SKULL AND BRAIN.

ridges, or gyri, being more complicated in the higher races of man than in the lower; which are, in this respect, intermediate between men and apes. But no

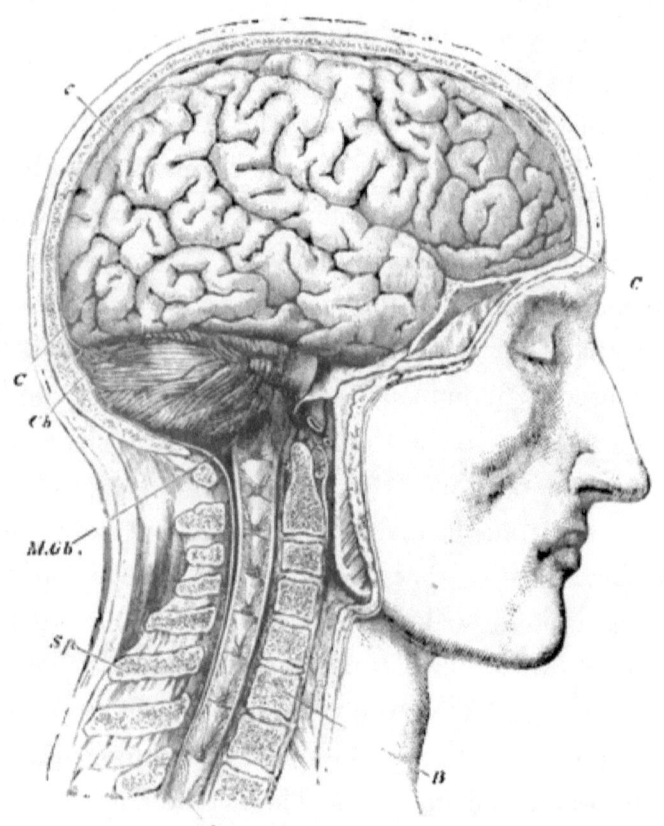

Fig. 125.—Convolutions of the brain.

doubt these complicated gyri of the brain in men are only the external indications of a structure which our present means of investigation have not yet completely succeeded in elucidating. They are simply like the case of a clock, which may contain either the simplest mechanism, or the most complicated contrivance which it is possible for man to devise.

The fundamental differences in the acts of men which distinguish them from all the lower animals, have been said to be the power of cooking and the power of drawing. Man is the only animal able to light a fire, and man is the only animal capable of indicating his thoughts to his fellows, either by pictorial representations or by written signs. Other animals are able to communicate with each other by a language of their own, and although the ideas they thus convey may be few and simple, yet the method by which they do convey them seems quite as intelligible to them as our language is to us. But none of them, even the most highly developed, can draw a figure, or write a line, whereas some of the lowest tribes of mankind, such as the Bushmen, draw figures with considerable accuracy, and group them together so that their fellows who come afterwards may understand the history or train of ideas which the draughtsman meant to communicate.

Even in the early stages of the world, while men were still unacquainted with the use of metals and used implements of unpolished stone, they were able to draw pictures with no little artistic skill, as we see from the sketch of a battle between rein-deer scratched by one of them with a flint upon a slab of slate (Fig. 126).

The differences in appearance and anatomical structure between man and the highest anthropoid apes, are not nearly so great as between these apes and the lemurs. But in mental power there is a wide, impassable gulf between man and the highest apes, however

Fig. 126.—Sketch of a battle between reindeer.

much they may resemble him physically. Great are the differences between the civilised Englishman on the one hand, and the barbarous Australian or Bushman on the other, but they are not so fundamental as those between the lowest man and the highest ape. The words of Scripture are, "God made of one blood all nations upon the earth," and, great as may be the differences between them, we must regard them as springing from one common stock and migrating from one common centre. It is therefore of extreme interest, not only to observe the points in which they agree and those in which they differ, but also to try as far as possible to discover in what way they have spread from a common centre over the whole of the inhabited globe.

One of the great causes of the migration of man is scarcity of food, as we have already seen exemplified in the migration of the Jews into Egypt, and may see constantly going on in the present day. The want of corn in the land caused the Israelites to migrate into Egypt, where they could readily get it, and the want of money wherewith to buy it causes men at the present day to emigrate to America, Australia, or New Zealand, where, land being plentiful and men scarce, a livelihood can be more easily obtained than amongst the dense population and struggling masses of the mother country. But after a race has emigrated and settled in a new land, the population rapidly increases, as we can now see in the Western States of America, and by and by the land becomes too small for them, and new swarms leave their homes, and go off to other countries as their forefathers did. During this time, however, the population of the original parent home, although lessened by the emigration of the first swarm, has gone on increasing, and after a while a second swarm follows the first and is not unlikely to settle, or attempt to settle, in the same country. Here, however, they find the land already more or less occupied by the descendants of the first swarm, and with them they must combat for its possession. The consequence is usually a bloody war, in which the second swarm is either beaten by the first, and driven back to the country whence it came, or it proves more powerful than its antagonists, and after defeating them, occupies their country. It may either drive many of them out to seek an easier existence in other lands, where the same war may be repeated, or it may drive them up into parts of the country which are not easily accessible, such as mountainous ranges. Or, finally, great numbers of both races having fallen in the struggle, the survivors may make up their minds to live amicably together, and may possibly found a new race.

The various races of man have been divided according to the nature of their hair, the colour of their skin, the formation of the skull, and the size of the jaws. In some races the skull is longer than it is broad, and these are called long-headed, or **Dolichocephali**; in others it is broader than it is long, and these are called short-headed men, or **Brachycephali**. In others, the form of the head is between these extremes, and these are called medium-headed, or **Meso-cephali**. The most marked examples of the long-headed class are

Negroes and Australians, while the Chinese and Tartars are types of the short-headed men; the Red Indians are between the two.

Men have also been divided into those with projecting teeth, or **Prognathi**, and those with straight teeth, or **Orthognathi**; but these two forms are found combined with every form of skull, so that men may thus be divided into six types.

It is found more convenient, however, to divide them, not according to the form of the skull, or projection of the jaw, but according to the nature of the hair. Men may thus be divided into two groups,— those with woolly hair, the **Ulotrichi**, in which each hair, when cut across, presents an oval section, and has therefore a disposition to curl, like the wool of a sheep; and **Lissotrichi**, in which the hairs are cylindrical, so that they present a circular section; and the hairs are consequently more or less straight, and they are therefore called straight-haired men. Amongst the lissotrichi the hair may sometimes become frizzled and curly, but is never actually woolly.

Woolly-haired men, or **Ulotrichi**, are further subdivided into two groups, the **Lophocomi** and **Eriocomi**, according as their hair grows in tufts, or covers the head entirely.

There are two tribes of tuft-haired men, or **Lophocomi**, the Papuans and Hottentots; the former inhabit New Guinea, and the islands lying near it, and formerly occupied the island of Van Diemen's Land, or Tasmania, although now they are extinct there, having vanished before the white man in the same way that the natives of New Zealand and Australia are now disappearing. There are also a few isolated groups of Papuans to be found in the peninsula of Malacca, and also in some of the mountainous parts of other islands of the Malayan Archipelago. This indicates that they formerly lived over a much larger area, whence they have been driven by another race, just as the Maori and American Indians have been driven into mere corners of the countries which they once roamed over. The Papuans are black, with low, narrow foreheads, large turned-up noses, and thick, protruding lips.

The Hottentots and Bushmen, like the Papuans, have tufted hair, but their skin is much lighter in colour, being yellowish-brown, and the nose is small, with large, dilated nostrils.

The next two groups of woolly-haired men, Kaffirs and Negroes, have the hair covering the whole head like a fleece, and are therefore called fleecy-haired, **Eriocomi.**

The Kaffirs are very widely distributed over Africa, and their colour, as might be expected, varies very much, from yellowish-black to pure black. The face, instead of being broad and flat, is long and narrow; the forehead high, the nose prominent, and the lips do not project very greatly.

The Negro tribe was formerly supposed to include a great number of varieties which are now classed with the Kaffirs and Hottentots, and the term is now limited to the races which live around the eastern and southern parts of the great desert of Sahara, and the west coast of Africa between the Equator and the tropic of Capricorn. The skin is pure black, oily, and velvety, and emits a strong, disagreeable odour. The forehead is low, the nose broad, and the lips very large and protruding. Their arms are long, and the calves of their legs very thin.

The group of straight-haired men, or **Lissotrichi**, is larger and more important than that of the Ulotrichi. It contains eight tribes, in five of which the hair is more or less stiff (**Euthycomi**), and in three somewhat curly (**Euplocomi**).

The stiff-haired tribes, or **Euthycomi**, are the Australians, the Malays, the Mongols, the Polar men, and the Red Indians.

The Australians, or Austral Negroes, somewhat resemble true negroes in appearance, having black skins, an offensive odour, long and narrow skull, projecting jaw, protruding lips, broad nose, and receding forehead, and also in the want of calves; but they are much

RACES

Ulotrichi or woolly-haired men.	Lophocomi, or tuft-haired.	Papuans. Hottentots.
	Eriocomi, or fleece-haired.	Kaffirs. Negroes.
Lissotrichi or straight-haired men.	Euthycomi, or stiff-haired.	Australians. Malays. Mongols . . . Polar men . Red Indians.
	Euplocomi, or curly-haired.	Dravidas. Nubians . . . Mediterranean . .

OF MAN.

Chinese.
Tartars.
Finns.
Turks.
Hungarians.

Esquimaux.
Greenlanders.
Hyperboreans.

Nubians.
Foulahs.

Basques.
Caucasian.

Semitic.
- Egyptians.
- Assyrians.
- Jews.
- Arabs.

Indo-Germanic.
- Aryo-Romanic.
  - Indians.
  - Persians.
  - Greeks.
  - Romans.
- Sclavo-Germanic.
  - Sclaves.
  - Goths.
  - Scandinavians.
  - Germans.
  - Norsemen.
  - English.
  - Americans.

smaller and weaker, and their hair is either lank, or slightly curled, and not at all woolly.

The Malays are a much higher race than the Australian. They are widely spread over Malacca, the islands near it, and the greater portion of the Pacific Islands. Their hair is black, their skin generally brown, though varying from a yellowish to a dark colour; their heads, instead of being long, like those of the Australians, are generally short, though medium and long heads are also found among them. The face is generally broad, the nose projecting, and the lips thick. The eyes are somewhat slanting—but less so than in the Mongols—and larger, in which respect they more resemble the Mediterranese.

The Mongol race is distinguished by the yellow colour of the skin, stiff black hair, narrow, slanting eyes, short head, broad face, prominent cheek-bones, and thick lips. It includes the Chinese, Tartars, and indeed the inhabitants of the whole of Asia with the exception of its north-east point, the Malay peninsula, and a considerable portion of the southern part of the continent. The parts just mentioned are inhabited by the Mediterranese, but the Mongols, on the other hand, extend over a good part of the north of Europe. The Finns and Lapps of Scandinavia and Russia, the Osmanlis of Turkey, and the Magyars of Hungary, are Mongols.

The Polar men are considered by Haeckel, from whom this description of the races of men is taken, to be a branch of the Mongols. This tribe includes the inhabitants of the Arctic Polar lands of both hemispheres, the Esquimaux and Greenlanders in America, and the Hyperboreans in north-east Asia. Like the Mongols they have narrow slanting eyes, prominent cheek bones, and wide mouths, black hair, and skin which is yellowish or brown, but sometimes inclines to red. Their stature is low and square, and their skulls medium or long.

The Aborigines of America, called from the more or less coppery tint of their skin, Red Indians, have, like the Mongols, prominent cheek bones; but the nose is large, prominent, and often aquiline, and their lips are rather thin than thick. Their skull is generally medium, being rarely either short or long.

In all these tribes of Lissotrichi the beard is either scanty or absent altogether, but in the next three groups it is well developed, and the hair has a tendency to curl more or less, instead of being completely lank or stiff, as in the tribes already described. They are therefore classed together as curly-haired men (**Euplocomi**). The three tribes in this class are the Dravidas, the Nubians, and the Mediterranese.

The first tribe—the Dravidas—is very limited in its distribution, inhabiting only the Deccan in Southern

Hindostan, and the mountains in the north-east of Ceylon. It is supposed by Häeckel to be very closely related to the primary form of curly-haired man, and perhaps even to the primary form of the whole race of Lissotrichi. "On the one hand," he says, "it is related to the Australians and Malays, and on the other to the Mongols and Mediterranese. Their skin is either of a light or dark-brown colour, in some tribes of a yellowish-brown, in others almost black-brown. The hair of their heads, as in the Mediterranese, is more or less curly, neither quite smooth as in the Euthocomi, nor actually woolly like that of the Ulotrichi. The strong development of a beard is also like that of the Mediterranese; the oval form of face seems to be partly akin to that of the Malays, partly to that of the Mediterranese. Their forehead is generally high, their nose prominent and narrow, their lips slightly protruding."

The next tribe is that of the Nubians, including the real Nubians who inhabit the countries of the Upper Nile, and the Foulahs who have migrated to the westward, and now live to the south-west of the Sahara. Their skin is yellowish or reddish-brown, their hair curly, but never woolly, their beard strongly developed, their faces oval, with high and broad foreheads, prominent noses, and thick, but not projecting lips.

The last tribe is the most important of all—the Caucasian, or, as it is now more generally called, Mediterranean; the shores of this inland sea having been the chief scene of their activity. The skin is light, though varying much in shade, the hair thick, and more or less curly, the beard well developed. The skull is large and wide, the head is neither broad nor long, but medium, though both short and long heads are frequent.

It is this race which has made the history of the world. The Mongolian Chinese have records stretching far back into antiquity, perhaps farther back than any records of the Mediterranese, and Mongolian irruptions have from time to time immensely affected the history of Europe and Asia, but still the records of this race are as nothing compared with those of the higher Mediterranean race.

The Mediterranese are subdivided, according to the nature of their language, into the Basque, Caucasian, Semitic, and Indo-Germanic groups.

The Basques now inhabit only a small portion of the north of Spain, and the Caucasians are likewise pent up in the valleys in and around the range of the Caucasus, but it is probable that at some earlier period they were spread over a much wider district. These two groups, also, have no great historical importance.

The other two groups, the Semitic and Indo-Germanic, are important, both on account of their wide distribution and their history.

To the Semitic races belong the Egyptians, Assyrians, Jews, and Arabs, which must have branched off from one another at a very early date, as the affinities which exist between such languages as the Egyptian and Hebrew are very slight.

The Indo-Germanic branch divided at a very early period into two, the Aryo-Romanic and Sclavo-Germanic.

The Aryo-Romanic was the first to become civilised, and to it belong the Indians, Persians, Greeks, and Romans.

To the Sclavo-Germanic belong the Sclaves, Goths, Scandinavians, Saxons, and their descendants—Germans, Norsemen, English.

The latter race is now foremost in the van of civilisation, and the former, the Aryo-Romanic, although richly gifted, seems at present to be standing still, or making but little progress. The same thing appears to have occurred with other races, for ancient Rome and Greece were both indebted for the germs of their civilisation to the Semitic Phœnicians and Egyptians, but while Greece and Rome rapidly developed, their instructors made almost no advance, and were soon left far behind.

LECTURE XIV.

DISTRIBUTION OF PLANTS AND ANIMALS IN TIME.

At the time when Abraham left Babylonia and went down into Egypt he found there a fully developed civilisation, an established government, arts and manufactures, and all the provisions for comfort and luxury of life as well marked as we now find them in the capitals of modern Europe. And this civilisation was no new one, as we learn from the monuments that it must have existed for more than a thousand years before Abraham entered the country, and possibly for a very much longer time.

We find no trace in Egypt of a gradual development. The civilisation seems to have arisen at once, full fledged, although this could scarcely have been the case, for we know that everywhere else civilisation has been a matter of slow growth requiring long periods for its perfection. In our own country we can trace it backwards from its present condition to the time when great parts of this island were inhabited by men who simply stained their bodies with wood, or went about clad only in the skins of animals, whose weapons and implements were only made of stone, and who were perfectly ignorant of the art of smelting or working in metal. Amongst them, too, we find suddenly starting up a full-grown civilisation, that of ancient Rome, whose troops, urged by the lust of conquest, left their homes in the sunny south to invade the naked hills and the bleak moors of the far north, who tore the barbarians from their families to send them to the wild-beast fights and gladiatorial shows of the Coliseum, and rendered the lives of those who were allowed to remain bitter with hard bondage, but who, after all, more than repaid them for all their sufferings, by the civilisation which they brought to them, and which it would otherwise have taken them ages to acquire.

In such a case as this, where barbarian tribes are invaded and subdued by civilised people, or as at the present day, when English traders visit the South Sea Islands and exchange knives and tools of Sheffield manufacture for fruits and shells, we may find existing together the use of implements of iron and stone.

In most other instances, we find three stages of

STONE AGE—PALEOLITHIC AND NEOLITHIC. 257

civilisation, which are distinguished as the **stone-age**, the **bronze-age**, and the **iron-age**.

The first tools that a man makes are of the very simplest construction. His only weapon is the pebble which he picks up and throws, or the sharp stone which he holds in his hand, and with which he wounds his enemy whether man or beast. He next finds that by striking one stone against another he is able to chip it into a particular form, and give to it a

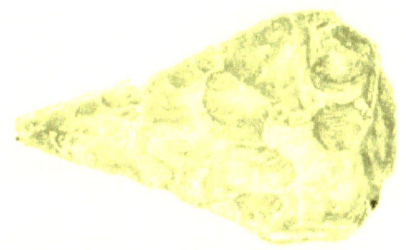

FIG. 127.—Celt or axe head of flint, rudely chipped (Paleolithic).

sharp cutting edge, but yet rough and angular. This period is called the **Paleolithic** or old stone age.

He next attempts to improve the weapon or tool which he has thus obtained by chipping it more finely, and by grinding it smooth; and weapons of this sort are said to belong to the **Neolithic** or new stone age.

After this he acquires a knowledge of the fact that copper, which he finds near the surface of the ground, may be melted and worked so as to form weapons more convenient than those of stone, and may be still further

S

improved by the addition to it of tin. The age, or stage of civilisation, in which this occurs is termed the

Fig. 128.—Lance-head of finely-chipped flint (Neolithic).

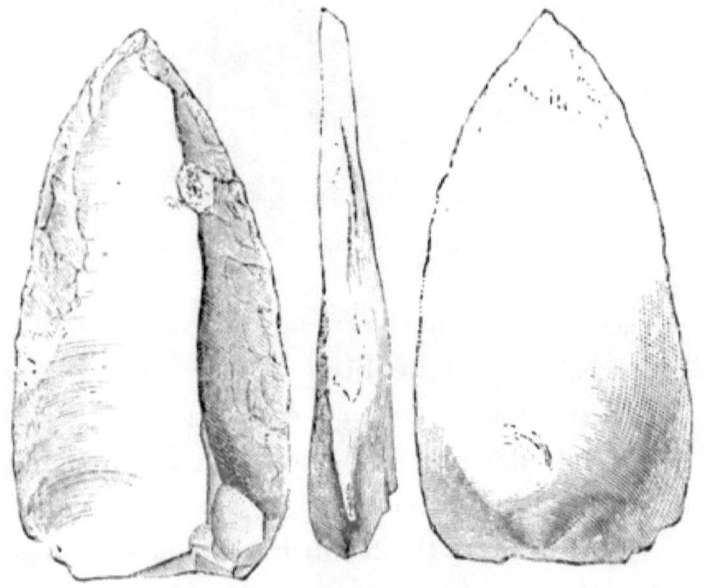

Fig. 129.—A flint lance-point, showing two sides and edge.

Bronze epoch, and not till afterwards is he able to surmount the greater difficulties involved in the smelting

IRON AGE.

and working of iron, which is less easily fused, less easily wrought, but when once manufactured furnishes him with implements immensely superior even to those of bronze.

This stage is called the **Iron epoch**. These three stages of civilisation may all co-exist upon different parts of the earth's surface, and the use of iron, as in the South Sea Islands at the present day, may succeed to the age of stone without the intervention of

Fig. 130.—Celt or axe head of polished stone (Neolithic).

a bronze age; but in former times, when the facilities for intercourse between remote nations were not so great as now, bronze has usually succeeded stone, and bronze has been superseded by iron, the implements of the better sort being gradually introduced, and slowly displacing those of the inferior order.

In ancient Egypt also stone implements were once used, although we have no historical record of the fact from the monuments, and do not know what race it was that employed them. The sudden appearance of a complete civilisation would lead us to believe that the ancient Egyptians whom we know from the Bible, and from the records they have left upon their monuments, were not the original dwellers on the soil, but had, like the Romans in Britain, come from elsewhere and taken possession of the land, destroying or subjugating its former inhabitants. Deep below the surface of the ground, in a well near Cairo, have been found flakes of flint, evidently fashioned by the hand of man. How long ago it is since these chips were struck off from the parent block by one of the savage dwellers in the Egyptian valley, it is impossible to say, but it may have been as far remote from the age of Abraham as his age is from ours.[1] Yet, strange to say, this period of time, immense though it be, is as nothing compared with the age of the world in which we live.

The Egyptian valley, as I have already mentioned, owes its fertility to the rich mud deposited by the Nile. When we walk across the Nile valley, we come, at either side, upon sea sand fringing the base of the hills which inclose it, and spreading away from the edge of the Delta, over the long expanse of the desert, on to the Red Sea. If we were to dig through the Nile mud

---

[1] The use of stone implements in sacred rites continued up to the time of Moses (Exod. iv. 25) in countries adjoining Egypt, if not in Egypt itself. But, notwithstanding this fact, the use of stone implements for the purposes of every-day life may have ceased for centuries, for it is in religious ceremonies that traces of ancient customs survive longest.

GEOLOGY OF EGYPT. 261

we should find that lying underneath it is this same sea sand, so we know that before the mud was deposited,

FIG. 131.—Geological map of Egypt. The Nile mud mentioned in the text is white in the map. The sand (miocene) is indicated by cross hatching. The map is too small to show the fringe of sand at each side of the Nile valley. The nummulitic (Eocene) and Cretaceous limestone is indicated by parallel lines.

the sand was already there. Now sea sand implies a sea, and therefore we conclude that long, long ago, the Nile valley and the desert of the Red Sea were at the bottom of an ocean whose waters were not confined to the narrow limits of the present Mediterranean and Red Seas, but stretched over the whole of ancient Egypt, and probably over the vast expanse of the Sahara also.

But as we walk still onwards towards the steep ridges which inclose the Nile valley, we leave the sand and find underneath it a limestone rock, just as we find the sand underneath the Nile mud. On examining this rock, we notice that it presents regular layers or bands, running horizontally, and that in it are embedded some curious fossils, which are round and flat, like pieces of money, and hence have been called nummulites. Close inspection shows us that these fossils are the calcareous cases of some of those lumps of protoplasm, which we have already learned to know under the name of foraminifera. As we know that these led an oceanic life, they must at one time have been swimming about in the sea, and only have sunk to the bottom after their short life was over. Small as those animals are, the limestone cliffs which their chalky skeletons form, are hundreds of feet high, so that a stupendous period of time must have elapsed before the accumulated remains of successive generations of foraminifera could possibly have built them up.

Here, then, we have evidence of the existence of a primæval ocean which rolled its waves over northern Africa into Asia Minor and across Persia and India on to the borders of China. The upheaved bottom of this ocean formed the cliffs, against which was dashed the spray of that sea whose sand now lies around their foot, and which, gradually receding as the land still rose, allowed the waters of the Nile, as they poured onwards, to deposit, inch by inch, the mud which forms the brown land of Mizraim.

Back, and yet further backwards, from age to age we seem to go, until the mind refuses to grasp the time required for these occurrences. And yet we are still but on the threshold of geological time. For although the time which elapsed between the deposition of these rocks from the waters of the ancient sea, and the first appearance of man upon the globe, was many times greater than that which has elapsed from his appearance until now, yet those strata belong only to the tertiary epoch, as it is termed, of geology.

The immense ages which have been required to give the earth's crust its present form have been divided by geologists into five epochs. The first is the **Archeolithic**, the second the **Paleozoic** or **Primary**, the third the **Mesozoic** or **Secondary**, the fourth the **Cainozoic** or **Tertiary**, and the fifth the **Post-tertiary** or **Recent**.

Each of these again may be subdivided into three.

The **Archeolithic** into the **Laurentian**, **Cambrian**, and **Silurian**.

The **Paleozoic** or **Primary** into the **Old Red Sandstone** or **Devonian**, the **Carboniferous**, and the **Permian**.

The **Secondary** or **Mesozoic** into the **Trias**, **Oolite** or **Jura**, and **Chalk** or **Cretaceous**.

The **Tertiary** into the **Eocene**, **Miocene**, and **Pliocene**.

The **Quaternary** or **Pleistocene** may be divided into **Diluvial**, **Post-Diluvial**, and **Alluvial**.

These divisions by no means represent periods of equal length. If we judge by the thickness of rocks deposited during them, the archeolithic or primordial period alone occupies more than a half, the paleozoic or primary period another third; the mesozoic or secondary period about a tenth; the cainozoic or tertiary period about a fiftieth; and the quaternary period, during which man has existed, only a mere fraction of the whole time required for their deposition.

But these divisions are simply made for the sake of convenience, and it must not be understood that each of them marks any great break in the history of the world.

In each of them, however, we find evidences of life in the presence of fossil remains, and these are of such a character as to show the predominance of certain living forms in each of the divisions before mentioned.

In the **Archeolithic** period we find traces of **seaweeds** and of those low protoplasmic forms of life which we have already found even in the rocks of Egypt, and which still appear at the present day—the **foraminifera** as well as of other invertebrate animals.

In the **Paleozoic** we find higher types, both of vegetables and animals, the characteristic forms being **ferns** and **fishes**.

In the **Secondary** we get yet higher forms, the **gymnosperms** and **reptiles**.

In the **Tertiary** we find **angiosperms** and **mammals**.

In the **Quaternary** we find evidences of the existence of **Man**, either in human bones or in tools or weapons.

These forms of plant and animal life may be looked upon as distinctive of the different periods, but in each of them we also find other forms, which occupy, however, a mere secondary place.

The groups of strata belonging to each epoch, or **formations**, as they are termed, are distinguished from each other, and their ages are determined, by their relative positions, and by the fossils which they contain.

One reason why we believe that one formation is older than another, is simply that we find it lying underneath the other when we drill through them, as in sinking a well or coal-pit, or in cutting a tunnel. The greatest number of these formations consist of sedimentary rocks, or, in other words, of rocks

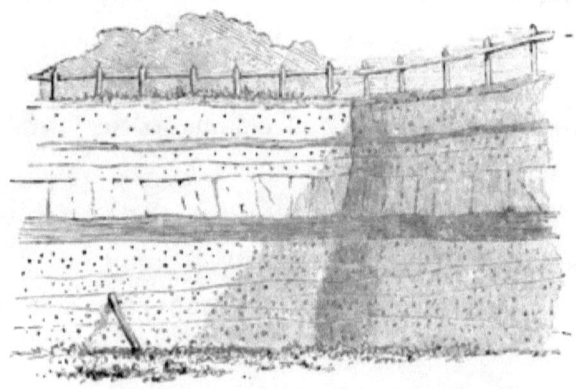

FIG. 132. Quarry in sedimentary rocks.

which have been deposited from water, and when they are lying flat and undisturbed those strata which lie undermost are necessarily the oldest, for otherwise the higher strata could not have been deposited upon them. Sometimes their position is disturbed, and instead of lying horizontally, they may have been forced up by volcanic action into a slanting or perpendicular position, so that the edges of the

DETERMINATION BY POSITION. 267

strata appear on the surface, or crop out, as it is termed. In such cases, as we walk across the country, we find first one kind of stone and then another. We notice the slope at which they lie, and see that one appears to pass under the other, and as we often find,

Fig. 135.—A view of contorted strata.

either by artificial shafts, or by the cuttings which are made by streams, that this is really the case, we conclude that strata having such a relative position at the surface lie upon one another even when we do not confirm our belief by cuttings or shafts. When rocks assume a nearly perpendicular position, it may be almost impossible to say which was orginally undermost, and in such cases we may be forced to rely upon the contents to settle the point. If we find that one of them contains broken up particles of another, we may be quite sure that the latter is the older of the two, for unless it had been previously deposited, particles of it could not come to be present in the other.

Fig. 134.—Vertical strata.

In this way we may settle the relative age of the strata in one spot upon the earth's surface, but how are we to determine the comparative ages of the rocks in different countries? This can only be done by a comparison of the fossils which each contains.

In former ages, just as at the present day, various structures, animal and vegetable, such as sea-weeds, bones of fish, shells of foraminifera and mollusca, branches and leaves of trees, bones of animals, &c.,

DETERMINATION BY FOSSILS.

fell into and became mixed with the sand of the sea or ocean bed, or of the sea-shore, and the mud of estuaries, lakes and rivers. These gradually became firmly embedded or encrusted in the sand or mud, which was by and by converted into stone by age and the pressure of subsequent accumulations upon it, and these remains, animal and vegetable, constitute fossils.

By comparing the shells found on the shores of different seas at the present day, the naturalist is able to decide whether the waters in which a certain shell-fish has lived belong to a tropical, temperate, or arctic climate, for the animals found in each clime differ from one another.

On going backwards in the earth's history we also find that there are differences between the animals now living at any particular place, and those which formerly lived there, and which are now found as fossils in the rocks. We also notice that the animals which are found in the older and deeper differ from those in the newer and more superficial strata. By a comparison of these we are not only enabled to form some conclusions regarding the climate of the place at different geological epochs, but we can decide upon the position and age of each formation from the fossils it contains. For while certain fossils are found in almost all formations from the oldest to the newest, others are limited to particular strata and are absent from the strata above or below them, so that the existence of some of these latter fossils in a certain formation enables us to fix the particular epoch in the earth's history during which the rocks composing this formation were deposited.

The comparative age of the fossils found in different strata at any one place having been determined by the relative position of the strata containing them, these fossils help us to determine the age of the strata as compared with that of strata in other parts of the same country, or in other countries; and it is by this means that we are enabled to arrange in regular order the various formations which compose the earth's crust. At no one place can we find the whole of them together, but we find some in one place and some in another. Unless they possessed something in common, we could not compare them or fix their relative age; but if we find that the fossils contained in the uppermost or newest of the strata in one locality are the same as those in the lowest or oldest of the strata found in another locality, we conclude that all the strata lying above those contained in the second group are newer than those in the first group, and that if we were to dig through the second group of strata we should in all probability come upon those of the first group, although the depth at which they may lie in the second locality may render them practically inaccessible. It is by such a knowledge as this that a geologist is able to say beforehand whether coal is likely to be found in a particular locality or not. If he finds that the strata which lie on the surface belong to a formation only slightly more recent than the Coal Measures, he knows that it is probable coal will be found at a moderate distance below the ground. If the surface strata are very much more recent, it is probable that while coal may be found by boring to a sufficient depth, it will be so far below the surface as to render the operations unprofitable. But if the surface strata belong to an older formation than the Coal Measures, the geologist knows at once that, however deep he may sink a shaft, he will not succeed in finding coal.

When the geologist finds the same fossils in a particular strata in different parts of the earth's surface, he assumes that these strata are of the same age. Now this may not be absolutely true, because it may have happened that strata containing particular fossils were deposited in one place somewhat before or after strata containing similar fossils elsewhere. But still we find that in a general way the assumption is correct, because the great periods of geological time are distinguished from each other by sufficient differences in the fossils they contain to allow us to determine the age of the respective strata with very considerable certainty.

The fossils which are generally chosen to distinguish the strata are the shells of mollusca, because these are found everywhere over the earth's surface. They afford, too, a means of comparing strata which have been formed in the sea at one place with strata deposited from a river or lake at another. For it is evident that it would be of no use for the geologist to compare the shells of one place with the fish-bones found in another. He must compare shell with shell, fish-bone with fish-bone. Nor can he compare the shell-fish and fish-bones of marine origin with the skeletons of land animals and the leaves of land plants. We cannot compare strata containing seaweed or bones of marine fish only, with strata containing leaves or the bones of land animals, but we may do so by using the shells of molluscs as a means of comparison. Usually we find the shells of marine mollusca along with seaweeds and fish-bones; and along with the leaves of trees and the bones of land animals we find the shells of fresh-water molluscs which lived in the rivers into which the leaves and carcases fell, and in whose bed the shale containing them were deposited. We could not compare the marine with the fresh-water molluscs if they were always found separately, but the shells of fresh-water mollusca are often deposited along with those of marine ones at the estuaries of rivers. Thus we find fresh-water and marine shells mixed together at some

particular place, and we thus know that they are of the
same age. At another place we can only find fresh-
water shells, and at a third only marine ones. We
could not have compared the fresh water and marine
shells, unless we had had a mixture of the two at the
third place. Without the shells it would have been
impossible to fix the date of these three strata, because
along with fresh-water shells we should have had fresh-
water or land plants and fresh-water or land animals

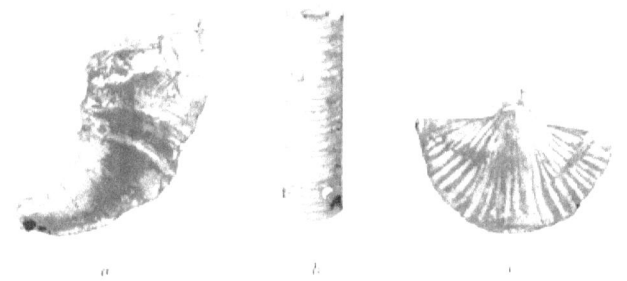

Fig. 15.—Fossils. *a*, coral; *b*, part of encrinite; *c*, spirifer, a marine shell.

while in the marine strata we should have had the
remains of marine plants and animals, and these of
course could not have been compared with each other,
but by using the shells as a means of comparison
we get out of this difficulty altogether.

The archeolithic period, as we have said, is that of
sea-weeds and headless animals, the paleozoic of ferns
and fishes, the mesozoic of pines and reptiles, and the
cainozoic of angiosperms and mammals. But besides

T

these we have other secondary forms, which we will now proceed to consider more closely.

The **Laurentian,** or first subdivision of the **Archeolithic** rocks, was long supposed to be destitute of life, but some years ago a kind of structure was observed in it by Sir William Logan, which seemed to him to indicate the former presence of a living animal. The rock has been much changed by the action of heat, and still some people are disposed to deny that this structure is that of an animal at all, but Dr. Carpenter's investigations render it extremely probable that it consists of skeletons of foraminifera.

It is impossible to say how long before this epoch life existed upon the globe, because any animals lower in the scale than the foraminifera, such as the naked amœba or monera, would leave no trace behind. Only hard structures, such as the foraminiferous shell, could be preserved.

As we ascend into the **Cambrian,** we find the burrows of certain worms and crustaceans, nearly allied to the wood-louse, which, from their appearance, have been called trilobites, and there are also a few molluscous shells and markings which possibly indicate the presence of sea-weed.

In the **Silurian** we find representatives of the hydrozoa, in the form of graptolites, which are the hard cases of compound hydræ. These are supposed to have differed from the sertularians or sea-firs of the present day by being able to swim about instead of being fixed. Star-fishes and encrinites, or sea-lilies, as well as sea-urchins, appear. Trilobites continue, and in addition to the lower molluscs, such as the brachiopoda and lamellibranchiata, the highest forms of the molluscous sub-kingdom, viz., the cephalopods or allies of the cuttle-fish, may be seen.

It is only in the very highest strata of the Silurian that we find traces of fishes, but in the next formation, the first of the **Paleozoic** rocks, the **Old Red** or **Devonian**, we find large fishes of very peculiar forms, and covered with an armour of hard enamel. Coral, ferns, and pieces of wood also occur.

It is in the next, the **Carboniferous** formation, or **Coal Measures**, that we find the greatest development of plant life. The seams of coal, to which, in great measure, England owes her wealth and power, consist of the stems, roots, and leaves of trees, Lepidodendrons and Sigillarias. The former bore no resemblance to the trees of our present forests, but belonged to the same class of plants as the club-mosses, which we now find growing about our Scotch heaths and near our peat mosses. Sigillarias are the stems of a kind of gigantic mare's tail. The roots of Sigillaria were once supposed to be the stems of a different plant, and were called Stigmaria.

T 2

During this formation, the climate must have been warmer than at the present day, and the same land on which this luxuriant vegetation grew must have been gradually subsiding, so that the accumulations grew

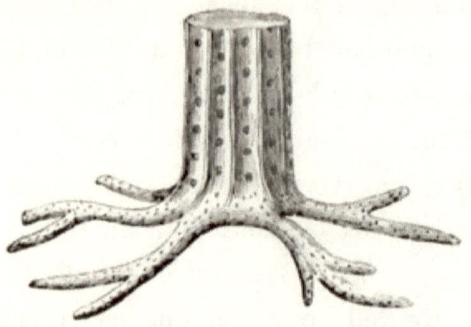

Fig. 136.—*Sigillaria* attached to stigmarian roots.

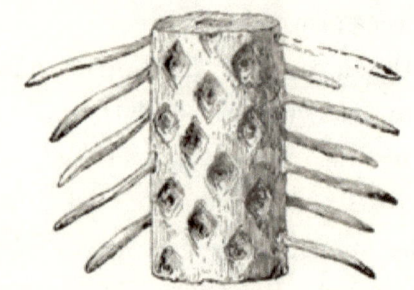

Fig. 137.—*Stigmaria ficoides*, a carboniferous fossil.

deeper and deeper, and at length, descending below the sea-level, were covered with salt water, where a coat of limestone gradually formed over them.

Pine trees grew on the land around those swamps, air-breathing reptiles and centipedes crawled along the ground, and insects hummed through the air. In the deep rivers, near the mouths of which many of those swamps probably lay, were great fishes.

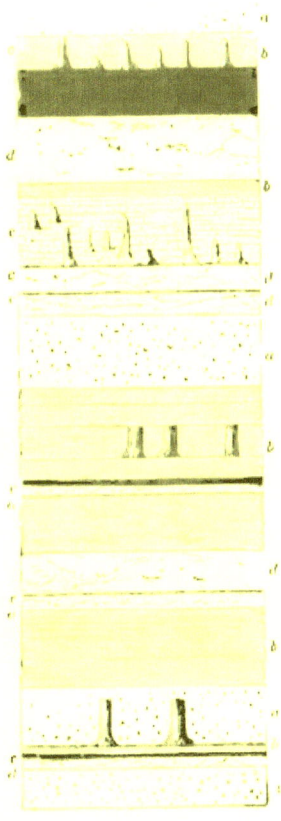

Fig. 138.—Section of a part of the Cape Breton coal-field, showing seven ancient soils, with remains of as many forests. (R. Brown.) *a*, sandstones; *b* and *c*, shales; *e*, coal-seams; *d*, underclays, or soils.

In the next formation, the **Permian**, so-called from its being found much developed near the town of Perm, in Russia, comparatively few fossils have been found,

278   MESOZOIC OR SECONDARY FOSSILS—TRIAS.

and it is distinguished by the footprint of a creature like an enormous toad, but with a very remarkable formation of teeth, so complicated that the name of Labyrinthodon has been given to the animal.

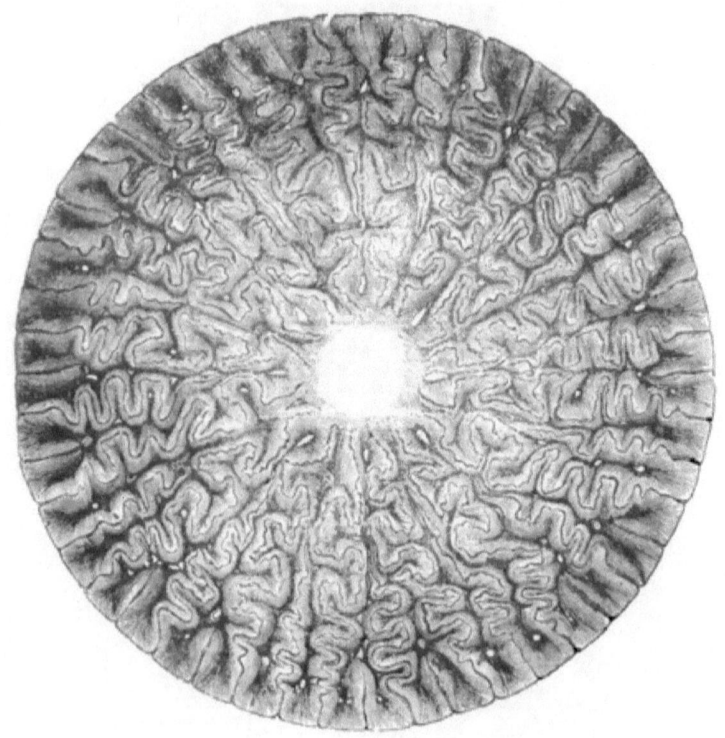

Fig. 139.—Section of tooth of Labyrinthodon.

About this period there seems to be a long break, and then comes the first formation of the **Secondary** or **Mesozoic** period, the **Trias**. Here, in addition to the labyrinthodon and huge saurians, we find the first traces of mammalia, in the teeth of a small animal, the microlestes, belonging to the same tribe as the kangaroo.

In America large foot-prints have been discovered of animals with three toes, and walking on two legs, which were probably either enormous birds, four or five times as high as the present ostrich, or reptiles which had assumed this bird-like character.

Fig. 130.—Cycad.

Amongst the plants of the Trias we still find the enormous lycopods and horsetails which characterize the carboniferous formation, but they are reduced in number. Pines become more plentiful, and cycads, which look somewhat like palms, but are in reality naked seeded, like the pines,—make their appearance for the first time.

In the next formation, the **Jurassic** or **Oolitic**, we find plants resembling those of the trias. The lower classes of the animal kingdom are abundant. But the most characteristic molluscs of this period are two forms of the cuttle-fish tribe—ammonites and belemnites. The ammonites first appear in the trias, but it is in the Jura formation that they attain the greatest development. Both ammonites and belemnites had shells like the Portuguese man-of-war of the present day, but that of the ammonite was curved so that it had the appearance of a ram's horn, while that of the belemnite was straight. Beetles, butterflies, and dragon-flies crept and flew amongst the trees, spiders fed upon them, and worms and crustaceans crawled about the banks or lived within the waters of the seas and rivers. Amongst fishes we find a number of the ganoid or mailed fish, but sharks and rays have now become very abundant. Lizards crawled about on the land, crocodiles and turtles swam near the shore, but the most characteristic reptiles of this age were huge saurians, the ichthyosaurus, plesiosaurus, and pterodactyl. The first was shaped somewhat like a whale or a dolphin, with four paddles, a long tail, short neck, long head, and a mouth armed with rows of long conical teeth. The eyes were of enormous size, protected by a ring of bony plates. The plesiosaurus had a much smaller body than the ichthyosaurus, long paddles, a short tail, and a small head, with a long, swan-like neck. The pterodactyl was a curious lizard, with a large head, and a wing somewhat like that of a bat. Its skin, teeth, and claws were like those of a reptile, but its bones were hollow like those of true birds.

In this formation we first meet with the remains of a true bird, the archaeopteryx, but this was more like

Fig. 141.—Skeleton of Ichthyosaurus.

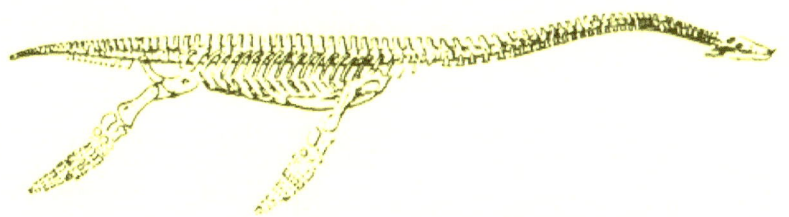

Fig. 142.—Skeleton of Plesiosaurus.

a lizard than any bird of modern days. In this formation we again find the remains of mammals, but only those belonging to the low order of marsupials. Both plants and mammals which then inhabited Britain appear at that time to have been more like those of Australia now than of any other country.

The next formation is the **Cretaceous** or **Chalk**, of which the southern English coast is formed. Enormous as its cliffs are, they consist almost entirely of shells of very minute species of foraminifera, and

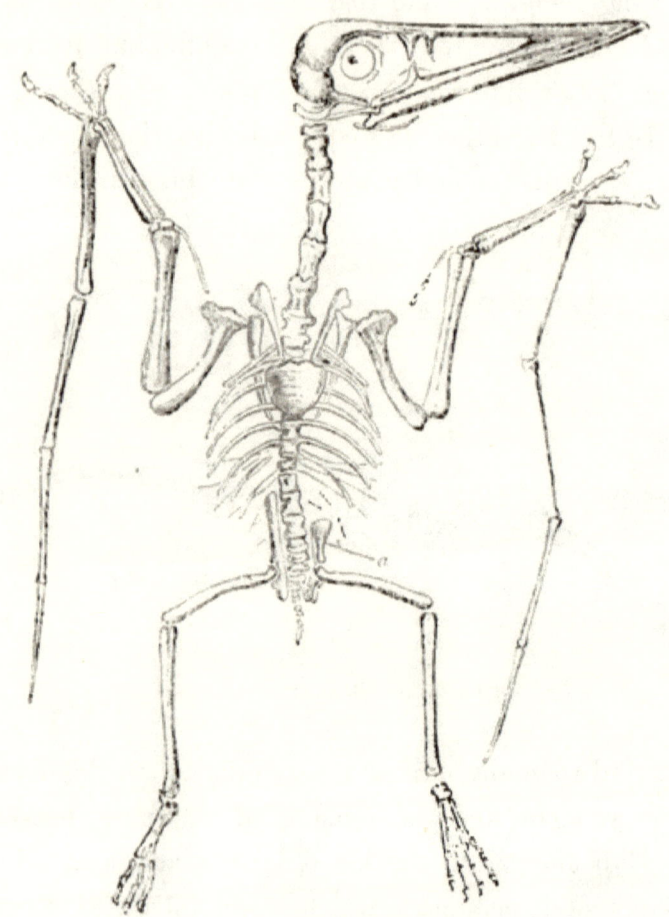

Fig. 143.—Skeleton of Pterodactyl.

have been deposited at the bottom of a deep ocean. At the present day the same sort of deposit is going on at the bottom of the Atlantic. The foraminifera live upon the surface of the water, but after their death the shells gradually sink until they reach the bottom, and there form a thick layer. As this deposit cannot be distinguished from that forming the cliffs of Dover,

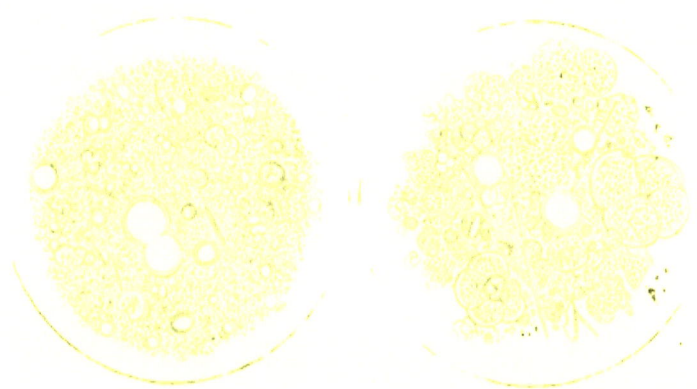

Fig. 114.—Microscopic section of chalk from Sussex. Magnified about 220 diameters.

Fig. 115.—Atlantic ooze from a depth of 2,250 fathoms. Magnified about 220 diameters.

for example, it has been said that we are still living in the cretaceous period, but this is not correct, for though these chalky animalculæ or globigerinæ still exist, yet other forms of life with which they were associated during the cretaceous epoch have entirely vanished. For, in the cretaceous seas, ammonites were still plentiful, the ichthyosaurus and plesiosaurus still swam about in their waters, and huge lizards, like the Iguanodon, bird-like reptiles like the Compsognathus, or reptilian birds like the Hesperornis, still walked about on the shores. Pterodactyls, also, still flew about, but many shells, somewhat resembling those of our present seas, began to appear, and the myrtle, fig, walnut, and oak began to grow side by side with Banksias and other plants resembling those of Australia.

Fig. 146.—Compsognathus longipes, a reptile resembling a bird in its long neck, small head, and partially-erect posture.

With the chalk closes the secondary, or mesozoic period, and between it and the tertiary a long break occurs. The first formation in the **Tertiary** is the **Eocene.**

During this period an enormous ocean stretched from the Pyrenees to the borders of China, and we find the large, coin-shaped foraminifera, or nummulites, of which

CAINOZOIC OR TERTIARY FOSSILS—EOCENE. 285

we have already spoken, in the Egyptian hills and the peaks of the Alps and Himalayas. In these seas fishes were numerous, and amongst the American fossils of

Fig. 147.—*Hesperornis regalis.*

the period have been found the bones of a huge whale, but the saurians of the cretaceous period have completely disappeared.

During a portion, at least, of the eocene period, parts of England and France were raised above the surface of the seas. The climate must have been warm, almost tropical, for the plants which flourished at that period near the present mouth of the Thames resembled those of Polynesia at this day. At that time a great river must have emptied itself into the sea near where the Thames now meets the ocean. Beside it grew fir-trees, palms, and plants like some of the Australian ones; turtles and crocodiles lived near the banks, and in the waters swam sharks, sword-fishes, saw-fishes, and sea-snakes, one of which, measuring thirteen feet long, has been found.

Near Paris have been found the bones of a bird as large as an ostrich, and animals of the hog tribe, but differing from any now living, walked about on the site of the present Isle of Sheppey. Amongst these were the anoplotherium, and the paleotherium, which was formerly supposed to resemble the living tapir in the form of its head and in the short trunk, but has now been shown to be lighter and more elegant.

Some of these animals seem to stand half way between the pachydermata and ruminants, and some were probably light and graceful, like the gazelle. Marsupials still occurred, and carnivorous animals, the hyena, dog, weasel, as well as the squirrel and ape.

In the next period, or **Miocene**, the climate in the

Fig. 148. — Palæotherium magnum, from plaster quarry at Vitry-sur-Seine, from *La Nature*.

northern hemisphere must have been very warm, because the deposits of this period in Greenland, Iceland, and Spitzbergen, show that beeches, oaks, magnolias, walnuts, and vines then flourished within the Arctic Circle. At the same period, however, huge icebergs must have been floating about in Northern Italy. Amongst the animals, marsupials still occurred in Europe, and, along with the carnivora, we find the dinotherium and mastodon, huge creatures allied to the elephant, as well as the rhinoceros, hippopotamus, giraffe, and now, for the first time, monkeys.

During the next period, the **Pliocene**, the climate seems to have been getting colder, although the elephant, mastodon, and rhinoceros still inhabited Britain at that time. With the pliocene ends the tertiary epoch.

We now come to the **Quaternary**, or **Recent** epoch, during which man made his appearance upon the earth. This period is distinguished in Europe by the evidence of extensive glaciers. In the preceding period, that of the pliocene, the climate, at least in Britain, was warm. In the **Pleistocene**, or **Post-pliocene**, the first of the quaternary periods, this warm climate seems to have alternated with cold, for we find a mixed arctic and tropical fauna. The elephant, rhinoceros, and hippopotamus, ranged as far north as England, where we have at the same time the reindeer,

RECENT FOSSILS—PLEISTOCENE. 289

musk ox, and mammoth, natives of cold climates.

Colder and colder the climate seems to have grown

ar after year the snow accumulated on the hills, forming huge glaciers, which descended to the valleys, and perhaps covered the greater part of Europe. Onwards and onwards they pushed, carrying on their surface or embedded within them huge blocks of stone, which rasped and grated against the bottom and sides

Fig. 150.—Floating icebergs.

of their channels, planing the surfaces both of the channel itself and of the glacial boulders, and then, descending to the sea, the ends of the glacier finally broke off and sailed away as icebergs, until by and by they gradually melted and dropped upon the spot over which they happened to be, huge boulders, which they had conveyed many miles from the parent rocks.

ICEBERGS AND GLACIERS.

At this time Scotland was probably much higher above the sea-level than it is now, and much more like Greenland, which near the sea rises from 4,000 to 6,000 feet, and inland is much higher still. Its level then gradually sank until a part of it was again submerged below the sea, when another gradual rise joined it for a second time with the continent of Europe. At this

FIG. 131.—Boulders deposited from an iceberg.

time glaciers lay upon its hills and filled its valleys, but no longer of the same size as the first. Traces of those glaciers are very common in Scotland. Over a great part of it is to be found a stiff blue or yellow clay, usually called till, which is the mud produced by the grinding action of the glaciers upon the rocks. In the Grampians, and in the hills of the west of Ireland, traces of glacial action may be seen, as plainly as by the very side of a glacier in Switzerland.

In Mareschal College, Aberdeen, lies a large stone found in digging the foundation of a house in the town. This block bears evidence of glacial action, for it is planed and scarred by the friction it has undergone against other blocks or against the sides or bottom of the glacier bed while being carried along imbedded in the ice of the glacier. The spot where

Fig. 152.—Boulder planed and scarred by glacial action.

the town now stands must therefore have been itself covered by a glacier, or more probably by a sea, on which the detached iceberg floated away from the glacier, carrying the huge stone with it, and dropping it as it melted over the site of the town.

As each glacier moves down from the hill-tops, it carries with it stones and mud. When it gets down to the valley, and there melts away with the heat, it leaves at its end a heap of round stones

Fig. 133.—Glacier of Zermatt.

termed the moraine. Such heaps are to be seen to-day in many of our highland valleys, running across their mouths like a wall, through which an opening has been cut by the stream which drains the glen.

Fig. 154.—Skull of old man of Cromagnon; vertical view.

After the melting of the great glaciers, Scotland England, and Ireland were probably all united to the continent of Europe, but then another partial submergence took place, by which the shallow Northern Sea was formed, separating them from the continent, and

FIRST APPEARANCE OF MAN IN BRITAIN. 295

then another, by which Ireland was divided from England.

It was probably before the ice began to cover Europe so extensively that man first appeared in Britain. How long a period elapsed between the time

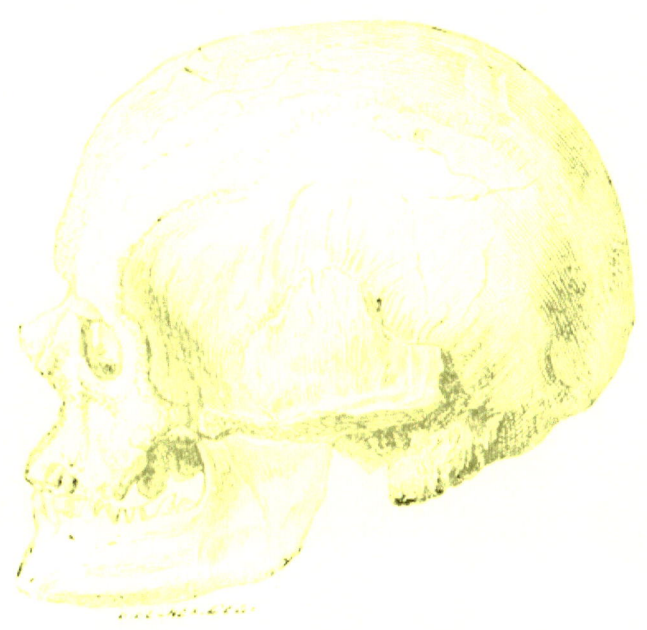

Fig. 155.—Skull of old man of Cromagnon; profile.

of his first creation in the east and his migration into these northern latitudes we cannot say, but the first inhabitants of Britain appear to have been a savage race, using implements of chipped flint of the rudest possible shape. Very few, if any, bones of these men have been found, but their flint axes, chipped in such a manner as could only be done by the hand of man, have been found along with the bones of the cave hyæna, cave lion, woolly rhinoceros, and mammoth, in such a way as to leave no doubt whatever that men

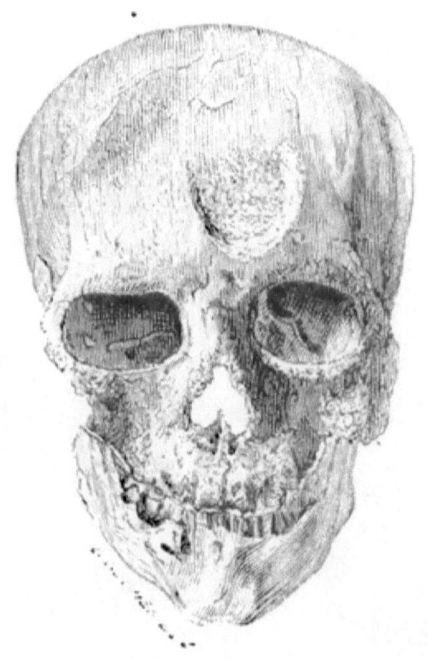

Fig. 156.—Skull of old man of Cromagnon; front view.

were living at the same time as these animals. When England again became united to the continent, when the climate had become warmer, and the glaciers had contracted within narrower limits, another race seems to have crossed the broad plain covered with forest

FIRST INVASION OF BRITAIN.

trees, where the German Ocean now rolls, and to have brought with them implements, still of stone, but of

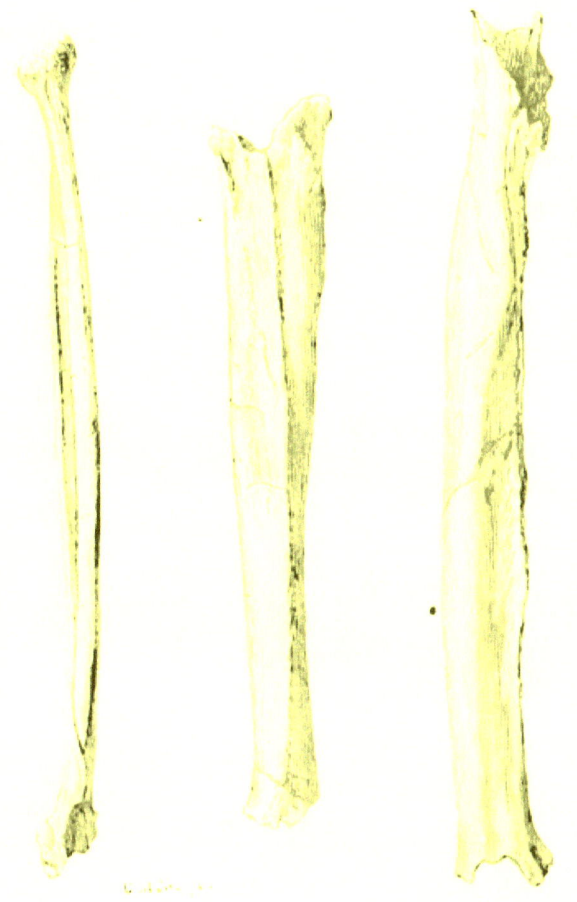

Fig. 157.—Bones of old man of Cromagnon; shin-bone; flattened tibia; femur: profile view.

much finer workmanship, to which the term neolithic has been given.

Although no skulls of the palæolithic age have been found in Great Britain, one or two skulls of that period have been discovered in Germany. They are, no doubt, of a somewhat low type as regards their shape, resembling in certain respects the skulls of savages, such as the Australians, but still they differ very widely from those of apes, and, as Huxley remarks, so far as capacity goes, they might serve to contain the brain of a modern poet or *savant*. Some

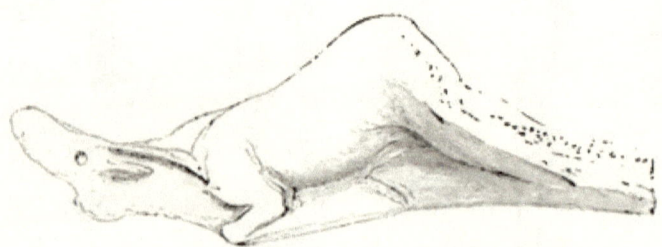

Fig. 158.—Sculptured bone handle representing a reindeer.

skulls belonging to the neolithic period are not even of a low type (Figs. 154, 155, 156). The men of the neolithic period have left behind them evidence of no mean artistic power in their drawings and sculptures of such animals as the cave bear and mammoth, with which they were contemporary, but which have now vanished from the face of the earth (Figs. 158—160).

A man, even in these days, far removed as they are from the present, *was* a man, and not a monkey.

Fig. 138.—Mammoth carved in ivory.

If man has been developed from any being lower in the scale of existence than himself, it is not in the

Fig. 160.—The Mammoth (*Elephas primigenius*).

West at least that we are to look for the missing link which is to connect him with the lower forms of life.

LECTURE XV.

GENERAL SUMMARY.

We have now made a general survey of the plants and animals living at the present time, and of those which have existed during previous periods of the world's history.

We find that the relations of the animal and vegetable kingdom to each other cannot be expressed by parallel lines; that the lowest and highest members of each kingdom respectively do not correspond to each other, but that the highest members diverge farthest, while the lowest are closely united, and, indeed, we might almost say are identical.

We find the same thing in comparing the different members of each kingdom amongst themselves. The palm and the oak are totally unlike in the nature of their foliage and the appearance of their trunks, in the growth of their stems, in the number of parts of their flowers, and in the germination of their seeds.

We cannot bridge over the difference between them by intermediate forms as highly developed as themselves, any more than we can connect the elephant with the palm-tree. To unite the elephant and the palm we must trace their affinities backwards to the lowest forms of animal and vegetable life, and to connect the palm with the oak we must also trace the affinities of these plants backwards, first through the lowest forms of monocotyledons and dicotyledons to the gymnosperms, cycads and pines, and thence to the lycopods.

But there is this difference in tracing the relations of animal with plant and of plant with plant, of the elephant with the palm, and the palm with the oak, that in the case of the animal and plant we must follow their affinities backwards until we come to the very lowest forms of life, to the protista, whereas in the case of plant with plant we do not require to descend so low in the scale. In the case of the palm and the oak we must trace their affinities through the gymnosperms to the lycopod, but in the case of the gymnosperms themselves, pines and cycads, which are more nearly related to one another than are the oak and the palm, we do not require to go any further back. The same link which connects the oak and the palm connects the pine and the cycad. In both instances we find a connection in the lycopod.

All through the vegetable kingdom it is the same. The more nearly allied the plants are, the less distance have we to go backwards or downwards in the scale of development to find their relations to each other. We are thus able to represent the **relations** of all the members of the **vegetable kingdom** by a branching tree, whose root represents the lowest forms of vegetable life, and whose topmost twigs represent the highest developments. Some of the twigs are completely united to one another, and to the main branches; others, however, must remain apart, the branch which should connect them being absent.

In the same way, on comparing the members of the animal kingdom, we find that the members of the various sub-kingdoms diverge far from one another at their highest extremities, and that it is only when we take the lowest members of one sub-kingdom that we can find their affinities with those of another.

We can see little or nothing in common between the lion, the bee, the cuttle-fish, and the sea-anemone. It is only when we trace the lion down to the lowest member of the vertebrate series, the amphioxus, and the cuttle-fish down to one of the lowest members of the mollusca, the ascidian, that we see the vertebrata and the mollusca, so different in their highest developments, closely allied in their lowest.

We cannot trace the relation of either the vertebrates or the molluscs with the bee, and the articulate sub-kingdom to which it belongs, without going down as low as the annuloida, but when we have once done this, the relation of all to the sea-anemone is not far to seek.

But in tracing all these classes of animals down to their lowest forms, we find, as we did in the vegetable kingdom, that we do not progress uninterruptedly, for now and then we meet with breaks in the chain, missing links which we cannot supply, and here, as in the vegetable kingdom, if we represent the **relations of animals** by a branching tree, we must leave blanks here and there between various groups, the forms which would unite them being nowhere to be found.

On looking at the distribution of animal and plant life during the various ages of this earth's history, we see that here, too, the **relations of animals and plants in time** can be represented by an irregularly branching tree, in the same way as the relations between the animals and plants now living.

In the lowest paleolithic rocks we find nothing but the traces of an amœba-like animal, but the existence of such an animal renders it probable that similar animals, yet lower in the scale, and not provided, like it, with a distinct shell, but merely composed of naked protoplasm, were living along with it.

It is possible that along with the eozoon other animals of higher types, but unprovided with soft parts, were in existence. We might, indeed, have representatives of almost every sub-kingdom which would entirely disappear and leave no trace behind them. Hydrae, and sea-anemones amongst the Coelenterata,[1] various soft-bodied worms amongst the Annuloida, and soft-bodied marine slugs and ascidians amongst the Mollusca, as well as such creatures as the amphioxus amongst the Vertebrata, might all have lived and died in those primitive seas without any possibility of our ever knowing it.

As we proceed upwards we find that the first plants whose traces have been preserved were of the very lowest forms, viz., algae, and these were succeeded by plants, allied, it is true, to the club-mosses of the present day, but yet resembling pines in their size and in the nature of their foliage.

Amongst the first animals which we find to succeed the foraminifera were hydrozoa such as graptolites, annuloida such as crinoids and star-fishes, and low forms of the mollusca and annulosa.

As we ascend, we find higher forms of these orders

---

[1] In the lecture on the Coelenterata, pp. 133-142, or animals in which the body cavity and digestive canal are not completely separated from each other, the subdivisions Hydrozoa and Actinozoa were given, and the name of Coelenterata was omitted by an oversight.

X

gradually replacing the lower ones, for in the secondary age the crinoids diminish, while the sea-urchins and star-fishes become more numerous. The brachiopods are no longer the dominant molluscs, for higher forms of molluscous life, the gasteropods and lamellibranchs are now on the increase, and cephalopods begin to appear.

The lowest forms of fishes, also, such as sharks and ganoids, are at first masters of the ocean, but after them come the higher teleostian fishes.

The earlier reptiles, such as the ichthyosaurus and plesiosaurus, although of enormous size, were of a type intermediate between fishes and reptiles, for while their general characters were reptilian, their paddles resembled the fins of fish in the number of the bones composing their skeleton. Others, like the pterodactyl and ornosaurus, were reptiles possessing bird-like characters, and creatures like the archæopteryx and hesperornis were true birds, but with reptile-like characters.

As we ascend still higher we find pines and cycads taking the place of the lycopods, and these again are succeeded by angiosperms, until we come up to the present day with all its varied vegetation.

Amongst the mammals, the first that we find belong to the lowest groups of the marsupials. Then we find forms, such as the palæotherium and anoplotherium, which present characters common to the tapir, pig, and horse; and as we go higher still we find these replaced by more specialized forms more nearly resembling still-existing animals, and it is not until we come nearly to the top of the series that we find traces of the highest groups of the animal kingdom, viz., monkeys. Last of all come the bones and handiwork of man.

We thus observe a **gradual progression** in the **life history of the earth**, both in the **type** dominant at particular periods, and in the **development** of the animals belonging to that type.

It is true, indeed, that we do find examples of animals which have lived on generation after generation almost unchanged from the beginning of the world's history until now, but these have always been low in type. It would appear that they found a groove which suited them, and had run on constantly in it, whilst animals higher in the scale of existence had changed or disappeared, just as we find that the lowest of the population, the hewers of wood and drawers of water, go on unchanged for many generations amidst all the revolutions of a country's history, and all the changes of dynasty or race in its rulers.

We have seen that in order to find a **relationship** between the various groups of the animal kingdom we have had to go to the **lowest forms** of each. We have seen also that in tracing groups backwards in time we find **intermediate forms which no longer**

exist, and are thus able to supply the missing relations between them.

We find also that in the **life history of individuals** we get something like the life history of the earth, and that where we are unable to trace any great likeness between the adult individuals, we can still find a great **resemblance** between them in their youthful, or still more in their **embryonic**, condition.

Two embryos, perfectly alike in their earlier stage, seem to start on different tracks, and to go on until at last they grow into forms utterly unlike each other.

Two railway trains, starting from the same station for distant towns far apart from each other, may run for a considerable time on the same line, or on two lines quite close together, so that there may be some little difficulty at first in determining to which destination either train was bound. But as they proceed further and further onwards, their directions become more and more unlike, so that at last it is easy to tell in what directions they are going, though, perhaps, hard to believe that they both started from the same point, so utterly do their courses now diverge. The further apart their destinations, the sooner does the divergence between their courses begin, though, where the destinations are close together, the courses may be the same for a long time. Something like this is found in the life-history of animals. In the adult condition the leg of the bird is quite unlike that of the lizard, but, as a reference to the adjoining figures will at once show, there is considerable resemblance between them in the embryonic condition.

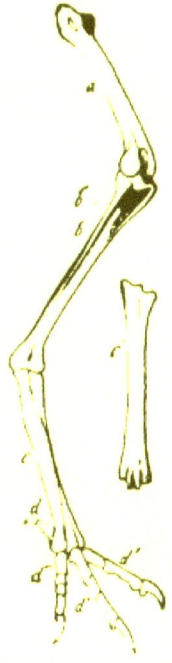

Fig. 101.—Hinder extremity of bird (*Buteo vulgaris*). *a*, femur ; *b*, tibia ; *b'*, fibula ; *c*, tarso-metatarsus ; *c'*, the same piece isolated and seen from in front ; *d d' d'' d'''*, four toes.

The frog and newt are nearly allied to each other, and we should therefore expect that the divergence between them would not begin until later on in the animal's development, and so we find it. In most frogs the newt-like stage is passed through after the creature has emerged from the egg, but in some frogs the process of development takes place com-

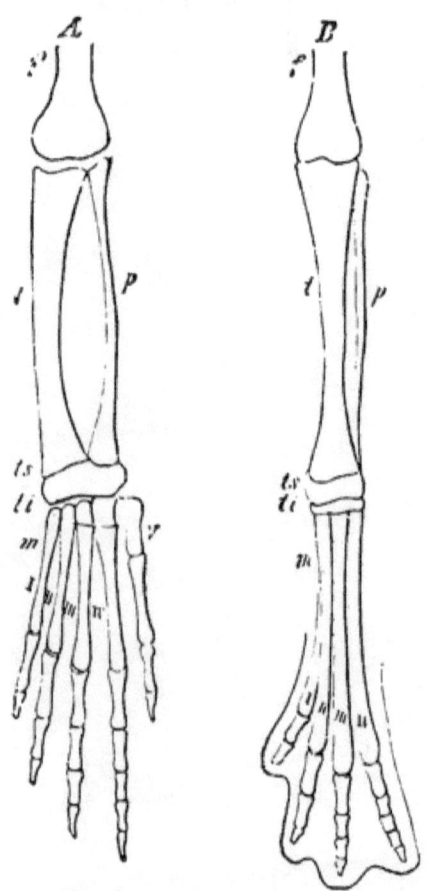

Fig. 162.—Skeleton of the foot of a reptile (lizard) (A) and a bird (B). The latter is in its embryonic state, in which the resemblance to the reptile is much greater than in the adult state (cf. Fig. 103); f, femur; t, tibia; p, fibula; ts, upper, ti, lower piece of the tarsus; m, metatarsus; i-r, metatarsalia of the toes.

pletely within the egg, and the animals are hatched as tailless frogs. The process of development has, in the latter case, taken place completely within the ovum, and the animal quits the ovum as a frog, and not, as in the ordinary case, in the form of a newt which is afterwards to develop into a frog. We are reminded here, although the analogy is a very loose one, of the difference between the spore of the lycopod

FIG. 163.—1. Egg of *Hylodes martinicensis*, twelve days old, lower surface; 2. Young of *Hylodes* as it leaves the egg; *c*, tail. 3. Adult male *Hylodes*, natural size.

and that of a fern. The spore of the fern develops first into a prothallus, from which a plant resembling the parent arises, whereas in the lycopod the prothallus is developed in the spore itself, so that the plant resembling the parent springs at once from the spore.

In figs. 164 and 165 we have diagrams representing the development of an ascidian and of an amphioxus.

MOLLUSC.

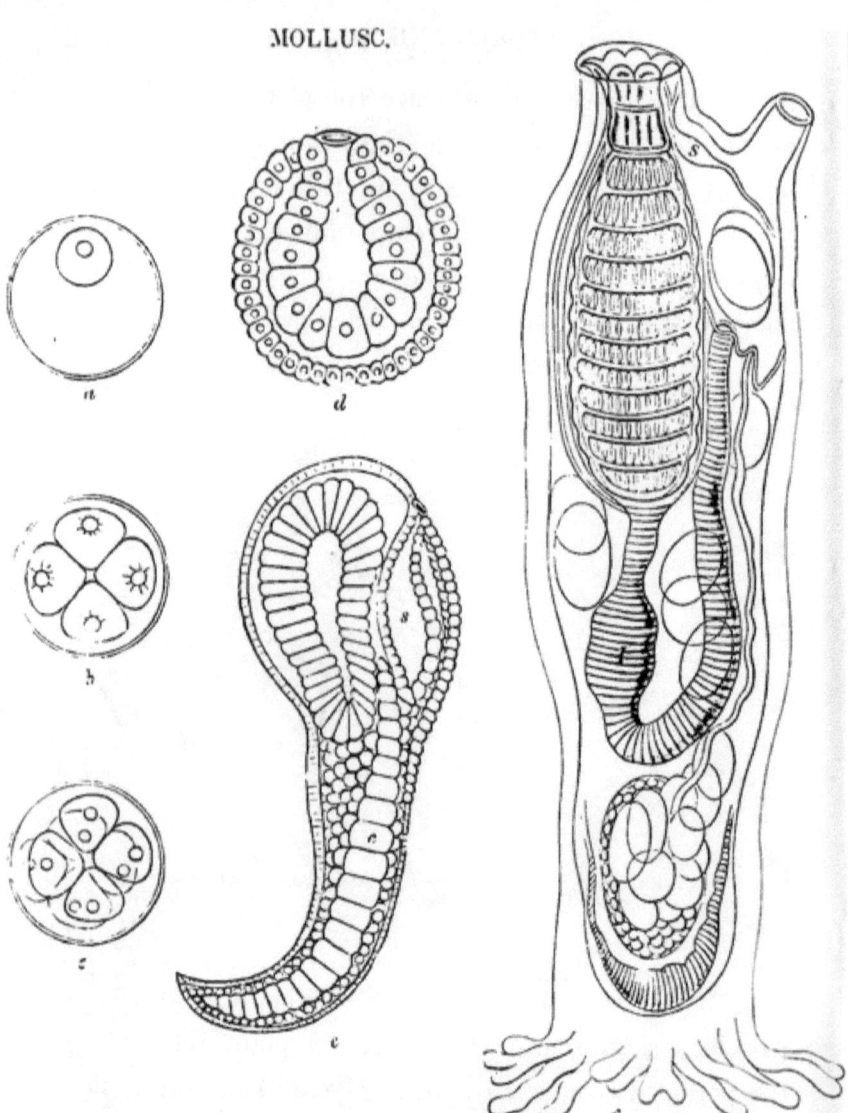

FIG. 164.—Development of an Ascidian. *a*, the ovum. *b* and *c*, fissure of the ovum with endogenous formation of cells, ending in the formation of a spherical cellular mass. Inside this, fluid collects so as to form a bladder with cellular wall. Part of the cell wall becomes inverted like the finger of a glove, and this inversion forms the rudimentary intestinal canal. At this stage the embryo reminds us of the coelenterata. *e*, Here the neural tube, *S*, the beginning of the spinal marrow, is being formed, its cavity still opens externally in front. Between it and the intestine (*I*), the chorda dorsalis (*c*), the axis of the inner skeleton has appeared. In the larvæ of ascidians this rod passes along the tail which is cast off at a later stage. There are some very small ascidians (appendicularia) which retain it through life, and swim about by its means.

VERTEBRATE.

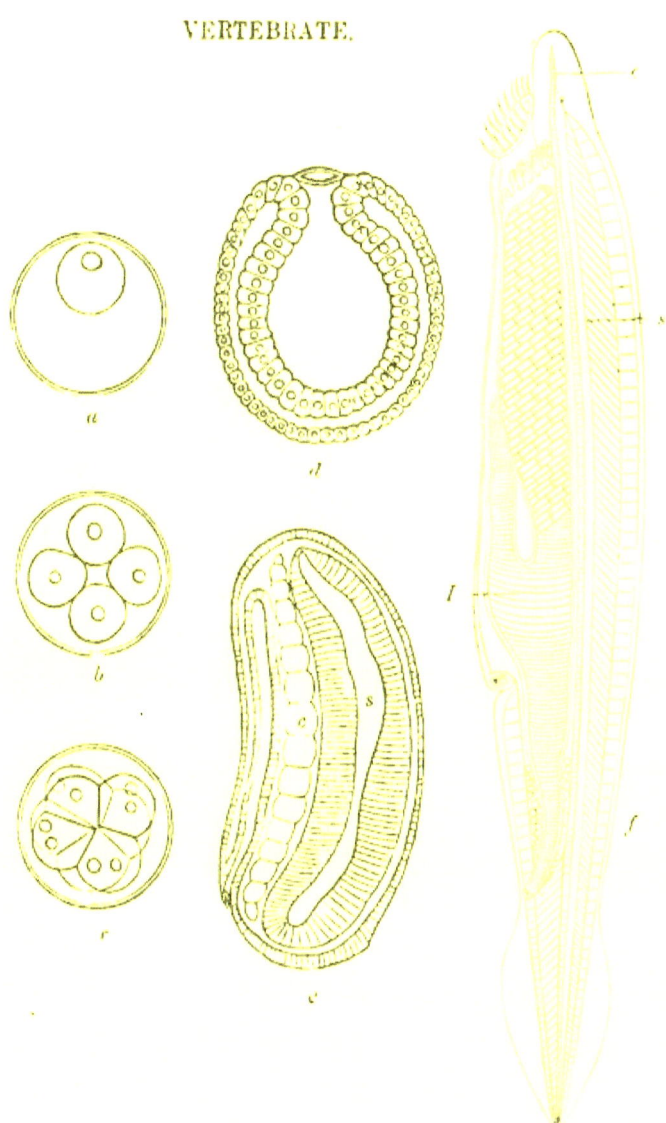

Fig. 165.—Development of Amphioxus. *a*, the ovum ; *b* and *c*, fissure of the ovum with endogenous formation of cells ; *c*, formation of a spherical cell mass. Inside this fluid collects so as to form a bladder with cellular wall. This bladder is inverted at one side so as to form a cavity—the intestinal cavity. *e* represents a further stage, and *f* the fully developed Amphioxus. The letters indicating the different parts are the same as in fig. 164.

I have already mentioned the points of resemblance between them, but you see that in the adult condition they differ very considerably. Yet as we trace them backwards, at each step they resemble each other more and more, until we find that they are absolutely identical.

Nor is this merely the case with low forms of life. It occurs also in the very highest. It was formerly imagined that every embryo, in its development from an ovum, passed successively through the different types of the animal kingdom, that it was successively protozoon, hydrozoon, mollusc, annulose, and vertebrate. But it has now been shown that this is not the case—each embryo does not move from type to type; it retains always its own type, but it undergoes specialisation in function. A vertebrate animal, during its development, does not become a starfish, a worm, an insect, or a snail; but at one stage or another of its growth it is much more closely related to these than when fully developed. In its first condition it is a simple cell, and may thus be looked upon as related to the lowest forms of protozoa. It next becomes an agglomeration of cells, and may then be regarded as related to the higher protozoa, or metazoa, and, through them to the molluscs, and annuloids; and as development goes on, we come to a stage when the embryo, for aught one can tell, may be that of a fish, amphibian, reptile, fowl, or mammal. At successive stages we can distinguish the fish from the others, then the amphibian, next the reptile, next the bird, while still we could hardly say whether the embryo was to develop into a pig, an ox, a rabbit, or a man. At each successive stage as the characteristics of the individual become more and more marked, we can distinguish between the animals more and more closely allied, until at birth there can be no possibility of mistake. (Figs. 166 to 173.)

But even after birth, as development goes on, we get greater and greater differentiation. Not to mention such cases as that of the axolotl amongst the lower animals, we find that at a comparatively early period in embryonic life man becomes differentiated as a vertebrate from the other animal sub-kingdoms; later on he is differentiated as a mammal from the other classes of vertebrata, and later still as a man from the other orders of mammalia.

But it is only after birth that the racial differences of men appear. For the first few days of its life the negro infant has a reddish-brown skin, and then the pigment which gives the black colour characteristic of its race makes its appearance. Later on, individual characteristics appear, and distinguish the men of one country from another, and one individual from another.

We thus see that all living beings, however

EMBRYOS OF FOUR VERTEBRATES.

Showing their close relationship at an early stage of development and gradual divergence as development proceeds.

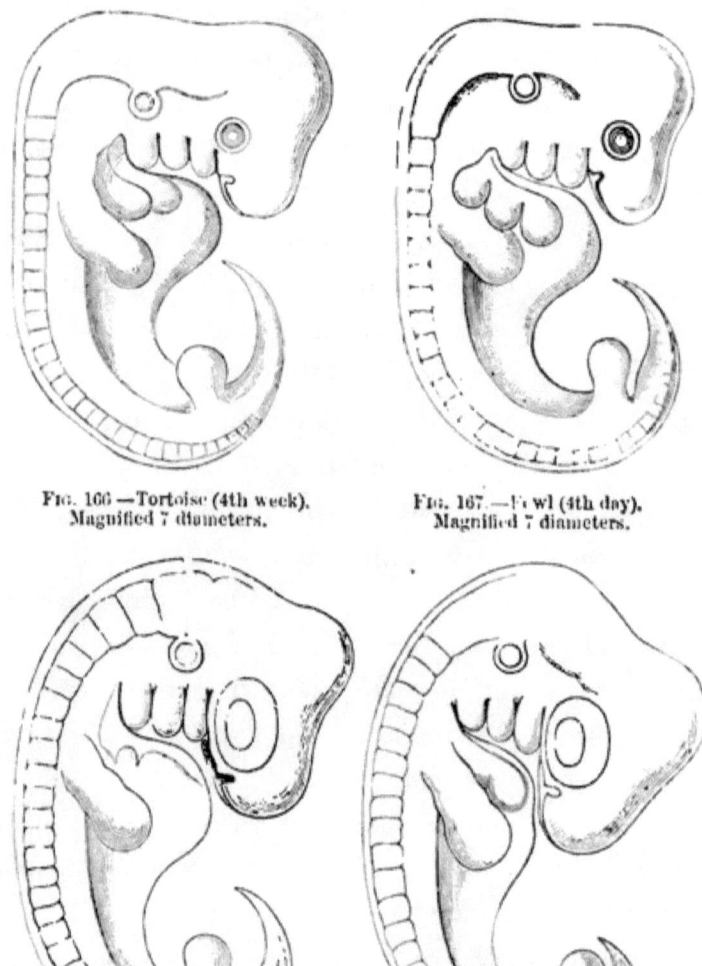

Fig. 166.—Tortoise (4th week).
Magnified 7 diameters.

Fig. 167.—Fowl (4th day).
Magnified 7 diameters.

Fig. 168.—Dog (4th week).
Magnified 5 diameters.

Fig. 169.—Man (4th week).
Magnified 5 diameters.

EMBRYOS OF FOUR VERTEBRATES.

Fig. 170.—Tortoise (6th week).
Magnified 4 diameters.

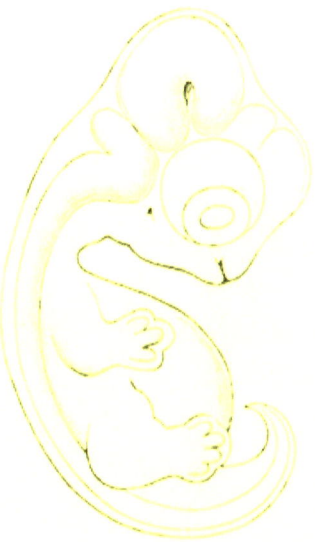

Fig. 171.—Fowl (8th day).

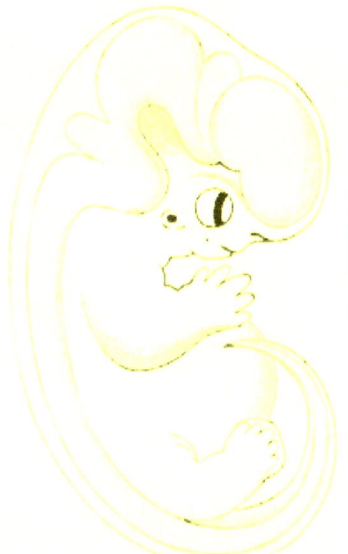

Fig. 172.—Dog (6th week).

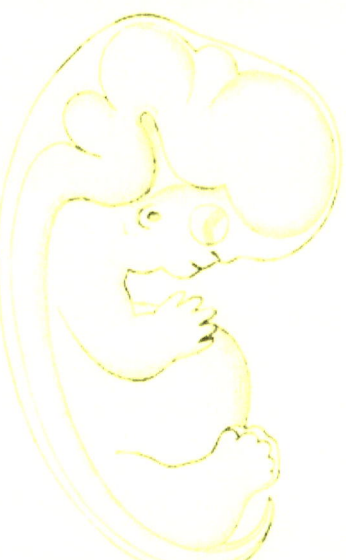

Fig. 173.—Man (6th week).
Magnified 4 diameters.

different their appearance may be, or however diverse their qualities and endowments, have this in common, that they are built up of simple masses of protoplasm, or cells. They are related, though many links of relationship are wanting, by various forms which connect them, running from the highest plant to the lowest animal, and thence to the highest animal. They are also related in time, for, as we trace the world's history backward, we come upon forms which have long ago disappeared from the earth's surface, but fill up the blanks amongst those now existing; and we find, too, that all animals, however different in their adult condition, are not merely alike, but are indeed almost indistinguishable from one another, at the earliest period of their development.

All statements which I have hitherto made are facts, discovered by careful observation, tested, tried and confirmed by hostile criticism and renewed observations of various naturalists, and may be verified by any one who likes to take the trouble for himself; but these facts have led to a disagreement of opinion regarding their interpretation. We cannot look at the animal and vegetable kingdoms, and all their relations, without asking, How did they come here, and why should they present these relations to each other? And around this question there is at present raging a controversy regarding **Special Creation** and **Evolution**.

SPECIAL CREATION.

According to the doctrine of special creation, each species of plant and animal was created at once, and has undergone no change since. According to this, some animals have gone on reproducing their kind from the Silurian age until now. Others have completely died out, and new ones have been created in their stead. All the higher forms of plant and animal life belonging to the earlier epochs, the huge lepidodendrons of the coal age, the enormous reptiles of the lias and oolite were created, lived for a while, and were then swept from the face of the earth; while their places were taken by those animals which we have already mentioned as resembling, yet differing from, those of the present day. These again were swept away wholesale, and new ones, those which we now see, were created. The ideas entertained by many persons regarding the mode of creation have probably been derived from the great epic poem, and cannot perhaps be better given than in the very words of Milton, as quoted by Huxley in his American Lectures:—

> "The sixth, and of creation last, arose
> With evening harps and matin; when God said,
> 'Let the earth bring forth soul living in her kind,
> Cattle, and creeping things, and beast of the earth,
> Each in their kind.' The earth obeyed, and, straight
> Opening her fertile womb, teemed at a birth
> Innumerous living creatures, perfect forms,
> Limbed and full-grown. Out of the ground up rose,

> As from his lair, the wild beast, where he wons
> In forest wild, in thicket, brake, or den—
> Among the trees in pairs they rose, they walked;
> The cattle in the fields and meadows green:
> Those rare and solitary, these in flocks
> Pasturing at once and in broad herds, upsprung.
> The grassy clods now calved; now half appeared
> The tawny lion, pawing to get free
> His hinder parts—then springs, as broke from bonds,
> And rampant shakes his brinded mane; the ounce,
> The libbard, and the tiger, as the mole
> Rising, the crumbled earth above them threw
> In hillocks; the swift stag from underground
> Bore up his branching head; scarce from his mould
> Behemoth, biggest born of earth, upheaved
> His vastness; fleeced the flocks and bleating rose,
> As plants; ambiguous between sea and land,
> The river-horse and scaly crocodile.
> At once came forth whatever creeps the ground,
> Insect or worm."

According to the hypothesis of evolution, on the other hand, the animals and plants now living are simply the descendants of those which have gone before them. Each generation, perhaps differing only a little from that which preceded it, has transmitted a slightly altered form to that which succeeded it, and this again another alteration to its successors, until by successive slight alterations the form has come at length to be entirely altered.

Let us take a single instance,—that of the horse:[1]

---

[1] For this account of the pedigree of the horse the author is indebted to Huxley's American Lectures.

In typical vertebrates we have in the fore-arm two bones, the radius and the ulna; and in the leg, also, two bones, the tibia and fibula. In the hand and foot we have five digits.

We find, however, that the horse differs from the typical vertebrate in having only one bone, the radius, in the fore-leg, and one bone, the tibia, in the hind-leg. Instead of having five digits it has only one— the middle finger or toe—which is immensely elongated and very strong, the nail covering it being converted into a hoof. In these particulars the horse differs very much from other vertebrates, and if the doctrine of evolution be correct, and the horse be really descended from a common ancestor with the other vertebrata, we should expect the progenitors of the horse to have characters more nearly allied to the typical vertebrate than those which he now presents. As we go backwards in the course of the horse's development we should find its ancestors gradually getting nearer and nearer to the typical vertebrate, and this, in fact, we find to be the case.

The single bone of the horse's fore-leg is not a radius only, but consists of the radius and ulna fused together, the upper part of the ulna being distinct, and the lower end traceable, even in the adult horse, and separable in the young horse, but the shafts of the two bones are completely fused. In the hind-leg we find a somewhat similar characteristic, for the head, and the lower end of the fibula also, are united to the tibia, only here the shaft of the fibula, instead of being completely united to the tibia, as the ulna is to the radius, seems to have simply disappeared, leaving, however, an indication of its presence in the shape of a small splint at its upper end.

In the fore-foot there seems at first sight to be only one finger, but on looking at it more closely we notice

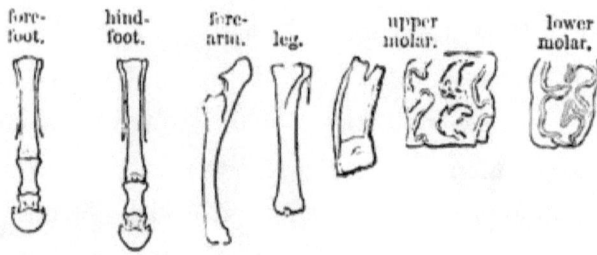

Fig. 174.—Recent Equus.

at each side of it a splint-shaped bone which is the rudiment of another finger.

In the hind-foot we see the same thing.

The teeth of the horse are also peculiar, as in them three substances; viz. hard enamel, somewhat softer dentine, and still softer cement, are arranged in complicated folds, the consequence of which is that the softer part, being more quickly worn away in the process of mastication, the more the horse eats the more do the ridges of enamel project and form a grinding apparatus admirably adapted for the purpose of masticating the food, just as, in the rodent, the more the animal gnaws, the sharper do its teeth grow. The remains of horses found in all the formations

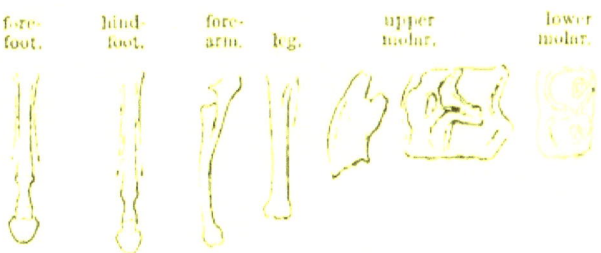

Fig. 175.—Pliocene Pliohippus.

above the middle of the Pliocene epoch entirely resemble the animals now living; but in the earlier part of the Pliocene epoch we find a horse resembling that of the present day in many particulars, yet having

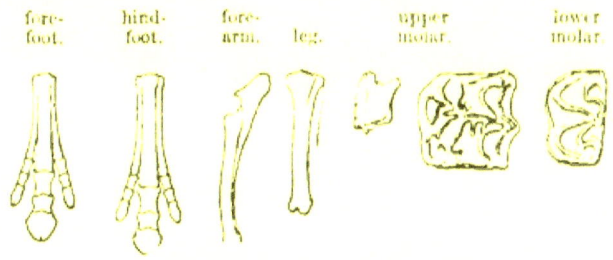

Fig. 176.—Protohippus (*Hipparion*).

on both the fore- and hind feet a distinct digit at either side of the large middle one, in place of the small splint-bones of the horse. These toes, however, though distinct, were too small to be of much use.

On going back to the Miocene period, we find in the Miohippus that the toes are large enough for the animal to have rested upon them. The ulna in the

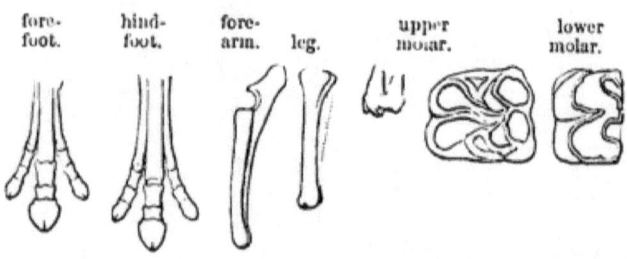

Fig. 177.—Miocene Miohippus (*Anchitherium*).

fore-arm is distinguishable in its whole length from the radius. The teeth are simpler, and have more distinct double roots.

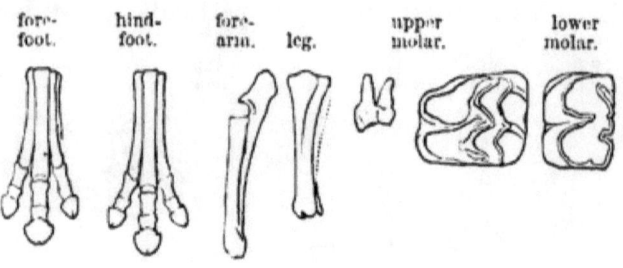

Fig. 178.—Mesohippus.

In the earlier part of the Miocene period we find the Mesohippus, which has the radius and ulna entire, and the tibia and fibula distinct. It has three digits on the fore-foot, and the rudiment of a fourth, and the teeth are simpler still.

On going back still further, to the Eocene period, we find the oldest form of the horse known—the Orohippus. In it we have a well-developed ulna and fibula, four complete toes in the fore-foot, and three in the hind, and simple teeth with double fangs.

Here, then, we find distinct evidence of the kind we should expect if the evolution theory be true, and, considering how small a portion of the earth's surface has yet undergone a thorough geological examination,

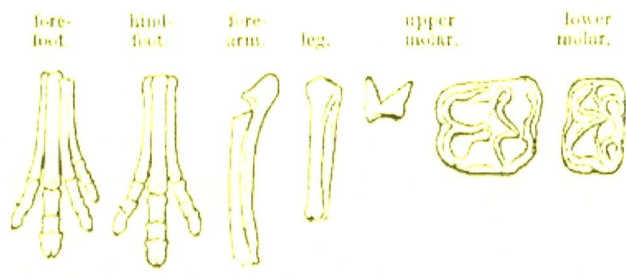

Fig. 179. Eocene Orohippus.

and also the necessary imperfection of the geological record itself, the wonder is that we have got so much evidence of this sort, and not that there is so little of it.

According to the doctrine of special creation we must imagine that during the Eocene period particles of earth became united together into a form like, and yet unlike, that of the horse and the tapir of the present day—the Orohippus; and that those particles were not merely agglomerated so as to assume the form of this animal, but that they were converted into flesh, blood, and bone, and then sprang from the earth a living animal. At the end of the Eocene period, these animals all died out, leaving behind them only their bones, which we still find in a fossil condition. During the next period, the Miocene epoch, a similar process was repeated no less than three times, each successive race of animals, the Mesohippus, Miohippus, and Protohippus, resembling the horse more and the tapir less. Again must we imagine these animals swept off the earth at the end of the Miocene period. Again, during the Pliocene period, another new creation takes place, and the Pliohippus of this epoch in many particulars very closely resembles the horse. Again, however, we must assume that the Pliohippus, like all its predecessors, was removed from the face of the earth, and that particles of mud again aggregated together to form the horse of the present day.

On the other hand, the believers in evolution, instead of imagining that the horse was specially created in the way that Milton describes, and that the animals similar to it, but not specifically resembling it, died out and left no successor, consider the horse of the present day to be descended from the Pliohippus and the Protohippus of the Pliocene, the Miohippus of the Miocene, and the Orohippus of the Eocene, all of which somewhat resembled the horse, the resemblance growing less, however, as we recede from the present time, while at the same time the structural peculiarities which distinguish the horse from other vertebrate animals disappear, and the relationship between what the evolutionists call its ancestors and other vertebrates becomes closer.

Such arguments as these, together with the general facts of classification and development in the animal and vegetable kingdoms, have led many thoughtful men of late years to believe in the hypothesis of gradual evolution, rather than that of special creation.

One great objection to the doctrine of evolution is that if it were true we ought to find evolution going on at the present time; and another is, that we ought also to discover intermediate forms between the different animals and plants now living as we go backwards in the history of the world.

Now it is quite true that we do not find all the links in the geological record that we ought. There are yet very many blanks, but, as I have already mentioned, intermediate forms do occur, and the number of these is increasing every day, as new parts of the rocks on the earth's surface are being examined, so that this argument against evolution is daily becoming weaker. The distinguished geologist, Sir Charles Lyell, who at first opposed the doctrine of evolution, was led by the accumulation of evidence to change his mind and finally to give in his adherence to it. It has also to be considered that the geological record is very imperfect, not merely on account of our lack of knowledge of it, but on account of the incompleteness of the record itself. We can understand this if we remember that all these rocks do not represent new matter on the earth's crust, but that each one was formed from those preceding it, just as the increase of the heap of sand in the lower bulb of the hour-glass corresponds to the diminution in the upper bulb. We must take from the one before we can add to the other.

The second great objection is that we do not find evolution going on at the present day.

But we do find evolution going on at the present day. The Shetland pony, the race-horse, and the dray-horse are all classed by naturalists simply as varieties of horse, and yet how different are they. By selecting and breeding from individuals of his stock presenting different qualities or peculiarities, the breeder is able to produce a race of animals having the properties which he desires. Perhaps this is seen even more markedly in the dog than in the horse. To an ordinary eye, there certainly seems to be a much greater difference between a pigmy Italian greyhound or a King Charles's dog, and an enormous bloodhound or St. Bernard, than between a shepherd's dog and a fox or wolf, and, had their bones been found by us simply as fossils, we should in all probability have ranked them as distinct species, if not as distinct genera, although we now consider them to be only varieties. In pigeons, too, we find the same thing. All the different kinds of domestic pigeons are derived from the ordinary rock-pigeon, and yet there is a much greater difference between the fantail or the pouter and the rock-pigeon than there is between it and most other wild species of pigeon. Yet we know that the fantail and the pouter have been produced by breeders simply selecting birds which possessed certain slight peculiarities, and choosing from each successive brood only those which presented those peculiarities in the most marked form, until, in the course of successive generations, they had succeeded in completely altering the appearance or habits of the bird.

We find also that races of men differ very much from one another at the present day, that the Englishman is immensely higher in point of development, bodily and mental, than the Australian or the Bushman; and yet all are agreed that Englishman and Australian have sprung from a common stock, and spread from a common centre. How is it, then, that Englishmen and Australians or Bushmen, are so different from each other? The most natural answer to this question seems to me to be that they have been living under different conditions for many generations.

We can see how these conditions would tell if we take a hypothetical case, and I take this especially because it illustrates the **struggle for existence** on which so much stress has been laid in the doctrine of evolution.

Supposing that a ship sailing on the southern seas were wrecked, and that the men and women built themselves two rafts and tried to make for land. On both rafts provisions were scanty, and gave out before they reached the shore. Let us suppose that, maddened by hunger, the stronger men snatched from the weaker all the eatables they possessed, and left them to starve.

When the whole provision had been exhausted the rafts grounded on land, but one of them stranded on a barren shore where there was very little to eat, and the other, driven by a contrary current, reached one where there was abundance of food. In each case the survivors who stepped on shore would be divided into two classes. There would be a few of the stronger men who had wrenched the food from the others, and there would also be in all probability one or two others, perhaps small and physically feeble, not strong enough to hold their own in a struggle with the most powerful of their competitors, but who were yet capable of

much endurance, and had been able to sustain life
without food for a longer period than some of their
fellows who were larger and more muscular than they.
Amongst this latter class would in all probability be
one or two women.

The struggle for bare existence begun on the raft
would now be continued in the case of those who had
landed upon the barren island, but here they would
all be forced to separate in search of food. Berries
might be found here, shell-fish there, and upon these
the small but tough and enduring individuals could
manage to find an existence of which their stronger
neighbours could no longer deprive them, as they
would have dispersed in search of food for themselves.
Here the stronger, no longer able to support themselves, would die off. The small individuals would
marry and propagate, and of their children only the
toughest would be likely to survive. Hence would
arise a small race, capable of subsisting upon little
food, although probably ready to gorge themselves,
like the Australians and Hottentots of the present day,
whenever an opportunity occurred.

On the other island the case would be different.
Here the stronger, finding abundance of food, would
gain an easy livelihood, and, marrying the women,
drive away their weaker fellows, who would thus live
and die childless. In the next generation the same

thing would be repeated, and thus we should get a large and powerful race such as we find inhabiting the South Sea Islands at the present day.

The effect of natural selection was well seen in the American Civil War. It is usually supposed that if you take a number of men from the country, and an equal number of townsmen, the countrymen would be stronger and more enduring than their urban neighbours, but in the American War it was found that the latter, although often smaller and apparently weaker than the countrymen, endured the fatigues and privations of campaigning better than they. At first sight this seems astonishing, but a little reflection will show that it is just what might have been expected. It has been calculated that the wear and tear of town life would in the course of a generation or two kill off all the townspeople if they were not constantly recruited from the country. All townsfolk are therefore descended from country folk, and it is evident that in the course of a generation or two only those will survive who are best fitted to resist the deleterious influences of town life, or, as we put it for simplicity's sake, only the descendants of the toughest will survive. If we then take a batch of townsfolk and a batch of countryfolk, and subject them to privation and fatigue, it is evident that the townsfolk ought to have the advantage, because amongst the countryfolk are a number of those whose parents or grandparents would have succumbed to the conditions of town life and left no progeny behind them. These persons owe their very existence to the favourable conditions under which their ancestors have lived; they inherit less robust constitutions than the townsmen, and therefore break down before them in a campaign where the conditions of life are unfavourable.

The reason why we now find breeds of fantails and pouters amongst pigeons, and Italian greyhounds, bloodhounds, and St. Bernards amongst dogs, is that the ancestors from which these breeds are descended possessed certain peculiarities which caused them to be preserved by their owners when the other members of each successive brood were destroyed. In the case of these breeds of pigeons, and also in the cases of some of the dogs, the selection was an artificial one, certain qualities having been arbitrarily chosen by the owners of the animals, and the individuals possessing them preserved and allowed to propagate, without reference to their fitness for obtaining sustenance for themselves in the event of their being cast adrift and compelled to wander, without a master, alone in the wide world. In many cases, the peculiarity nurtured artificially by breeding would be a fatal drawback to their ability to sustain themselves, and the breed would probably die out so soon as the food supplied to them by their masters was stopped, and they had to struggle for themselves.

The cases of the men whom we have fancied to be cast adrift upon a desert island, and of those brought up in town and country, are quite different from those of the animals just referred to. The selection of the men is not artificial and arbitrary, but natural; in other words, it depends upon the fitness of the individuals to fight the battle of life, and to survive amidst the circumstances by which they are surrounded. The reason why we get races differing in physical strength or in power of endurance is that men multiply quicker than their means of subsistence, that some, consequently, must die off, and that those die who are least fitted to obtain a livelihood in the circumstances which surround them. In the barren desert island of which we have spoken, the small and enduring race survived in the fertile island the large and strong, and if we suppose that a part of the population from each island were shipwrecked in the same manner as their ancestors, but that the small and enduring people from the barren island were cast upon the fertile coast, and the large and muscular people from the fruitful country were wrecked on the barren soil, the members of each race would undergo modifications, the toughest among the large and muscular people surviving on the one hand,

ADAPTATION TO CIRCUMSTANCES.

and the largest of the enduring and tough race on the other. But the populations resulting from the modifications of each race might be very different from those descended from the original inhabitants. The small and tough people would grow larger and more muscular, but they might never reach the size and muscularity of the primitive population descended from the original sailors of the raft; after a residence of many years on the barren island the large and muscular people again would become smaller and more enduring than before, though they might never become so small, or attain to the power of endurance of the original individuals descended from the small sailors.

Let us suppose, again, that some members, from whatever cause, were forced to migrate from any of these settlements into an unhealthy district. There some of them would die off, and others would survive. Let us suppose that from some reason those who were able to withstand the miasms were of a darker complexion than were those who had died. Their colour would then gradually grow darker and darker, until at length they might become perfectly black, when they would enjoy almost perfect immunity from the fever poison, just as is the case amongst negroes.

In all these instances the large men, the tough men, and the dark men, survived because they were best able to obtain the means of living, and to resist most successfully the causes of death amidst the circumstances in which they were placed.

This same struggle for existence goes on, not merely amongst men, but (as has been the case for innumerable ages), amongst the lower animals and plants, and is supposed by Darwin to be the chief, though not the only cause, of the gradual evolution of the forms of animal and plant life which exist upon the earth's surface at the present day.

LECTURE XVI.

THE MOSAIC RECORD AND EVOLUTION.

WE have now seen that the various forms of plant and animal life are linked together, and that the embryos of all animals pass through various stages, in which they resemble lower forms of life before they reach the one which they shall finally assume.

Now, the question arises, How did these things all come to be so? Is it not because animals and plants are all derived from one simple, common form of life, and present these resemblances to each other because they are members of one great family, all descended from the same parent, and all more or less closely related to each other? We are accustomed to despise the inquisitors who tortured Galileo in order to make him assert that he had been mistaken in believing that the earth went round the sun, instead of the sun round the earth. The old philosopher is reported to have said, even after he had been forced to sign a recantation, "It moves for all that."

Here the accused was wiser than his judges, who had before them an example which they disregarded, but which we ourselves would do well to follow. Eighteen hundred years ago, when the new doctrines of Christianity were beginning to be talked about, a number of the Jewish rabbis were greatly exercised in their minds regarding them, and thought it their duty to put a stop to them. But the aged Gamaliel, at whose feet Paul had sat, wisely warned them. "Let them alone, for if this counsel or this work be of men, it will come to nought; but if it be of God, ye cannot overthrow it; lest haply ye be found even to fight against God."

Then, as now, the proverb was true, "Great is truth, and it will prevail." If the doctrine of evolution be false, it will ere long be destroyed by the advance of knowledge and the acquirement of new facts, but if it be true, it will prevail, whether we like it or no.

And now let us see what difference it will make to us if it be true. One great objection to it is that it is said to be atheistical, and that it ousts God from His own universe. But is this so?

The question is, how animals and plants now living around us came to be here. Few, I presume, will deny that if God pleased to make them by one grand process of gradual evolution, instead of by numerous acts of special creation, it was in His power to do so; and the question for us is, not whether the animals and plants in question were made by God or not, but how He made them.

Even when we consider the doctrine of evolution in its very widest sense, including, not merely evolution of living beings, but of matter in the form in which we are acquainted with it, the doctrine is not atheistical, as some would have it to be. According to the notions now generally accepted by physicists, there was a period at which the solid masses of the earth, sun, planets, and stars did not exist, and when the matter composing them was widely diffused, in a nebulous condition, through space. Nay, more: if the speculations of Lockyer be correct—and the accumulated evidence which he brings in support of them almost forces us to believe that they are—the very chemical elements themselves must be looked upon simply as one kind of matter under differently aggregated forms. In the very beginning, then, of this universe, so far as our knowledge goes, matter was diffused equally through space. Then atom coalesced with atom, singly or in groups, and then the most primitive of our elements, such as hydrogen, were formed. Further and further aggregation took place, the equally diffused matter became more and more condensed, in certain parts forming distinct nebulæ, which went on shrinking more and more, and increasing in density as they diminished in size, until, to take a single instance, the matter which uniformly filled a space much greater than that now occupied by the entire solar system became condensed into the bodies of the sun and planets, leaving between them only that thin, impalpable substance to which we give the name of æther. The shock of the atoms, as they struck against each other, not only gave them a motion of revolution, but raised them to a temperature of which we have scarcely any conception, and which rendered the very existence, not only of compounds, but of many of the actual metals themselves, impossible. Gradually the smaller planets cooled down, and as the cooling process went on the higher metals were formed; compounds of carbon, oxygen, and hydrogen became possible, steam condensed into water, organic matter appeared, and, by and by, in the course of long ages, some of these developed into living protoplasm. After this began the process of the evolution of the animals which we now see.

But now let us follow the same process into the future. The sun, which is now the source of light, and life, and energy to its subsidiary planets, will in time grow cold; but if there be, as experiments seem to show, some friction in æther, the rate at which the planets revolve around the sun will gradually diminish, they will approach nearer and nearer to it, and ultimately fall successively into it, the impact of each again raising its temperature to an enormous extent. Untold ages may be necessary for this process, but by and by the end will come and the whole of the solar system will be swallowed up in the sun. Nor is this all. The sun itself, and all its attendant planets, appear at present to be circling round some point in the Pleiades. The same process will go on with them until the whole of the matter in the universe shall be collected into one huge ball.

A similar change is going on with regard to energy. No energy is lost any more than matter; but yet, at every change of form a certain amount is converted into radiant heat. When we transform heat into light, or heat into electricity, or heat into motion, or electricity into motion or chemical action, or chemical action again into heat, however we change its form we never get back the whole of the original energy which we transformed—a certain portion is always converted into radiant heat. We may compare this to the process of changing money. Each time that we convert pounds into francs, francs into dollars, dollars into piastres, we lose a little by the exchange. The money-changer always retains a certain percentage for his trouble, and such percentage is lost to us. If we went on changing our money sufficiently often, we should finally have none left, as the percentage of the money-changers would have absorbed it all. In the same way, at each change of energy in the universe, some is converted into radiant heat. By and by the whole of the energy in the universe will be converted into radiant heat, and the whole of matter into one huge ball. Here, then, we seem to have an arrangement which we may compare to an enormous clock set going ages and ages ago, which will go on for ages and ages to come, but, at some remote period, will certainly run down. And now the question naturally arises, Who wound it up? Matter and energy, such as we know them, appear to be practically coming to an end, and we seem almost forced to believe that their original position and properties must have been impressed upon them by some power apart from either. Supposing this to be the case, the Power who gave the atoms their position and properties must, from a knowledge of these, almost necessarily have been able, not only to declare the end from the beginning (Isaiah xlvi. 10), but to know what was going on in every space and at every time, and must indeed be not only omnipotent, but omniscient.

Thus, in the doctrine of evolution, carried to its very remotest limits, there is nothing atheistic, but the very reverse.

The next objection is that we are told in the Bible that God did make animals after a certain fashion, and that it was the fashion of special creation, and not of evolution. Here then, the Bible, and what seems to be the evidence of the Book of Nature, are in contradiction. Here, again, we must ask, Is it so? What we read in Genesis is this, "And God said, Let the waters bring forth abundantly the moving creature that hath life, and fowl that may fly above the earth in the open firmament of heaven. And God created great whales, and every living creature that moveth, which the waters brought forth abundantly, after their kind, and every winged fowl after his kind: and God saw that it was good. And God blessed them, saying, Be fruitful, and multiply, and fill the waters in the seas, and let fowl multiply in the earth. And the evening and the morning were the fifth day. And God said, Let the earth bring forth the living creature after his kind, cattle, and creeping thing, and beast of the earth after his kind: and it was so. And God made the beast of the earth after his kind, and cattle after their kind, and everything that creepeth upon the earth after his kind: and God saw that it was good." This, it seems to me, is a wide, general description of creation, and the only argument that can be drawn from it in favour of special creation of species, is from the words "after his kind." But what does "kind" mean? Does it mean species, or does it signify type? I believe the word to be a general one, and that we have no right to limit it to species. If we say that it means type the statement is generally correct, and here

I can see no discrepancy between the first chapter of Genesis and the doctrine of evolution.

But by far the most serious objection to the hypothesis is its necessary extension to man. If we accept it, we must give up the belief which we all learned in our childhood, that a single man was created out of lifeless mud, became a living soul, and was the progenitor of the whole human race. We must believe, instead, that men are descended, not from any of the species or genera of monkeys now living, but from creatures which were the common ancestors of man and monkeys, and much lower in the scale of existence than either. If such progenitors existed, they were probably somewhat like the lemurs of the present day, though still lower in the scale of existence than they. From these hypothetical common ancestors of man and monkeys, two different races started. Man developed onwards towards greater and greater intellectual power; he learned to light fires, and gained all the power which this could give him; learned to communicate with his fellows, not merely by verbal signs, but by visible ones, either in the way of drawing or writing, and thus was enabled to pass on the accumulated knowledge of one generation to another. The monkeys, on the other hand, developed rather physically than intellectually; they became admirably adapted for an arborial life, but the satisfaction of their hunger, or the gratification of their other appetites, were the utmost ends to which their mental development enabled them to attain. Believers in evolution do not, however, fancy that a monkey can now become a man, or that monkeys of the present day can ever develop into men; for between men and monkeys there is a great gulf fixed. They may have started from a common point long ago, but the races have now diverged so far that it is perfectly hopeless for the one ever to pass into the other.

The doctrine of a common descent of man and monkey from some lower animal seems at first sight to cut at the root of all religious beliefs. But again we must ask the question, Does it do so? Many people seem to believe that, according to the theory of evolution, men are monkeys, because men and monkeys are descended from a common ancestor. But this is not the case. A man is a man, and not a monkey, whether his first progenitors became men by special creation from a lump of clay, or whether they were developed from a man-like animal. We are not pagans, robbers, murderers, manstealers, living by rapine and dealing in bloodshed, and yet it is almost certain that we are descended from ancestors who were pagans, robbers, murderers, and manstealers. Nor does it matter now whether these our ancestors were suddenly changed from heathen pirates to Christian herdsmen and agriculturists, or whether a generation or two elapsed during the change. The change has taken place, and that is enough.

But it may be said that this is no true analogy, for this was merely a change of manners—the men were still men, the pagans and robbers had souls as well as the Christians, whereas the monkey and lower animals have no soul. If we believe that man was created from a lump of clay, we can clearly see how he could have a soul, and an animal not, whereas upon the hypothesis that he was developed from a monkey this is impossible.

But is it so?

We are reasonable beings, responsible for our actions, knowing good from evil, and awarding praise to one and punishment to another, but **we were not always so.** We were not responsible to the civil law for our actions until we had attained the age of twenty-one, though we were responsible to the criminal law long before; and even at an age when a court of justice would hold us irresponsible, our parents and teachers regarded us as knowing good from evil, and punished or praised us as our actions deserved. But even they would regard us as irresponsible at one period of our existence. No one blames or

EMBRYOS OF FOUR VERTEBRATES. 347

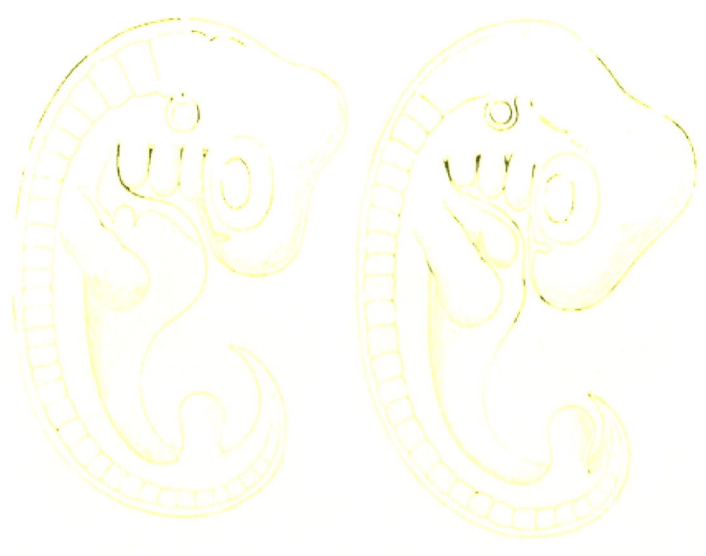

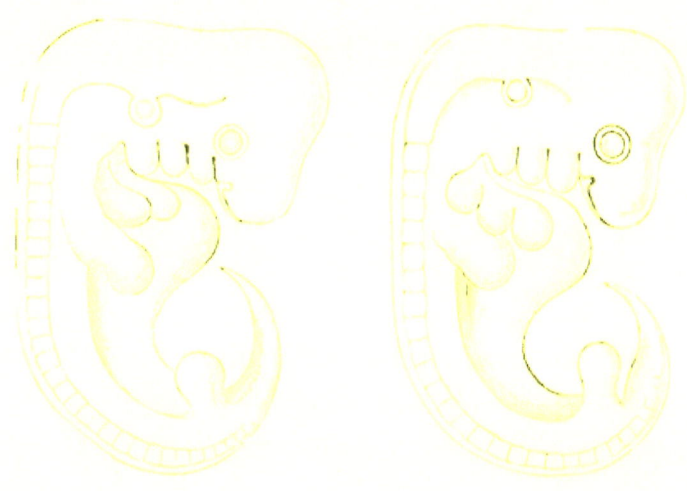

348 EMBRYOS OF FOUR VERTEBRATES.

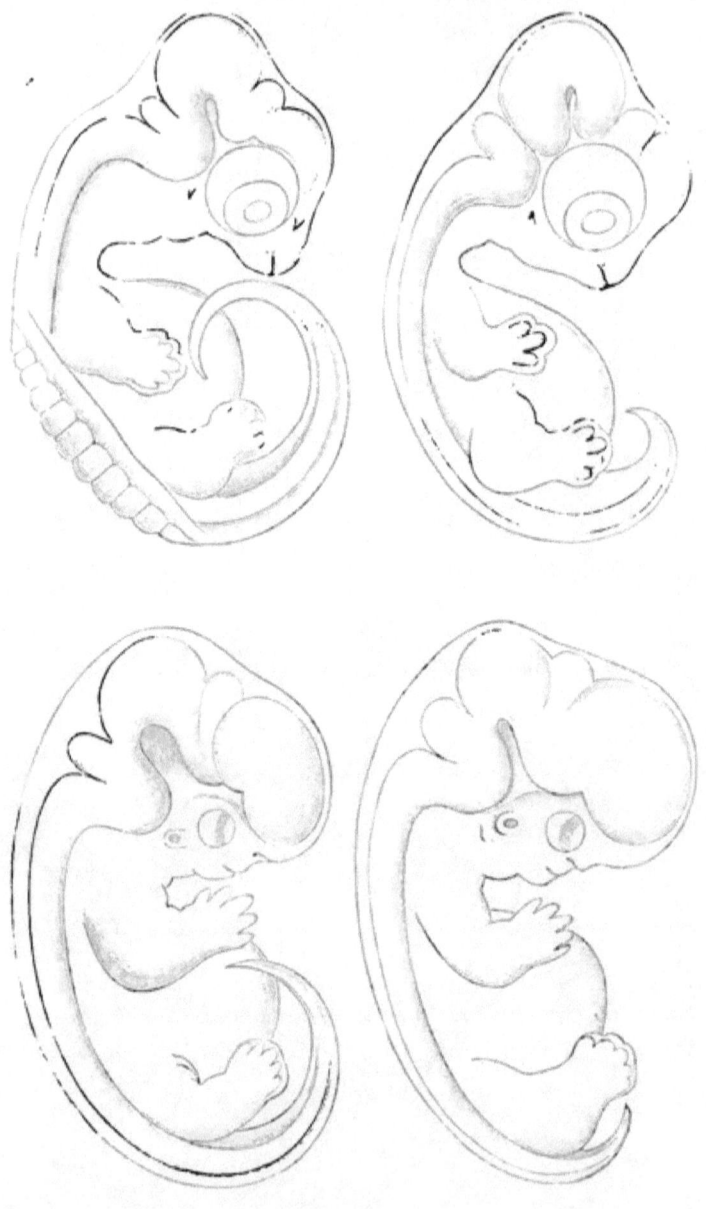

praises the new-born child for its actions. Every one blames and praises the same child when it has grown up.

The man is responsible though the child was not, and at some point in his life he passed to the condition of responsibility from that of irresponsibility, although it would be difficult to say where the point was.

In the existence of every man there is a point at which he becomes a living being, at which he is regarded as passing from death to life. A child born some months before its time is not looked upon as a living child, yet it would be hard, or impossible, to fix the precise period at which the child passes from death to life.

Nay, more, there is a point in the existence of every man in which he becomes a human being. The ovum from which he is developed is not a human being; the embryo which succeeds the ovum is, at certain stages of its development, undistinguishable from that of a fish, a tortoise, or a bird, and, at a later period, from that of a dog or rabbit (Figs. 166-173).

It cannot be said, then, that the embryo which afterwards develops into a man is a man, or has a soul, and yet by and by it will so develop, although we cannot fix the exact point at which it becomes a human being.

Now the question of evolution is simply whether the race of mankind has been developed in the course of time in the same way as that in which every individual man has developed from an embryo, and the difficulties regarding the passage from an animal to a man and the possession of a soul are the same in the case of the individual man as they are in the case of the race.

The fact that each man has been developed from an embryo like that of the lower animals, and was at one period of his existence a lifeless, irresponsible being, does not lessen his responsibility now, nor would it in the most infinitesimal degree alter man's duties or responsibilities if it were proved that his first ancestors were descended from apes, or animals lower than apes, instead of being formed from a lump of clay. There is a point in every man's life at which he becomes a human being, and similarly, if men were developed from animals, there was a point in the existence of the race at which the beings composing it ceased to be lower animals, and began to be men, although it might be impossible to fix the exact point.

But the next difficulty is that this assumption as to the evolution of man from the lower animals is thought by many to be in direct contradiction to the Bible narrative, although, in the case of the lower animals, the Biblical account and the record of nature may be readily reconciled. But let us read the Bible narrative again: "And the Lord God formed man of the dust of the ground, and breathed into his nostrils the breath of life, and man became a living soul." Here, again, it seems to me that this account is so general that it may coincide equally well with evolution and with the doctrine of a special creation, for the statement is simply that God formed man out of the dust of the ground. It does not say how He made him; and out of the dust of the ground man certainly is formed. Even supposing that evolution be true, it was out of the elements which existed on the earth's surface long before the advent of life that the first amoeba-like creature was created, and every succeeding being, beast, bird, fish, or reptile, was equally formed out of the dust of the ground, and to the dust every one must sooner or later return.

Again, it may be objected that, according to the evolution doctrine, primitive man was an ape-like animal, and that, according to the scriptural account, he was higher and better than his descendants. But here, just as in the case of our notions regarding the mode of creation of the lower animals directly from the earth, we have, to a great extent, drawn our conclusions, not from the Bible, but from Milton's *Paradise Lost*, where the poet describes Adam and Eve walking about in the garden:—

> "All kind
> Of living creatures, new to sight and strange.
> Two of far nobler shape, erect and tall,
> God-like erect, with native honour clad
> In naked majesty, seemed lords of all,
> And worthy seemed; for in their looks divine
> The image of their glorious Maker shone,
> Truth, wisdom, sanctitude severe and pure—
> Severe, but in true filial freedom placed,
> Whence true authority in men: though both
> Not equal, as their sex not equal seemed;
> For contemplation he and valour formed,
> For softness she and sweet attractive grace;
> He for God only, she for God in him.
> His fair large front and eye sublime declared
> Absolute rule; and hyacinthine locks
> Round from his parted forelock manly hung
> Clustering, but not beneath his shoulders broad:
> She, as a veil down to the slender waist,
> Her unadornèd golden tresses wore
> Dishevelled, but in wanton ringlets waved
> As the vine curls her tendrils—"
>
> * * * * * *
>
> "So passed they naked on, nor shunned the sight
> Of God or angel; for they thought no ill:
> So hand in hand they passed, the loveliest pair
> That ever since in love's embraces met—
> Adam the goodliest man of men since born
> His sons; the fairest of her daughters Eve."

This is a very beautiful picture, but it is not at all the one given in Genesis, for there we find that man, after the fall, was a being in the condition of the savages of the Stone age in Europe, clad in skins, and tilling the ground with implements made either of wood or stone, the use of metals being unknown until generations afterwards. And yet this being, low in the scale as we would term him, is represented as being so much higher in wisdom than Adam before the fall, that he was to be reckoned almost as a God in comparison, for in Genesis, iii. 22, we read that "The Lord God said Behold! the man is become as one of us, to know good and evil." So that, although the Miltonic account of primitive man is an absolute contradiction of the notions of evolution, the Mosaic account is in conformity with them.

But a still more serious difficulty yet remains. Even supposing that we reconcile the Scriptural account of the creation of man with the theory of evolution, how are we to reconcile the account of the creation of woman? For it is said that "The Lord God caused a deep sleep to fall upon Adam, and he slept: and He took one of his ribs, and closed up the flesh instead thereof; and the rib, which the Lord God had taken from man, made He a woman, and brought her unto the man. And Adam said, This is now bone of my bones, and flesh of my flesh: she shall be called Woman, because she was taken out of Man! Therefore shall a man leave his father and his mother, and shall cleave unto his wife; and they shall be one flesh." If we are to take the words of the Bible as an accurate account of the creation of woman, I do not see how we are to reconcile it with the hypothesis of evolution. If this be a true history, of which every word has a literal signification, that hypothesis must be false, but, if evolution be really a fact, we must consider whether the interpretation we have been accustomed to place upon this account be really the true one.

First of all, let us consider what practical end was to be served by the account given of the creation in Genesis. The Scripture is profitable for doctrine, for reproof, for correction, for instruction in righteousness, that the man of God may be perfect, thoroughly furnished unto all good works. The use of Scripture is explained by St. Paul as a practical one, and we know that the practical doctrines which are drawn in the Bible from the first chapters of Genesis are the observance of the Sabbath day and the sanctity of marriage. Because God made the earth in six days, therefore man is to remember the Sabbath day to keep it holy; and because woman was taken out of man, therefore man and wife shall cleave together, and shall be no longer twain, but one flesh.

Some years ago a fierce controversy raged regarding the age of the earth, and the date of the appearance of man. It was considered that the days mentioned in Genesis must needs have been of the same length as our days, and that therefore the accounts of Scripture were irreconcilable with the teachings of geology, but, thanks in great measure to Hugh Miller, people

IS OUR INTERPRETATION CORRECT?

have now generally come to accept the days of Genesis, not as periods of twenty-four hours, but as long epochs of thousands, perhaps millions of years.

The time has now arrived when we must consider whether our interpretation of the story of the creation is true or not. We are accustomed, too much, perhaps, to consider the Bible as written entirely for us, and to judge it exclusively by our own standards. We forget that it was not written *even chiefly* for us; that the books of Moses were first of all written for the chosen people, and were for them sacred guides for a very much longer period than they have ever been to us of the western nations. It is marvellous how wonderfully they do suit us, belonging to a different race, living under different circumstances, and having a very different degree of knowledge from the ancient Jews; but we must always remember for whom they were written, and consider that what was written was primarily for their instruction in righteousness.

But Paul, in teaching the Corinthians, did not begin by telling them everything at once. He "fed them with milk, and not with strong meat, as they were able to bear it, for strong meat belongeth only to them who are of full age, even those who by reason of use have their senses exercised to discern both good and evil."

Now, supposing that the hypothesis of evolution be

true, what good would it have done to have taught the early Jews all these things that we hear of now? What did it matter to them whether rocks were sedimentary or igneous, whether they contained fossils or not? What use was it for them to know that the first forms of life were simple protoplasm, which afterwards became developed into higher types until at length man was reached? It would simply have confused them. The great lesson for them was that in the beginning God created the heavens and the earth; that He created man, and therefore they must obey Him; that He had rested when His work was over, and therefore they must keep the seventh day; and that He had made woman out of man, and therefore man and wife must cling to one another.

One of the first questions that every child asks its parent is, "How did baby brother come?" and the parent answers, not by giving a full explanation of all the mysteries of birth and development, but by saying, "God gave baby brother to papa and mamma, and therefore you must be kind to him." A full explanation would to the child be unintelligible, and if intelligible injurious; and is it not possible that the Bible account of his own creation, given in his childhood to man for his guidance, is like the account given to children now of the baby brother's birth for their guidance?

It may be said that this is playing with Scripture; that the words of the Bible must be taken literally, or else we may give up the whole book.

But it is impossible always to take the language of the Bible literally; we must, in some instances at least, take it generally. As an example, in the book of Judges we find, "And the Lord was with Judah; and He drove out the inhabitants of the mountain; but could not drive out the inhabitants of the valley, because they had chariots of iron." If we take the verse literally we must believe that the power of the Lord was unable to overcome the chariots of iron. In the fifth chapter of Genesis also we read, "In the day that God created man, in the likeness of God made He him; male and female created He them, and blessed them, and called their name Adam, in the day when they were created." Here we find that Adam appears as a plural noun, whereas in the next verse it seems to be a singular one; but we find that singular and plural nouns are used indiscriminately. In the tenth chapter we find, "And the sons of Ham; Cush, and Mizraim, and Phut, and Canaan. And Canaan begat Sidon his firstborn, and Heth, and the Jebusite, and the Amorite," and so on.

Here we find individual names, and names of tribes, mixed up promiscuously. In the first chapter of Judges, too, we find it written: " And Judah said unto

Simeon his brother, Come up with me into my lot, that we may fight against the Canaanites; and I likewise will go with thee into thy lot. So Simeon went with him." Here we seem to have a very definite account of two brothers speaking to one another, but in the next verse we find that the brothers Judah and Simeon were not meant at all, as they had been dead hundreds of years, but the tribes of Judah and Simeon were meant. In all these passages the words cannot be taken in their literal signification.

Another objection, however, may be raised—that because the Bible is the Word of God, it must be perfect; and that, therefore, it must be perfectly adapted not only to those to whom the record was first addressed, but for us also living in later times.

This assumption, however, is incorrect; because we find that the laws given by Moses to the children of Israel in the name of God were not perfect, but were adapted to them in the condition in which they were at the time. For Christ says: "Moses, for the hardness of your heart, gave you this precept, but from the beginning it was not so."

Seeing, then, that Paul graduated his instructions to the people whom he was addressing, first giving them milk, and afterwards strong meat; that Moses modified his laws to the people whom he was ruling, giving them laws which were not perfect, but suited

OBJECT OF THESE ARGUMENTS. 359

to their circumstances; that in some parts of Scripture at least we cannot assign a literal meaning to the words without destroying the meaning of the passage; may it not be allowable to believe that the account of the creation of woman given in the first chapter of Genesis is not a literal description of fact, but a parable, such as those so freely employed by Christ in His teachings to those whom He addressed? For though Christ gave full explanations to His disciples when alone and apart, He spoke to the multitude only by parables, according as they were able to bear it.

To many a one the explanations and arguments I have just adduced will seem perfectly inadequate, and they will unhesitatingly reject the doctrine of evolution; to others they may seem very doubtful, and not to be accepted at present—at the very utmost to be looked upon only as provisional. If this doctrine of evolution be false, they are not required; but if the facts already accumulated, and which are being added to every day, should lead some to believe it to be true, what I have just said will show that they need not therefore cast aside their former religious beliefs, any more than they have done so because they may now believe the seven days of creation to be long epochs, and not periods of twenty-four hours each.

Now it is very remarkable that the doctrine of evolution, be it true or no, exactly agrees with the

Mosaic account in reference to the place where man was created, whether this creation took place by special act, or by evolutionary process. It took place in a paradise, where the air was balmy, where fruit-trees were plentiful, and where there were no furious carnivorous animals to prey upon or attack man. For man differs from the lower animals in the absence of a furry or hairy coat (although curiously enough such a coat is possessed by unborn children). Now, if for a moment we suppose ourselves driven to conclude that, in respect of his physical nature, man was evolved from a lower form of life, he could not have lost his hairy coat unless the air had been soft and balmy, for the essence of the doctrine is that the fittest only survive, and the fittest to survive exposure to heat or cold would not have been the naked, but the hairy individuals. Had not food been abundant and easily masticated, like the fruit of trees, man would not have lost the projecting muzzle and larger jaw of the apes, as a small jaw would be less fitted for the mastication of hard and innutritious food. Had man been liable to the attacks of wild animals in this paradise, he could not have lost the large canines which form such powerful implements of defence in the gorilla. Nor would he have remained so long helpless, and unable to take the least care of himself, unless in such a paradise as we have supposed,

SITE OF PARADISE.

where all the conditions of life were favourable. The children, which were long in developing, would have been at a disadvantage in the struggle for existence; they would have died off; and the progenitors of the human race could never have developed into men.

The site, too, of the paradise, according to the evolution theory, agrees exactly with that indicated in the book of Genesis, and, indeed, until I saw a map by Haeckel, the most prominent defender of the evolution theory in Germany, I was puzzled to understand the Mosaic account. It reads thus: "And the Lord God planted a garden eastward in Eden; and there He put the man whom He had formed. And out of the ground made the Lord God to grow every tree that is pleasant to the sight, and good for food; the tree of life also in the midst of the garden, and the tree of knowledge of good and evil. And a river went out of Eden to water the garden; and from thence it was parted, and became into four heads. The name of the first is Pison: that is it which compasseth the whole land of Havilah, where there is gold; and the gold of that land is good: there is bdellium and the onyx-stone. And the name of the second river is Gihon; the same is it that compasseth the whole land of Ethiopia. And the name of the third river is Hiddekel: that is it which goeth toward the east of Assyria. And the fourth river is Euphrates."

Now the river Euphrates to some extent fixes the position of the garden, but many commentators, unable to find the other three rivers, place the garden near the source of the Euphrates, although it does not there part into four. Other commentators, however, after a careful discussion of the former notions, have decided that Eden must have been somewhere near the place where the Euphrates emptied itself into the Persian Gulf, for the only river that could be identified with the Hiddekel is the Tigris, which, like the Hiddekel, "goeth toward the east of Assyria." The name also is nearly identical, for, cutting off the aspirate, we get Dekel, Diglath, Diglis, Tigris. My great difficulty, however, in accepting this explanation was that no river which joined the Euphrates before it entered the Persian Gulf could by any possibility compass the land of Ethiopia.[1] Let us suppose, however, that at the time when man was put into the Garden of Eden the continents of Asia and Africa extended much further than they do now; that they reached, in fact, to the line of islands which we see dotting the Indian Ocean, from beyond the Cape of Good Hope to Ceylon. Then the Euphrates and Tigris, continuing their course to the sea in the same direction that they do now,

---

[1] The position of the land of Ethiopia, or Cush, is by no means definitely settled, but the balance of evidence seems to point to a position south of Egypt.

might be met by such a river as the Zambesi, or one which, like it, might be said to compass the land of Ethiopia. Whether the Pison were the Indus or not does not greatly matter. It was probably either the Indus or some river passing down from the country of the Amalekites[1] through the present Red Sea, which would then be dry land.

The site thus indicated with the utmost precision by Moses is perhaps the only one upon the surface of the whole earth which fulfils the demands of the doctrine of evolution. For, as we have already seen, according to this doctrine man must have been developed in a genial climate, in a spot where abundance of food existed. Now such a place might perhaps be found in a similar latitude in America, but it is agreed by all evolutionists that man could not possibly have been developed in the new world, because his affinities are altogether with the monkeys of the old world and not with those of the new. This is the only point, too, from which man could have spread in such a way as would agree with the distribution of races which we now find.

But man did not always continue to live in this Paradise. He was driven out. According to the theory of evolution, he was probably forced to migrate from

---

[1] In exploring the Dead Sea, Lieutenant Maury found a valley like a river channel running southwards from the Dead Sea.

this sacred spot for the same reason that races have been forced to migrate ever since, namely, want of food due to increasing numbers. These increasing numbers would, first of all, consume the natural fruits of the trees; they would then be forced to till the ground, and, finally, some of them would be obliged to leave altogether. We read in Genesis that the woman was cursed by her conception being multiplied, and that the man was cursed by having to till the ground by the sweat of his brow. While in Paradise he was naked, but after he left it he wore coats of skin. He had not yet learned the use of metals, and his tools and implements must have been of wood or stone. For, according to Genesis, it was not until several generations afterwards that Tubal-Cain taught men the use of brass and iron.

However man was formed, then, the Mosaic account corresponds with what we find in the progress of civilisation—the Stone age precedes that of bronze and iron. The Paradise whose locality was indicated by Moses has now disappeared beneath the waters of the Indian Ocean. Whether its disappearance was preceded by some great volcanic eruption or not, and whether such an eruption is referred to in the mention of the flaming sword which turned every way, we cannot tell, but we have no indication in Genesis of the submergence of Paradise until the time of the flood.

THE DELUGE.

Although the waters of the deluge suddenly burst in upon man at the last, yet it was not a sudden event, for we are told that Noah had been preparing an ark for 120 years before. We read that God said unto Noah, "I, even I, do bring a flood of waters upon the earth, to destroy all flesh, wherein is the breath of life, from under heaven; and everything that is in the earth shall die;" but how He said this we are not told. We usually imagine, although there is no record whatever of it, that Noah was warned in a dream, but it may have been that he was made aware by the evident sinking of the land, which would sooner or later bring it beneath the level of the ocean. We are misled by the picture-books and narratives with which we become familiar in childhood. We are apt to think of the rain which fell for forty days and forty nights as being the chief element in the flood, but a little reflection will show that this is impossible, and that only the breaking up of the fountains of the great deep, or, in other words, the submergence of the land, and consequent rush of the waters of the ocean over it, could have produced such a deluge as is described. And this rush, according to the hypothesis which we have been considering, was just such a one as would carry the ark towards the point indicated by Moses, viz. Mount Ararat, for if the land on which we have supposed Paradise to be situated sank along with that part of Asia lying to the northward of it, Ararat is the first high land which would be likely to come at all near the surface of the water, and upon which the ark might therefore strand. After a certain period, the land again rose, until the face of it was dry, but we do not know that the whole of the submerged land again appeared above the level of the waters, and probably it was at this time that Paradise for ever disappeared from the eye of man.

Long afterwards, however, and even to our own day, traditions have survived of a paradise situated somewhere in the far east, and this paradise is nearly always spoken of as an island. You will remember, too, that in the account I gave you of the Egyptian funeral, the deceased was judged before he was allowed to cross the lake or river to his place of sepulture, and in our own day we speak of crossing the river of death before the soul can enter into bliss. Whether the expressions so common in our hymns are really remnants of the time when men talked of Paradise, from which they had once come, and to which they hoped one day to return, but which was separated from them by the deep waters, we cannot tell, but I think it is evident, from the Egyptian custom already alluded to (page 18), that they are not simply derived from the crossing of the Jordan into the Promised Land by the Israelites, but have come down from a still earlier period.

TRADITIONS OF THE FLOOD.

After the ark stranded on Ararat, and its occupants dispersed, men spread from a fresh centre over the earth. It is perfectly astonishing in how many different parts of the world we find traditions of the flood and of the ark, and it almost seems that all those nations at least which have spread to the north, east, and west of Mount Ararat, have preserved some such legend, but whether such is the case with the natives of Australia and Africa I do not know. If, however, they should have no tradition of the flood, this might, on the one hand, be put down to the low character of the race; but on the other hand, there is a possibility that these races might have migrated so far from the original site of Paradise as not to be involved in the deluge which destroyed it, and which swept from the face of the earth all the nations living around it.

LECTURE XVII.

DEVELOPMENT OF INDIVIDUALS.

Ethnologists and philologists are generally agreed that men have spread from a common centre, but they differ considerably in their notions regarding the geographical position of this centre. Some philologists at least are inclined to fix this point in the central tableland of Asia, not very far from the sources of the Euphrates, or from Mount Ararat; but if this be the centre from which man has spread, it is difficult to account for the presence of tuft-haired men in two districts only, and those so far apart as Papua and Southern Africa. But if we believe that man spread really from two centres, viz., the original cradle of the human race, or Paradise, from which early forms of man, such as the Papuans and Hottentots, had migrated before the deluge, and again from a second centre in the highlands of Armenia, the difficulty will disappear.

DEVELOPMENT OF INDIVIDUALS.

In discussing the early history of our race I have given much that is speculative, and we may now turn with advantage to a more practical view of the subject—the development of individuals, and the causes which affect such development. However much we may differ in opinion regarding the manner in which man was created, all are agreed that the different nations spread from a common centre, and rose from one common stock. The qualities which every individual possesses are ascribed, both by evolutionists and their opponents, to hereditary descent. Non-evolutionists must believe in this to a greater extent than evolutionists, for they hold that in all animals specific qualities have been transmitted from parents to children without variation, ever since the original creation of the species. Evolutionists, on the other hand, believe that while these qualities are transmitted from parents to children, they may be modified by external circumstances, and both evolutionists and non-evolutionists believe that external circumstances modify the qualities hereditarily transmitted, to such an extent as to lead to the formation of varieties at least, if not of species. In the case of mankind, some might call Negroes and Englishmen distinct species, while others would call them only varieties. The difference here is really in regard to the idea with which the word "species" is associated in the mind of each.

We have already seen how the conditions of life may lead to modification in the size, strength, and mental qualities of a race, and there can be no doubt whatever in the mind of any one, that external conditions have much to do with the development of every individual.

An alteration in the external conditions to which the egg of the fowl is subjected during incubation will modify the form of the chick so, that the local application of warmth to certain points on the surface of the egg will lead to the production of a monstrosity instead of to the growth of a well-formed bird. In human beings, also, external circumstances may exercise a powerful influence upon the individual previous to birth, and the fright of a mother during gestation has not unfrequently left its melancholy impress upon the character and mental faculties of her offspring. If the doctrine of evolution be true, and the various stages of development in men and animals before birth correspond to various stages in the evolution of the races to which they belong, it is only natural to believe that a similar process takes place, to some extent, after birth. We appear to see this, indeed, in the case that we have already mentioned, of the negro, where the black pigment, so distinctive of the race, does not exist in the skin at birth, but only appears afterwards. Before birth the changes which would correspond to enormous periods of time in t progress of the race are run through very rapidly in the individual. After birth the changes are much slower, and the slowness increases with increasing age. It may be pushing the analogy too far to say that an English boy, for example, corresponds in his mental characteristics to the pagan Saxon ancestors from whom he is descended, and yet, to some extent, we seem to find in boys the same delight in fighting, the same restless activity, and the same heedless cruelty which distinguished those old pagans. In a novel, called *The Guardian Angel*, Dr. Oliver Wendell Holmes has illustrated, with his usual felicity, the idea that a man's character is, to a great extent, compounded from that of his ancestors, modified, of course, by the conditions to which he himself has been subject. The heroine of his story, while floating down a river, passes an old burial-place, and is supposed to see, dancing around it, a number of ghostly figures. Some of them are solid and distinct, while others are so vague and shadowy as to be barely visible. Between these two kinds of figures are intermediate forms. All these are recognised by the girl to be her ancestors. They are more or less all represented in her own being, and, so to speak, live in her. The solid and distinct forms represent her immediate ancestors, whose individuality, transmitted to her, makes up a great portion of her whole being, while the vague and shadowy forms are her remote forefathers, whose qualities, diluted by much admixture through successive generations, take but a small part in the composition of her being.

A second idea illustrated by Professor Holmes in the same work is that the qualities of different ancestors predominate in a man's character at different periods of his life. One frequently notices this in regard to children, and sees also that such changes take place very rapidly in them. One week an infant may be said to be like his father, during another like his mother, and in another like his grandfather, or some other distant relation. If the doctrine of evolution be true, it seems probable that at this early period of the child's life the resemblances which he shows are not really to father or mother, but to distant ancestors from whom his father and mother have derived certain traits, and that later on in his life he approximates more and more nearly to his immediate ancestors. There can be no doubt that in many men the personal appearance at one period reminds one of their maternal ancestors, and at another of their paternal ones, and it does not seem unlikely that changes in the individual of which these are the outward signs may be transmitted more or less to any children they have during these periods, and that this may be one reason of the diversity in appearance and character between the children of one family.

EXTERNAL CIRCUMSTANCES AFTER BIRTH.

But external conditions, even after birth, have a great deal to do with the development of the individual, and may lead to the production of entirely different characters, even when they act upon individuals having characteristics almost exactly identical. Look at a chubby-faced boy and say, if you can, what he will turn out. Look at a venerable man, honoured and respected, whose hoary head is found in the way of righteousness, and at a decrepit beggar, crouching, squalid, and despised. How truly different are the two, and yet they may have started from the same point. But, supposing them to do so, we see that every step of their course leads them farther and farther apart. At the stage of boyhood you still feel that the reclamation of the one and the downfall of the other are alike possible. At early manhood you feel that though the one who has started fairly may yet fall, the one who has taken the wrong turning has not much chance of recovery, and that it is nearly impossible in complete manhood for the depraved sot to become the honoured citizen, and that in old age there is between the bad and the good a great gulf fixed, over which neither can pass to the other. The man who has sown tares cannot reap wheat. "For, as a man soweth, that shall he also reap; he that soweth to the flesh shall of the flesh reap corruption, but he that soweth to the spirit shall of the spirit reap life everlasting." Now, how has the man whom we have figured to ourselves sown to the flesh? He has yielded to all the merely animal impulses of his nature, he has lived for the present and not for the future. He is typified by Bunyan in *Pilgrim's Progress* as Passion, and not as Patience. He will have his good things now, and will not wait for them hereafter. In boyhood he will not learn because it involves confinement, attention, and labour, all of which are more or less disagreeable to him, and he will rather play about in the streets, an occupation which yields him pleasure for the moment. At first he may have had some slight power of self-control, but day by day he loses it, and his will grows weaker and weaker for want of exercise. His animal passions daily increase in strength, until his power of self-command is entirely gone, and he is no longer the ruler but the slave of his appetites. He now takes to drink, because it makes him feel stronger and happier for the moment, and he continues to take it, regardless of the consequences. He dislikes work more and more, and is only forced to it by want. The work which he occasionally does he gets through as perfunctorily as possible. He cares not for reputation, he recks not that he loses his chance of future employment by his negligence, all he thinks of is the present moment. And so from bad to worse he goes, becoming weaker, more demoralised, and more miserable at every step, until finally he sinks into a drunkard's grave.

The other, on the contrary, follows the example of Patience, and not of Passion; he is content with discomfort now in order that he may have pleasure hereafter. In his home he learns to submit to the lawful authority of his parents, to control his natural impulses in accordance with their commands. He sees cake on the table, and he knows that preserves are in the cupboard. His natural instincts lead him to take both, because they are very pleasant to his palate, and would give him momentary enjoyment, but he foregoes the present pleasure, not only for the sake of avoiding the pain of punishment, but for the greater pleasure of the approbation of his parents. At school he learns to sit still, although he would much rather be running about. He learns to fix his attention upon his lessons, although it would be very much pleasanter for him to draw pictures upon his slate, or propound riddles to his companions. He learns to rule his temper, and to keep quiet even when irritated. Day by day his power of self-control increases by exercise. Day by day he becomes more accustomed to act, not on account of the pleasure or pain of the present moment, but with an eye to future advantage or safety. He looks not only at his own things, but also at the things of others, and in doing this he realises the truth of the Scripture, "Give, and it shall be given unto you; good measure, heaped up, pressed down, shaken together, and running over, shall men give into your bosom. For with what judgment ye judge, ye shall be judged; and with what measure ye mete, it shall be measured to you again." He judges himself, he examines his actions whether they be right or wrong; he chooses the good, and refuses the evil; thus he escapes the condemnation of his fellows, and thus, loved and honoured, he passes through life, and his hoary head becomes to him a crown of glory.

How different have been the courses of these two men, starting, as they apparently did, from the same point. Why was it that the one took the wrong course, and the other the right one? Partly, no doubt, it was due to the force of external circumstances, and partly, also, to powers and deficiencies in the boys themselves, which were inherited from their parents.

In the instance we have just considered, we have supposed the child in each case to be exactly the same, and the different courses to be entirely due to external circumstances. In the one case the boy has a happy home, is well taught, is kept out of the way of temptation; at school he is well trained and has good companions. As a young man, circumstances are favourable; he is kept from vice by home influences, by the example of good companions, and still more by the influences of religion.

Trained up as a child in the way he should go, when he is old he does not depart from it. He passes through the temptations of youth, and the trials of business in middle life. Possibly, like Agur, he had neither poverty nor riches, but was fed with food convenient for him, so that he was neither full and denied God, saying, "Who is the Lord?" nor so poor, that he stole, and took the name of his God in vain. So he passed safely, successfully, and happily through life, because the external conditions under which he was placed were favourable to him; while, if they had been adverse, he would have taken the other road by which we see the chubby and innocent child, left to itself by no fault of its own, but, let us suppose, by the grievous misfortune of its parents' death, going down to disgrace and ruin. With no one to guide it, it seeks the pleasure of the present moment. Thrown with others like himself, or worse than himself, to play in the streets, he learns to steal, to lie, to swear; he knows that if he steals he may be imprisoned, but thinks it rather manly and noble to do so if he could only avoid detection. He learns to swear, to drink, to smoke, because he sees men around him doing the same, and wishes to be manly. He seeks the pleasure of the present moment, at first because he knows no better, and afterwards because by habit he has lost the desire to do otherwise. He has shirked the discomfort of learning and preferred the pleasures of play, and so as he grows up he can find no profitable employment. His labour is worth little, and what he does earn he is apt to expend in the pleasure of getting drunk. He may be married and have children, but he looks to his own things and not to the things of others; he selfishly cares for his own pleasures, and leaves them to exist as best they can. They in turn care nothing for him; his home is uncomfortable, his wife constantly quarrels with him, his very children despise him. He cared nothing for them while they were young and helpless, and so when he becomes old and decrepit they leave him to his fate. And now, to modify the words of one of the paraphrases—

> ".... mark his end: want doth assail
> When all his strength and vigour fail;
> Want like an armed man doth rush
> The hoary head of age to crush."

In these two examples we have been considering the case of two persons whom we have supposed to start with the same qualities, bodily and mental, and whose different courses and different nature have been entirely due to the effect of different external circumstances

But we must now consider that we very rarely find two persons with exactly the same bodily and mental constitution. One may start with strong passions, and may proceed through life without a corresponding increase in his power of self-control, and he will therefore be liable to succumb to many temptations. Another may likewise have strong passions, but, having a strong will and much self-control, he may successfully resist the temptations which prove too strong for the other. A third may have neither strong passions nor much self-control, and may therefore under favourable circumstances easily follow a correct course, while, if temptation arises, he has little or no power to overcome it. A moral jelly-fish, without backbone, he adapts himself to any mould into which he may be put.

The late M. de Metz, of Mettray, had a Reformatory for children belonging to the criminal classes, and his experience was that it cost more trouble to reform a lymphatic than an energetic ruffian. When once the latter got into the right groove he was not likely to leave it, but the sluggish nature was liable to relapse if left to itself or placed within the reach of bad influences. The will is a potent influence for good or evil, and its exercise and training is perhaps the most valuable lesson in education. As Tennyson says:—

> "O well for him whose will is strong!
>   He suffers; but he will not suffer long;
>   He suffers, but he cannot suffer wrong;
>   For him nor moves the loud world's random mock,
>   Nor all Calamity's hugest waves confound.

* * * * *

> But ill for him who, bettering not with time,
> Corrupts the strength of heaven-descended Will,
> And ever weaker grows thro' acted crime,
> Or seeming-genial venial fault
> Recurring and suggesting still."

As M. de Metz found, and as we see every day, some children have strong and others weak wills. But how is it that they thus come to differ? On inquiry we probably find that the parents of the one were likewise strong, and those of the other weak. Step by step backwards, when we know their ancestry, we are often enabled to trace the same thing, modified in one direction or another by the influences to which the child's ancestors have been subjected. As Mrs. Harriet Beecher Stowe remarks, in one of her works, "we are the sum of a number of factors, stretching back to all eternity." If we picture to ourselves what the children of the two men whose course we have mentally followed will be like, we shall at once see that the children of the good man are likely to be good, not only because they are placed in more favourable circumstances, but because his own good tendencies, strengthened by use, have been transmitted to them. And that the children of the bad are likely to be bad, not only because of their unfavourable surroundings, but because they have inherited from their father the evil tendencies which he has strengthened by custom, and the feeble will, which he has rendered yet feebler by want of exercise. If the children of each of these men were put into the very same circumstances from which each started, the children of the good man would have a chance of being even better than their parent, while the children of the bad man might become worse than he. Every day, looking around us, we see verified the words of Scripture, that the sins of the father are visited upon the children, even unto the third and fourth generations. It, perhaps, may never have occurred to us why God is said to visit the sins unto the third and fourth generations, whereas He is said to show mercy unto thousands of those who love Him and keep His commandments; but if we only look at the two faces, we shall see that the descendants of the sot are likely to become extinct in the third or fourth generation, whereas those of the good man may go on until the end of world, if each succeeding generation follows in the footsteps of its parents.

It may seem very hard that some are thus predestined, as it were, to destruction, while others are predestined to happiness, and that not for any fault or virtue of their own. It was not the fault of the drunkard's children that their father was a sot, nor is it any virtue in the children of the good man that their father has been good. However far we follow the race back, generation by generation, still we find the same thing, that each generation inherits from the preceding one qualities, mental, moral, and physical, which determine its power to follow any course, and the start in life which determines the direction of that course for good or evil, although such course may be afterwards modified by other circumstances. It may seem to us unjust that such should be the case, but so it is; and even now, when we seek to explain it, we can say no more than Paul did to the Roman with whom he was arguing, that so it is. The Roman says, "Why doth he yet find fault? for who hath resisted his will?" Paul answers, "Nay, but, O man, who art thou that repliest against God? Shall the thing formed say to him that formed it, Why hast thou made me thus? Hath not the potter power over the clay, of the same lump to make one vessel unto honour and another unto dishonour?" This is a hard saying, but still it is the teaching alike of physiology and of Scripture. Many a man is apparently doomed from his birth to a course of crime and of misery, unless some external force be applied which will change the direction of his career; and it is one of the great privileges of ministers of the Gospel that they have in such cases a great and exceptional power to effect this desirable result. But how are they to do this? There can be no doubt whatever of the power which a firm religious belief will exercise over man's conduct, but on this part of the question I will not enter. It is dealt with fully and completely by others more competent than I. I shall rather restrict myself to those points with which I am more particularly conversant.

And first let us take up the question of the use of strong drink, a custom which does more to ruin men, body and mind, than almost all others put together. Why does a man drink? We very frequently use the expression "thirsty soul," without thinking in the least of its meaning. I remember once reading a story of an old drunkard who complained bitterly that his neighbours "aye spoke o' m drinking, but they never spoke o' his drouth." Yet it was the drouth that impelled him to drink. Now this drouth is, I believe, of two kinds. The craving for drink may depend either on a condition of the body generally, or on a condition of the stomach alone. Where it is a condition of the stomach, a substitute may, I believe—nay, I know—sometimes be used in the form of a little sal-volatile with tincture of red pepper, which causes in the stomach a sensation of warmth like that produced by the action of alcohol, but lacks its ruinous after-effects. Where the craving proceeds from a condition of the body generally, and not of the stomach alone, we must try to find out the causes of it, and remove them if possible. Now the bodily condition which causes desire for alcohol is generally one of depression. It may be that a man at first takes it in order to stimulate him above his natural powers—to make him more witty, more attractive, more lively, more apparently intelligent than he naturally is; or he may take it simply for the sake of custom or companionship; but even in the case of these persons, and in many cases, from the first, the habit is generally due to their feeling below par—or not up to the mark, as they term it. They have a sinking at the pit of the stomach, a feeling of languor and depression, of melancholy, sometimes without apparent cause, and they take alcohol to cheer them up, and to remove or make them forget their misery, to do away with their apparently causeless despondency or their real misery. Where the habit of drinking has once been acquired, the only safety for the drunkard is for him to leave off entirely, and he may be aided in this by taking something, such as I have mentioned, to relieve the craving, and at the same time a tonic to strengthen his body generally. The case of the author of the *Sinner's Friend* is one of the most striking, and has not, I think, received the attention which it deserves. He struggled and strove in vain to break himself of the habit of drinking. Every now and again, in spite of prayers, tears, and penitence, he yielded to temptation; resistance seemed vain, until at length he began to take a simple tonic medicine, and from that time to the day of his death a drop of alcoholic liquor never passed his lips.

But another thing is to remove temptation. Some men are able to remain sober so long as drink is kept away from them; but when it is brought near them they cannot resist it, and even when they can do so, once, twice, or thrice, they may succumb to repeated temptation, as a poor woman complained, "I can get my husband past three public-houses, but I cannot get him past sixteen." We ought, I think, to do something to lessen the number of public-houses; but the mere diminution of public-houses will not stop drinking. So long as the wish to drink exists men will gratify it, and the chief thing is to remove the desire for drink. But this depends on several different causes. Many men go to public-houses because their homes are uncomfortable, and they have no amusement or employment there to occupy them after their hours of labour are over. Others are driven to these houses because they feel a want arising from ungratified appetite. Their food is, perhaps, good of its kind, but it may be badly cooked and unsavory, and they do not care, perhaps, to eat so much of it as they would otherwise do; and they resort to the public-house to supply the craving thus occasioned.

We cannot all at once make homes comfortable and teach wives to cook, but, as far as possible, we should at once set to work to do this. Classes for cookery ought, I believe, to be established in every school, and a knowledge of cookery should be as imperatively required in the education of every girl as a knowledge of A B C.

Much has already been done to make evenings comfortable by awakening in men and women new interests by the diffusion of useful knowledge, by cheap and at the same time interesting and attractive periodicals, magazines, books, and papers. Colportage has done much to carry these into homes where they would otherwise have been unknown, and much yet remains to be done in this way.

Lectures, too, are another most valuable means to this end. I know a clergyman in a wretchedly poor district of London, who, every week, if not oftener, has lectures for the men and women in his parish—lectures on various subjects, history, travel, chemistry, natural philosophy, natural history, various branches of science illustrated by experiments, diagrams, or the magic-lantern. By these he not only keeps numbers of men out of the public-houses for the time during which they are present at the lecture, but he awakens in them, to some extent, higher tastes.

But men are not to be raised all at once. Homes cannot be made all at once happy. Some men do not care for lectures or reading, but wish for social companionship. They like to smoke a pipe along with their neighbours, and drink a glass of beer. Now, for such men the establishment of coffee-houses and tea-taverns is most valuable. There they can smoke their pipes, and discuss with their friends either the occurrences happening in their own street or the politics of the kingdom.

But some of them will not be content with drinking either coffee or tea: they want beer. Now if they were supplied with beer alone, of good quality, and were prevented from drinking spirits, I believe they would be kept out of harm. In Germany I have seen men and women sitting for hours playing dominoes and drinking beer, while the men, at least, smoked; but the beer was light, not like our heavy ale, and they arose in two or three hours from their amusement and from their beer-jugs nothing the worse. I believe that while tea-taverns and coffee-houses will supply the wants of some, if we want to keep others from becoming sots we must establish for them beer-houses where they can have light sound beer to drink while they are smoking, where they can discuss politics, and where, possibly, they may have the intervals of conversation enlivened by music. We must, so far as it is possible, put down the drinking of whisky, gin, and brandy; and if we can only do so by replacing them by light, wholesome beer, let us have the beer-houses by all means. But let us not be content with them; let us seek to lead those that frequent them to something better. Remembering that Moses did not give to the Israelites a perfect law, but only one which was as good as they could bear, and that Solon did the same for the Athenians, let us lead them on step by step, not running the risk of utter failure by trying to make them all at once take a step towards perfection to which they are quite unequal.

But even if we partly succeed in reclaiming drunkards by these means, shall we be able to keep them from returning to their former habits? We have seen that M. de Metz could reclaim the energetic criminal, who had the vigour to continue the right course when once he was in it; but that those limp, lymphatic individuals—creatures without a backbone, as they are sometimes termed—were always liable to fall back. Now what makes people limp and lymphatic? They have, no doubt, more or less inherited the tendency from their parents, but in many instances this inherited tendency is greatly increased, and the limpness and weakness may even be generated by unfavourable conditions to which the child has been exposed.

Now, one of these is want of light. Even in frogs, light has an effect upon the changes which take place in their tissues. They live more quickly, they breathe more actively, when exposed to light than when kept in darkness. The same thing has been noticed in some of the lower animals, and light is really a true tonic.

Improper food is another cause. We sometimes see children, even of apparently healthy parents, growing up weak and flabby, and perhaps dying off in early manhood from consumption and other causes. One great cause of this is improper food, and notably a deficiency of fatty food. Fat meat implies abundant feeding in oxen, and fat meat is a dear article of food; but still more so is butter, and the dearness of butter is one of the most common causes of weakness in childhood and consumption in adolescence. Instead of butter, the child gets marmalade and jam, but these are not fat. Sometimes you will find that children will carefully cut away the fat from their meat, and refuse to eat it. They suffer in consequence, and yet the child's instinct is right. If it were able to run about in the open air the whole day, it might possibly take the fat with pleasure, but it finds that to eat solid fat is to bring upon itself nausea, harder to be borne even than pain. This tendency in the child is not to be counteracted by corporal punishment. Fat it ought to have, but it should have fat in the form in which it can digest it. If we were asked to eat a lump of butter without bread, we should probably say that we could not do so without being sick. But if we spread the butter upon bread, or mash it up with potatoes, we can eat it with enjoyment, and so it is with the child. It cannot eat the fat of meat because this consists of solid lumps, but if you take the same fat and make it up into a dumpling, or cut it into fine pieces and mash it with potatoes, the child may be able readily to digest it, and the more finely it is divided, the more easily will it be digested. Where one fat is not tolerated, another can sometimes be taken. If the fat of beef or mutton disgusts the child, it may still be able to take bacon fat with ease, and if the circumstances of the parents will not allow them to buy butter, they may still be able to afford dripping. Let bread-and-scrape be abolished, and let children have a free supply of fat; and if they do not thrive, despite abundance of ordinary food, give them cod-liver oil. Often, perhaps generally, children are irritable because they are ill, and the father goes to the beer-house because the children are fretful. If they were good-tempered, he might stay at home, and enjoy himself by his own fireside, and they would often be good-tempered if they were simply better fed. By having fat prepared for them in a proper manner, it may thus be possible to make home happy, and to keep the parents away from the public-house.

Another cause of depression, often unsuspected, is imperfect drainage. You will sometimes hear a man complain that he is feeling ill and out of sorts, without his being able to give a reason for it, and that not only he, but everybody in his house has been suffering in the same way, and the chances are ten to one that it never occurs to him that his drains are out of order. From imperfect drainage a man feels languid and weak, and for his languor and weakness he has recourse to stimulants. The proper plan is, not to take stimulants, but to remove the cause of the languor.

Now another cause of depression, generally unsuspected, is barometric fall, or an alteration in atmospheric conditions. The influence of atmospheric conditions upon mortality is very marked indeed, different diseases proving more fatal at one time of the year than another, and sudden alterations in the atmosphere being rapidly followed by an increased number of deaths. This is readily seen, not only from an examination of elaborate tables such as those of Mitchell and Buchan, but even from a cursory inspection of the daily papers. Let any one during the winter simply measure the length of the column of deaths in the *Times*, and he will almost invariably find that a few days after a severe frost the column is considerably lengthened. Most probably, too, he will observe that in this long column a large number of names are those of children or of aged persons, the two extremes of life being most readily affected by cold. Nor is it merely the death-rate that is affected by atmospheric conditions. Diseases which are not fatal are also influenced. In a poem on the signs of rain, two of the lines run—

> "Hark how the chairs and tables crack,
> Old Betty's joints are on the rack."

The same atmospheric alterations which caused the tables and chairs to crack by altering the length and thickness of the parts of which they are composed in the same way as in the well-known barometers in which one figure comes out in dry and the other in wet weather, likewise caused the rheumatic joints to ache and twinge. Corns, also, as almost everybody knows, become painful, and shoot and sting during atmospheric changes. It is curious, too, that sometimes pains may be felt when no change of atmosphere is to be observed, except by careful instrumental measurement. After the American Civil War the soldiers who had been engaged in it returned to their homes in all parts of the United States. In many cases nerves had been injured by gun-shot wounds, and Dr. Weir Mitchell noticed that a considerable number of such patients were liable to attacks of pain from time to time. A great number of them had been under his care, and afterwards communicated with him frequently. The information which he thus received from all parts of the States enabled him to come to the conclusion that every now and again a wave of pain swept over the continent, or, to put it very roughly, if one patient were suffering from pain at San Francisco on a Monday, another would suffer in Denver on the Tuesday, a third in St. Louis on Wednesday, and perhaps a fourth in Philadelphia on Thursday or Friday. On comparing this wave of pain with meteorological observations, he found that to a certain extent it coincided with the wave of rain, but that it was much more extensive, that is to say, that each area of meteorological disturbance might be divided into two parts, concentric with each other; the inner part is called by Dr. Mitchell the "rain area," and within this the patients felt pain in the sites of their wounds. They would see a connection between the pain which they felt and the change of weather. In the outer area, which he designates the "pain area," which was concentric with the rain area, but with a radius nearly one hundred miles greater, the patients likewise felt pain, but did not see the connection between it and the atmospheric disturbance, although such connection nevertheless existed. Already we have in our newspapers regular notices of approaching storms, and it seems highly probable that by the extension of such observations as Weir Mitchell's, we may have, before very many years, warnings to all rheumatic persons to "put on extra flannel, as a pain-storm is approaching." Animals are also affected by changes of atmosphere, as is seen in the frog and leech barometers. The frog barometer, which is more used in Germany than in this country, consists of a small glass jar in which a tree-frog is confined, and which contains a small ladder. So long as the weather is good, the frog sits quietly at the bottom, but when it is about to rain it walks up the ladder and sits at the top. The leech barometer is a tall glass jar about three parts full of water, in which a leech is placed. In dry weather the leech remains at the top of the jar, in dull and wet weather sits at the bottom, and when wind is expected it moves rapidly about from one part of the jar to another. Even the colour of frogs is altered by atmospheric change, as is also expressed in the poem above alluded to :—

"The frog has lost his yellow vest,
And in a russet coat is drest."

These changes in death-rate, in pain, and in the movements of animals, are probably not due simply to the increase of watery vapour in the atmosphere, nor yet to barometric pressure, but, **as** Dr. Weir Mitchell thinks, to a combination of these, along with alterations of an unknown character in the electrical conditions of the atmosphere.

But atmospheric conditions do not act only in

increasing the human death-rate, or in causing pain in diseased conditions,—they also affect, to a great extent, the feelings and acts of the individual.

Kingsley illustrates this most vividly in *Yeast*, where his hero makes the following entries in his diary:—

"*Monday, 21st.* — Wind S.W., bright sun, mercury at $30\frac{1}{2}$ inches. Felt my heart expanded towards the universe. Organs of veneration and benevolence pleasingly excited; and gave a shilling to a tramp. An inexpressible joy bounded through every vein, and the soft air breathed purity and self-sacrifice through my soul. As I watched the beetles, those children of the sun, who, as divine Shelley says, 'laden with light and odour, pass over the gleam of the living grass,' I gained an Eden-glimpse of the pleasures of virtue.

"N.B. Found the tramp drunk in a ditch. I could not have degraded myself on such a day—ah! how could he?

"*Tuesday, 22nd.* — Barometer rapidly falling. Heavy clouds in the south-east. My heart sank into gloomy forebodings. Read *Manfred*, and doubted whether I should live long. The leaden weight of destiny seemed to crush down my aching forehead, till the thunderstorm burst, and peace was restored to my troubled soul."

Goethe also, in his conversations with Akerman, remarks that when the barometer was high he could do his work with ease, but that when low, although by steady determination he could get through his work, yet it gave him much trouble. By watching the barometer we are able in some measure to foretell the probability of a series of colliery explosions, and it is just possible that by carefully observing atmospheric conditions we may by and by be enabled to predict an outbreak of drunkenness amongst those who are addicted to liquor. Should this be the case, it may prove a most useful means of prevention. For just as we take increased precautions in a coal-pit to prevent an explosion, when we know that barometric conditions are likely to lead to one, so in those who are liable to drunken fits we may use additional precautions when we suspect their advent.

In some men we find alternations between a perfect condition of temperance, lasting perhaps for many weeks or months, and outbreaks of the maddest drunkenness. After lasting a few days, these attacks pass off, and again the subject of them will remain sober for a time. He regrets and bewails his tendency, but seems unable to help himself.

In these cases a tonic, like that used by the author of the *Sinner's Friend*, may be useful, but often perhaps the best remedy is bromide of potassium. For these cases seem akin to epilepsy, and between this disease and drunkenness there is a close association. While a tendency to nervous derangement may appear in one member or branch of a family in the form of epilepsy, in others it may show itself as a tendency to inebriety. The children of drunkards are often epileptic, and *vice versâ*. If the parents are epileptic, additional care should be taken to prevent the acquisition of a taste for alcoholic liquor by the children. It has been noticed that the progeny of first cousins are often epileptic, and that among them also the tendency to inebriety is strong. Wherever we suspect this, we ought to watch the children, and prevent their nervous system from being weakened by overstraining their education at school, while we should endeavour to strengthen them by open-air exercise, and diminish the risk of their acquiring a taste for liquor by inducing them to take the pledge of total abstinence in childhood, and to keep it at least until they are twenty-one. Strength of body and soundness of mind go more or less together, and by weakening the one the healthiness of the other may be impaired.

But we are apt to forget sometimes that we cannot eat our cake and have it too; boys cannot work to the full extent of their powers and grow at the same time.

Many growing boys become apparently stupid while their bodies are growing, and if we try to force their minds at that time we may permanently weaken them. During growth we must remember that the great essentials are abundant food, open-air exercise, and not too much to do. After growth has ceased, we may allow children to work, and they will then work with both pleasure and advantage.

We are sometimes apt to forget this, and in the

hurry and struggle of modern life there is too great a tendency to force the education of children — to store their minds with facts and methods, by constant and assiduous teaching, to the great detriment of their bodies, and not only of their bodies but of their minds. This is shown by an interesting experiment of Mr. C. Paget, who made a portion of the children in a school work only half-time at their lessons and spend the other half in garden-work. In a short time these children completely outstripped the others in their school-work; so that they actually acquired more knowledge as well as gained in health and strength by the abbreviation of their tasks. And even after the body has apparently ceased to grow, we must remember that the brain has not yet attained to its full power, and that forcing the brain in youth may ruin the power which ought to be fully developed only in manhood.

It is strange how often teachers forget the old proverb that "you may take a horse to the water, but you cannot make him drink." Great harm is done by persistent attempts to force children to learn, which renders knowledge utterly distasteful to them. If, instead of cramming the child's mind with facts in which he is not at all interested, and which he will therefore soon forget, his curiosity be awakened, he will learn the facts for himself, and remember them with advantage.

It is well to give a child a slight knowledge of a range

of numerous and varied subjects, so that he may learn how wide the fields of knowledge are, and choose for himself those studies which he will afterwards prosecute; but at the same time it is necessary to give him a thorough training in one subject at least, whether a language or a science, in order to instruct him in the methods of learning. Nor is such thorough instruction as this useful only to train the child in the method of learning, although this is of very great importance indeed; it is also useful as a moral training. However much we may try to simplify the process of education, there will always be in it many things that are unpleasant to the child, and the training undergone by him in learning to face and surmount obstacles by patience and perseverance, and in doing things, disagreeable at present, for the sake of future advantage, cannot but be to him of great benefit as a preparation for the duties and trials of life.

The power of prevision is one of the great characteristics by which man is distinguished from the lower animals, and the power of acting in the present so as to secure future reward or avert future evil is a characteristic by which the wise man is distinguished from the foolish one. As Solomon puts it (Proverbs, xxii. 3), "A prudent man foreseeth the evil, and hideth himself; but the simple pass on and are punished." The laws of nature are invariable, and any breach of them is followed by punishment, whether such breach be intentional or accidental. If a man falls from a height involuntarily, he is just as much bruised as though he had purposely thrown himself down.

The advantage gained by the study of science, or, in other words, by the study of natural phenomena, is that by a more intimate acquaintance with nature's laws we are able to regulate our actions in more exact accordance with them. For many centuries the fisherman has studied the appearance of the clouds and the direction of the wind before venturing to leave the harbour, but all the knowledge so acquired could not secure him against a storm which might be crossing the sea, and might strike his boat in four or five days' time. It is only of late years that we have become able to predict the occurrence of storms some time before they arrive on our coasts, and even now, in planning an excursion in the country a week hence, we cannot foretell whether the day will be dull or rainy, dry or sunshiny. Ships about to sail for foreign lands now delay their departures in order to avoid being struck in mid-ocean by squalls which have been prophesied by the meteorologist, but we, because of the insufficiency of our knowledge, are liable to become drenched while out on a pleasure expedition. As knowledge increases, we may be able so to fix our plans as to avoid such a disappointment, but if we should wilfully disregard the information when once it had been obtained, we should suffer the same penalty as if we had remained in ignorance.

What is true of physical laws is also true of moral laws, and the penalties for the transgression of the latter, although, perhaps, less evident and not so immediate, are no less certain than are those consequent upon the breach of the former, and the benefits resulting from obedience are no less sure in the one case than in the other.

In these days religion is often sneered at; but the moral laws given in the Ten Commandments represent truths which cannot be disregarded without being followed by inevitable punishment, and one of the great advantages of a religious education is the habit which it induces of not weakly yielding to the temptation of a moment, but of regulating one's life each day in accordance with the good and the true, and thus day by day developing more and more unto the stature of the perfect man.

INDEX.

A.

ABRAHAM, 255, 260
Acid, carbonic, 99, 103, 104, 177
Acotyledons, 56
Acrogens, 70
Acrogenous stems, 60
Actinia, 137
Actinozoa, 137, 142 ; circulation in, 142
Actinosphærium, 127
Activity, functional, of animal tissues, 177
Actual energy, 102, 122
Adaptation in roots and flowers, 107
Adelsberg, 192
Africa, 246, 247, 363, 362
Age, bronze, 257-259, 364 ; iron, 257, 259, 364 ; neolithic, 257 ; paleolithic, 257 ; stone, 257 ; of formations determined by composition, 268 ; by fossils, 269
Ahab, 48
Ai, 35, 36, 40
Air tubes, 151
Ajalon, 39
Akermann, vide Errata and Eckermann
Alexander the Great, 5
Algæ, 70, 72, 80, 81, 305 ; cilia of, 116 ; ciliated embryo of, 117 ; reproductive power of, 117 ; subdivision of cells in, 76-78
Alimentary canal of molluscoida, 155
Almond tree, 47, 50
Alluvial epoch, 264
Alps, 285
Alternation of generations, 80
Amazon, 229
America, 243, 279 ; civil war in, 332, 392
American Indians, 246
Americans, 249
Ammonites, 161, 162, 280, 283
Amœba, 120-123, 125, 126, 128, 129, 143, 149, 274 ; colonies of, 129 ; differentiation in, 123, 124 ; in sponges, 131 ; differentiation of, in sponges, 131 ; vacuoles of, 142, 143

Amphibia, 180, 188-190, 194, 214 ; difference between mammalia, reptilia, and, 194 ; link between fishes and, 189 ; structure of, 190
Amphioxus, 162, 180, 181-183, 305 ; development of, 311, 313 ; notochord in, 183 ; structure of, 182
Anarthropoda, 148
Anatomical difference between man and apes, 242
Ancestors, resemblance to, 372
Ancestral influences, 371
Angiosperm, 87, 98, 265, 273, 306
Animals, cold-blooded, 179, 203 ; difference between plants and, 103, 115, 116 ; digitigrade, 231 ; distribution of plants and animals in time, 255 ; fish-like, 179 likeness between low plants and low animals, 116 ; lizard like, 179 ; plantigrade, 231 ; pinnigrade, 231 ; oviparous, 178 ; ovoviparous, 178 ; relation of plants to, 301-305 ; warm-blooded, 203 ; viviparous, 178 ; motion of, 122
Animal kingdom, 120, 179, 231, 304 ; distinction between vegetable and, 117
Animal tissues, 177
Annuloida, 143-147, 305
Annulosa, 148, 153, 154, 162, 305
Anoplotherium, 286, 306
Ant bear, 219
Ant eater, 218
Anthers, 86, 92, 107, 108
Antheridium, 78, 80
Anthropoid apes, 237, 238
Ants, 154
Apes, anthropoid, 238 ; anatomical difference between man and, 242 ; mental difference between man and, 241 ; feet of, 238
Aphides, 154
Apices of stamens, hairs of, 92
Aplacental mammalia, 217
Arabs, 249 ; encampments of, 36
Arachnida 153

D D 2

404   INDEX.

Archeolithic epoch, 263, 264, 265, 273, 274
Archeopteryx, 205, 281, 306
Arctic circle, fossils in, 288; polar lands, 251
Aristotle, his use of Solomon's writings, 5
Aristolochia, 92
Armadillos, 218
Armenia, 368
Arm bone, 168
Artesian well, 29
Arthropoda, 148
Articulata, 148
Artiodactyla, 220, 221
Aryo-Romanic, 249, 254
Ascidians, 117, 156-158, 162, 182, 183, 311, 312
Ascidian molluscs, 156, 157
Asenath, 8
Asia, 250, 251, 362
Asia Minor, 263
Aspidium filix-mas, 80
Aspidium fern, 76
Assyria, 361
Assyrians, 249, 254
Astronomy, Moses' knowledge of, 26
Atlantic, 283
Atolls, 139
Atoms, aggregation of, 339, 340
Australia, 243, 246, 281, 284
Australians, 242, 245, 247, 248, 250
Austral negroes, 247
Axil of branch, 85
Axolotl, 191

B.

Baboon, 237
Babylonia, 255
Banian, 75
Banksia, 284
Barak, 47
Barbery, stamens of, 91
Bark of trees, 57-59; tissue of, 60
Barometer, frog, 394; leech, 394; prediction by, 395, 396
Basal ganglia, 175
Bashan, oaks of, 96
Basques, 249, 253
Bats, 197, 233, 244
Bees, 45
Bee orchid, 94
Beech-trees, 69
Beer-houses, 387
Beetles, 280
Belemnite, 280
Béthel, 36
Bethlehem, star of, 47
Bible lands, 1
Bile, 176
Bimana, 218
Birds, 180; circulation of, 203, 204; classification of, 209, 212; climbing, 210; perching, 210; link between reptiles and, 204-208; of prey, 211; respiration of, 203, 204; running, 212; swimming, 210; scratching, 210; wading, 209; structure of, 200-203
Blade-bones, 167, 172, 173
Blood, 176; corpuscles, 177, 179, 203; vessels, 176; use of, 150, 176; circulation of, in branchiæ, 151, 153
Body cavity, of actinia, 138; of ascidians, 158; of molluscoida, 155
Bondage of Israelites, 24
Bones, of arm, 168; blade, 167, 173; breast, 173; collar, 173; foot, 172; of hand, 170, 171, 224; hip, 167; haunch, of bird, 208; of crocodile, 208; quadrate, 180; thigh, 168; of bird, 208; of crocodile, 208; of dinosaur, 208
Boulders, 290-292
Bracken, 57, 59
Brachiopoda, 156, 275, 306; shells of, 156
Brachycephali, 244
Brain, 175, 176; of man, 239, 240
Branch, 73; axil of, 85; of carices, 75; of horseradish, 75; of strawberry, 75
Branchiæ, 151
Brass, 364
Bread and scrape, 390
Breast-bone, 173
Brick-like cells, 69
Brick-making, 13, 14
Britain, 281; first invasion of, 297
Bronze age, 257-259, 364
Bruta, 218
Buchan, 391
Buds, of cellular plants, 76; growth of, 96, 97; of hydra, 135, 136; multiplication by, 77; propagation by, 75; of strawberry, 75
Bulbiferous lily, 76
Bunyan's *Pilgrim's Progress*, 374
Bushman, 242, 246
Buttercup, 89; root fibre of, 106
Butterflies, 280

C.

Cainozoic epoch, 264, 273
Cairo, 7, 8; flints in, 260
Caleb, 30
Calyx, 84
Cambium, 69
Cambrian epoch, 264, 274
Camel, 220, 228
Canaan, 30, 36, 49; wheat of, 51
Canaanites, 47
Canadensis, cornus, 91
Canal, alimentary, 155; digestive, 137, 142, 176; neural, 168; hæmal, 165
Canine teeth, 220, 228, 230, 233, 234, 360
Cape of Good Hope, 362
Capricorn, tropic of, 247
Carbon, 100, 103

INDEX. 405

C............ 99, ...
C............................
C...... 218, 230, 231
Carpenter, Dr., 274
Carpus, 170, 171
Carices, branches of, 75
Cartilaginous rod in ascidian, 183
Cat, 231
Catarhina, 237
Caterpillar, 153
Cattle stealing, 21, 22
Caucasian race, 249, 253
Caucasus, 253
Caudicle of orchis, 93
Cedar of Lebanon, 52, 96
Celandine, 86
Cells, 62-72, 96, 107; .... ; bricklike, 69 .... 81, 124 .... 81; of .... 68, 72, 99; .... 104, 105; .... of, ... ; spermatozoa, ... 67, 68; of stems, 60; ....
Cellular plants, 70, ... ; ... of, 76
Cellular tissue, 69; of style, 89
Cellular structure, the ovule a, 84
Cellulose, 96, 105, 116, 117, 156
Centipedes, 149, 276
Centres of distribution of man, 368
Cephalopoda, 160-162, 275, 306; branchia of, 160; mode of progression of, 160
Cerastes, 11
Cerebellum, 175
Cerebrum, 175
Cetacea, 218, 229, 230
Ceylon, 252, 302
Chalk animalculæ, 284; cliffs, 126; formation, 205; epoch, 264, 281-284
Channel of Jordan, 33
Cheiroptera, 218, 233
Chelonia, 196
Chemical energy, 100
Chemistry, Moses' knowledge of, 26
China, 284
Chinese, the, 245; Mongolian, 249, 250, 253
Chimpanzee, 237
Chrysalis, 154
Cilia, 78, 127; of sponges, 129; of ascidians, 158
Circulation, 121; in .... 190; in birds, 204; in .... in mammalia, 214; in .... of water in ascidians, 158
Cistus, 47
Classification of animals by placenta, 217; by teeth, 218; of birds, 209; of man by hair, 245-252; by skulls, 244, 245; by teeth, 245; of plants by root-leaves, 56

Cl.........
C.................. 269, 276, 286, 288-
C............................ of amphibia, ...
C.........................
C.........
C.................. 275; climate of, 276
C.................. 305
C.................. 268
C.........................
C.........................
C.........................
C.................. 164, 172, 180, 183, ... 185; of teleostei, 18..
C........., Italian, on Joshua's com......... to 38
C......... formations, 268; determi......... of age of formations by, 268
Compsognathus longipes, 207, 209, 284
Condyles, 180, 204; in mammalia, 180; in sauropsida, 180
Conferva, 77
Coney, 228
Connecting link between .... and fishes, 189; between .... lusca, 154; between .... brata, 162, 180-183; .... bird, 204-208
Conquest of Palestine, 41
Contractile tentacles, 138; vacuole, 123
Cookery classes, 386
Copper, use of, in weapons, 257
Coral, 116, 138, 139; islands, 138; reefs, 139-142
Cornus canadensis, 91
Corolla, 84, 91, 93
Corpuscles, blood, 176, 177, 179, 203; nucleus of, 179
Cotyledons, 55
Couch grass, 75
Countries, mutual relations of plants and, 51
Crabs, 149, 153
Creation, Milton ....; special, 318, 319; ....
Creeping stems, 75
Cretaceous epoch, 264, 282-284
Crinoids, 146, 305, 306
Crocodile, 195, 280; circulation of, 204; haunch bone of, 208; structure of heart of, 204
Crœsus, 39
Crustacea, 153, 274, 280
Cucumber, 50
Cursores, 212, 213
Cusps, 220
Cuttlefish, 154, 161, 162, 275
Cyaxares, 39
Cycads, 87, 279, 306
Cydippe, 141, 142
Cypress, 49

D.

Darkness, plague of, 27
Darwin on coral islands, 139; on evolution and natural selection, 336
Dead, judgment of, 18, 366; Sea, 43
Death of Moses, 31
Death-rate and weather, 391
Deborah, 47
Deccan, 251
Deer, 221, 224; horns of, 227
Degradation, process of, 374
Delta. 9, 10, 50, 260, 261
Deluge, 365; traditions of, 367
Description of Egypt, 9; of Palestine, 42-49
Development, downward, 377; of embryos, 308-317; of individuals, 369; upward, 376; and religion, 401; of type, 307
Devonian epoch, 264, 275
Diatoms, 76, 116
Dicotyledons, 55, 56; section of, 58, 59
Difference, anatomical between man and apes, 242
Differentiation of amœba, 123, 124; of amœba in sponges, 131; of embryos, 314, 315; of infusoria, 126; of plants, 81
Diffusion of information, 1
Digestion, 122, 123; in plants, 111
Digestive canal, 176
Digestive juices, 176
Digestive cavity, of infusoria, 127; of paramœcium, 128; rudimentary, 127
Digits, 172
Digitigrade animals, 231
Diluvial epoch, 264
Dinosaur, 207, 208
Dinotherium, 288
Dionea, 112, 113
Dislike to fat, 389
Distinction between animal and vegetable kingdoms, 117
Distribution of man, 368; of plants and animals in time, 255
Dividing waters of Jordan, 32, 33
Dogs, 231, 233
Dolichocephali, 244
Dolphins, 229, 230
Dover, cliffs of, 283
Dragon flies, 280
Drainage, imperfect, 390
Dravidas, 248, 251
Drosera, 111, 114
Drought, 48
Drunkenness and epilepsy, 397
Dugongs, 229

E.

Eagle, 211
Earth, life history of, 301-307
Earthquakes near Jordan, 33-35
Earthworm, 148
Eastern tours 6, 7
Echinodermata, 145-148

Echinus, 144
Eckermann, 395, *vide* Errata
Eclipse of sun, 38, 39; effect of, 40
Edentata, 217, 218
Education, 398, 399
Egypt, 50, 243, 255; ancient, 259, 262; colour in, 52; description of, 9; embalming in, 16; famine in, 10, 20; fossils of, 262; foreign embassies to, 14, 20; Hebrews in, 22; importation into, 14; irrigation of, 13; mourning in, 16, 17; pyramids of, 126; reaping in, 14; shape of, 9; use of stone in, 259; war in, 22; wheat of, 51
Egyptian funeral, 17-19; garden, 15, 53; hills, 285; houses, 15; religion, 26; tombs, 19; valley, 260
Egyptians, 249, 254; learning of, 26; length of year fixed by, 26
Ehrenberg, microscopist, 128
Electricity, 100
Elephant, 228
Elijah, 48
Embalming in Egypt, 16
Embassies, foreign, to Egypt, 14, 20
Embryo, 90, 97, 98; sac, 86, 90
Embryos, resemblance of, 308-317; development of, 308-317; differentiation of, 314-317
Encampments, Arab, 36
Encephalon, 175
Encrinites, 146, 275
Endogens, 69, 70, 81, 95, 99
Endogenous stems, 59
Energy, 100, 104, 122, 340; actual, 102, 122; changes of, 341, 342; chemical, 100; convertible, 100; mechanical, 100, 103; potential, 102, 122
England, animals of, 286; climate of, 286; in Eocene period, 286; glaciers in, 288; plants of, 286
English, the, 242, 249, 254
Eocene epoch, 264, 284-288, 325, 326
Eozoon, 274, 304, 305
Epilepsy and drunkenness, 397
Epochs, alluvial, 264; glacial, 290-295; geological, 263
Equator, 247
Eriocomi, 245, 246, 248
Esdraelon, 50; plain of, 44
Esquimaux, 249, 251
Ethiopia, 25, 361-363
Ethiopian king, conquest of, by Moses, 25; daughter of, 25
Euphrates, 361, 362
Euplocomi, 247, 251
Europe, 255
Euthycomi, 247, 248, 252
Evolution, at present time, 329; future of, 340; in dog, 328, 329; hypothesis of, 320, 326, 327-338; in horse, 328; in man, 329-336, 344; in pigeons, 329; in paradise, 360; Mosaic record of, 343; not atheistical, 338, 339, 356; of matter,

339; objections to, 327, 328, 338, 342, 344
Existence, struggle for, 330-332
Exodus, the, 25, 28
Exogens, 69, 70, 81, 95, 99, 114
Exogenous stems, 58
Expulsion of Hebrews from Egypt, 23
External conditions, influence of, before birth, 370; after birth, 373
Extinct reptiles, 198, 199

F.

FAMINE in Egypt, 10, 20
Famines, 49, 213
Fat, dislike to, 389
Fauna, 50
Fellah, 13
Fellaheen, hovels of, 7
Femur, 168
Fern, aspidium, 80; bracken, 57; bulbiferous, 76; leaf, 81; maidenhair, 57
Ferns, 52, 53, 55-57, 59, 70, 80, 81, 96, 265, 273
Fibula, 168, 169
Fig, 284; tree, 50, 52; Indian, 75
Fins of fishes, 180
Fish, 179, 180, 273; ganoid, 186, 280, 306, fins of, 180; gills of, 180; hag-fish, 184, 185; link between amphibia and, 189; lungs of, 188; myxinoids, 184, 185; ray, 280; shark, 185, 280, 306; sturgeon, 186; swimming bladder of, 188; teleostei, 186, 187, 306
Fleecy-haired men, 246, 248
Flora of Palestine, 50
Flower, 84; adaptation in, 107; classification of, 52; effect of rain on, 108; fertilization of, 91-94; formation of male organ of, 85; of china primrose, 88; of nettle, 92; of spotted orchis, 93, 94; of yew, 84; petals of, 85; placenta of, 88; protection from rain in, 108; structure of, 84, 85; style of, 85; sun, 107
Foot, bones of, 172
Footmen, running, 8
Foramen, 89
Foraminifera, 125, 126, 262, 263, 274, 282-284; shells of, 125, 135, 262
Forked veined leaf, 54
Formations, 265; chalk, 205; climate of, 269; composition of, 268; fossils of, 269, 270; Jura, 204; of vegetable tissue, 67; of vessels, 68; position of, 267; relative ages of, 265-268; Trias, 204
Fossils, 269; determination of age of formations by, 269, 270; of France in Eocene period, 286; of Mesozoic epoch, 278-284
Foulahs, 249, 252
Fox, 154
France, fossils of, in Eocene period, 286
Frog, 193

Frog barometers, 394
Fronds
Functional activity of animal tissues,
Funeral Egyptian, 17; feasts, 20
Furniture, 76, 78, 104, 116
Future life, 19, 20

G.

GALILEO, 337
Gamaliel, 338
Gamopetalæ, 95
Ganglion, 148; basal, 175; of ascidians, 158, 182; in cephalopoda, 162; in insects, 148
Ganoids, 186, 306
Gardens, Egyptian, 15, 53
Gasteropoda, 159, 160, 306
Gastric juice, 112, 176
Gemmæ in liverwort, 76
Genealogical tree of animals and plants, 303
Generations, alternations of, 80
Geological epochs, 263-265, length of, 263, 264; record, 325, 327
Geometry, Moses' knowledge of, 26
Germans, 249, 254
Germ cells, 178
Germination of monocotyledon, 55; of dicotyledon, 55
Gibbon, 237
Gibeon, 39
Gihon, 361-363
Gills, 151, 159, 178; of fish, 180
Giraffe, 228
Girdle, shoulder, 165, 167; pelvic, 165, 167
Glacial epoch, 290-294
Glaciers in England, 288
Glands, honey, 92
Globigerinæ, 283
Glutinous secretion in plants, 111, 112
Goats, 227
Goethe, 118, 395
Gonidia in lichens, 78
Gorilla, 237, 239, 300
Goths, 249, 254
Gourd, creeping, 99
Grafting, 71
Grains, pollen, 84
Grallatores, 209
Graptolites, 274, 305
Grass, couch, 75
Grasshopper, 47
Greece, 254
Greeks, 249, 254
Greenland, fossils in, 288; height of, 291; whale, 229, 230
Greenlanders, 249, 251
Growth, in children, 397; in summer, 69; versus work, 398
Gymnosperms, 83, 87-90, 98, 205
Gyri, 240

H.

Hæckel, 119, 251, 252, 361
Hæmal arch, 173; canal, 165
Hagfish, 184, 185
Hand, bones of, 171, 172, 224
Hair, classification of man by, 245-253; moss, 79; of apices of stamens, 92
Haunch bone, of bird, 208; of crocodile, 208; of dinosaur, 208
Haurân, 43
Havilah, 361, 363
Heartsease, 90
Heat, 101, 104
Hebrews, in Egypt, 22; expulsion from Egypt, 23
Hedgehog, 234
Hermon, 46-48
Herons, 209
Hesperornis regalis, 205, 283, 306; teeth of, 207
Heterocercal tails, 186
Hexagonal cells, 60-62
Hiddekel, 361-363
Hills, Lybian, 19; Syrian, 53
Himalayas, 285
Hindoo, 235
Hip-bones, 167
Hippopotamus, 220, 221, 223, 228
History, 2; of individuals, 308; of life of earth, 307, 308; of Moses, 25-31; natural, 2, 3, 50
Holmes, Oliver Wendell, 371, 372
Homocercal tail, 187
Honey, 46, 62, 94; glands, use of, 92
Horned snakes, 11
Horns, 227, 228
Horse, 220-224; in Eocene period, 325; in Miocene period, 324; in Pliocene period, 323; pedigree of, 321-326
Horseradish, 75
Horsetails, 279
Hottentots, 245-248
House of Joseph, 8
House of Egyptians, 15
Hovels of Fellaheen, 7
Hugh Miller, 354
Humanity, development of, 319, 320
Humerus, 168, 169
Humility of Elijah, 8
Humming-bird orchid, 94
Hungarians, 249
Hungary, 250
Huxley, American lectures, 319, 320; on sponges, 130; on vertebrata, 179
Hydræ, 155, 305
Hydra, 133; buds of, 135, 136; colonies of, 135; manubrium of, 136; reproduction of, 134-137
Hydroid polyp, 137
Hydrozoa, 103, 133, 143, 274, 305
Hyksos, 21, 23
Hylodes, 311
Hyracoidea, 218, 224

Hyperboreans, 249, 251
Hyssop, 5, 52

I.

Icebergs in Italy, 288
Iceland, fossils in, 288
Icthyopsida, 179, 180
Icthyornis, 206, 207
Icthyosaurus, 280, 283, 306
Iguanodon, 283
Ilium, 167
Imago, 154
Implements, coexistence of, iron and stone, 256
Importations into Egypt, 14
Indian fig, 75
Indians, 249, 254
Individuals, development of, 369
Indo-Germanic groups, 249, 253, 254
Indus, 363
Influences, ancestral, 371; external, after birth, 373, 376; before birth, 370
Information, diffusion of, 1
Infusoria, 126-128
Inherited constitution, 378
Insessores, 211
Insects, 149, 153, 154; fertilization of plants by, 114; resemblance of, to orchids, 113
Insectivora, 218, 234
Intemperance, causes of, 383; treatment of, 384, 385
Intermediate forms of life, 307, 327
Intestines, 176
Invasion, first, of Great Britain, 297
Invertebrata, 143; moral, 379
Invertebrate animals, 265
Irrigation of Egypt, 13
Irritability, 117-119
Irritable stamens, 91
Iron, age, 364; epoch, 257, 259
Iron implements, coexistence of, with stone, 256
Islands, coral, 139-142
Isle of Sheppey, fossils of, 286
Israelites, 243; bondage of, 24; journey of, 28, 41
Italy, icebergs in, 288

J.

Jaw, of man, 244
Jellyfish, 136; moral, 379
Jericho, siege of, 35
Jews, 243, 249
Jordan, 42, 43, 48; nature of channel of, 33; dividing of waters of, 32, 33; earthquakes of, 33-35; passage of, 32; valley of, 33
Joseph, house of, 8; marriage of, 14; journey of, 11-14; public life of, 20

INDEX. 409

Joshua, 30; his command to sun, Italian commentary, 37-39
Journey of Israelites, 28
Judea, 44
Judgment of dead, 18
Juices, digestive, 176
Jura, epoch, 264; fossils in, 280
Jura formation, 204

K.

KAFFIRS, 246-248
Kangaroo, 215, 216, 279
Kerner, 114
Khamâsin, 28
Kidneys, 178
King, Ethiopian, daughter of, 25; conquest of, by Moses, 25
Kings, shepherd, 21
Kingsley, Charles, 395
Kishon, 47

L.

LABYRINTHODON, 278
Lacertilia, 194
Lagoon, 139-141
Lake, salt water, 139
Lamellibranchiata, 159, 275, 306
Lampreys, 184
Lands, Bible, 1
Land of Promise, 35, 42
Lapps, 250
Larva, 153
Laurentian epoch, 264
Leaf, fern, 81; type of plant, 57; venation of, 53, 57
Leaflets, 84
Leaves, 52, 73, 104; classification by, 52, 54; root, 55; veined, 55, 56
Learning of Egyptians, 26
Lebanon, 44; cedar of, 52, 96
Lectures, 386
Leech, 148; barometers, 394
Leek, 50-53, 96, 99
Lemur, 234, 235
Lepidodendron, 275
Lepidosiren, 188, 189
Libyan Hills, 19
Lichens, 52, 53, 56, 62, 70, 96; gonidia in, 76
Life, development of, 349; future, 19, 20
Life history of the earth, 304-307
Light, 101, 104; effect of, 388
Lily, bulbiferous, 76
Links between amphibia and fishes, 189; between annulosa and mollusca, 154; between mollusca and vertebrata, 162, 180-183; between reptiles and birds, 294-298; missing, 325, 327
Lingula, 156
Linnet, 210

245, 247, 248, 251, 252
283; flying,
339
50,
151, 178; of birds, 204; of fishes, ; of mammalia, 215
Lycopods, 81, 82, 98, 279; prothallium in, 82, 83; spores of, 83
Lydians, 39
Lyell, Sir Charles, 327

M.

M 237
M
M 57
M
M 246
M
M 85
M 265, 273, 306; aplacental; circulation of, 214; contains 180; first traces of, 279, 281; 215; placental, 217; teeth in,

M
M of, 335, ape
and, a 346; of of

quaternary epoch
of, 344; feet of, 238,
ance of, in Britain,
246; jaw of, 244;
tween apes and, 241
in, 332-335; origin
242; races of, 244;
stiff-haired, 247;
248; teeth of,
245; woolly-haired, 245, 248
Manatees, 229
Manepthah, 27
Maori, 246
Maple tree, 69
Marah, 28; waters of, 29
Marriage of Joseph, 14
Marsupials, 215-217, 281, 286, 288, 306
Marsupium, 215, 216
Mastodon, 288
Mechanical energy, 103; power, 101
Moles, 39

Mediterranean, 42, 43, 48, 248
Mediterranese, 250-253
Medulla oblongata, 175
Medullary rays, 61
Medusæ, budding, 136, 137
Melon, 50, 52, 53
Mental difference between man and apes, 241
Mesohippus, 324, 326
Meso-cephali, 244
Mesozoic epoch, 263, 264, 273, 278, 284; fossils of, 278-284
Metamorphosis of amphibia, 190, 192
Metz, M. de, 379, 380, 388
Microlestes, 279
Microscopist, Ehrenberg, 128
Migration, causes of, 49, 243
Miller, Hugh, 354
Milton, on creation, 319, 320; on primitive man, 351, 353; *Paradise Lost*, 351-353; *versus* Darwin, 326
Miocene epoch, 264, 286, 326
Miohippus, 324, 326
Mitchell, Dr. Arthur, 391; Weir, 392
Mizraim, 263
Mole, 234
Mollusca, 154, 158, 162, 272, 305; ascidian, 156, 157; comparison of, 273; link between vertebrata and, 162, 180-183; nervous system of, 158; subdivisions of, 159, 160
Molluscoida, alimentary canal of, 155; body cavity of, 154-156; nervous system of, 155
Molluscous shells, 274
Monera, 119, 121, 123, 149, 274
Mongolian Chinese, 253
Mongols, 247, 248, 250-252
Monkeys, 162, 233-235; common descent of man and, 344, 345; development of, 344, 345; first appearance of, 288
Monocotyledon, 105; germination of, 56; section of, 59
Monotremata, 215-217
Moraines, 294
Mosaic record of creation, 351, 353; of evolution, 343, 344
Moses, 24, 225; death of, 31; history of, 24-31; his knowledge of astronomy, 26; of chemistry, 26; of geometry, 26
Moss, 53, 55, 56, 62, 70, 72, 76, 78, 79, 82; club, 81; lesser club, 83; reproduction of, 79
Motor nerves, 174
Mount Ararat, 365-367
Mourning, Egyptian, 16, 17
Mouth, 176
Movement, implies energy, 122
Mud fish, 188, 189
Mulberries, 45
Multiplication, by buds, 77; by cells, 64, 65
Muriform cells, 69
Muscle, 173-175

Mushroom, 78, 79
Musk-ox, 288
Mycelium, 78
Myrtle, 284
Myxinoids, 184, 185, 189

N.

NATATORES, 210
Natural history, 50; its nature, 2; its subdivisions, 3
Natural selection, adaptation of to circumstances, 335; effect of, in civil war, 332; Darwin on, 336; in man, 334
Nature of species, 369
Nautilus, paper, 161
Negroes, 246-248; Austral, 247
Neolithic age, 257; skulls, 298; race, 297
Nerves, motor, 174; sensory, 174
Nervous system of molluscoida, 155; of mollusca proper, 158
Netted veined leaf, 54
Nettle, flower of, 92; stamens of, 91
Neural canal, 165
New Guinea, 246
New Zealand, 243, 246
Nightingale, 211
Nile, 10, 50; mud of, 261, 262; valley of, 260-262; waters of, 263
Nitrogen, 63
Nitrogenous waste, 178
Norsemen, 249, 254
Northern Sea, formation of, 294
Notochord, of amphioxus, 183, of hagfishes, 184; of lepidosiren, 188; of teleostei, 187
Nubians, 248, 249, 252
Nucleolus, 63
Nucleus of blood corpuscles, 179; of protoplasm, 62
Nummulites, 284
Nummulite rocks, 262
Nutrition, 117, 118; in infusoria, 128; of plants by flies, 113

O.

OAK, 57, 58, 68, 69, 71, 284; of Bashan, 96
Observatories, pyramids astronomical, 26
Octopus, 160, 162; gills of, 160; nervous ganglion of, 162
Oil, 45
Old red sandstone epoch, 264, 275
Olive trees, 45, 50, 52
Onions, 50, 52, 53, 96
Oogonium, 78, 80, 84
Oolitic epoch, 264, 280; fossils in, 280
Ophidia, 195
Opossum, 215
Opposition of thumb and great toe, 236
Orchids, bee, 94; humming-bird, 94; resemblance of insects to, 113

INDEX. 411

Orchis, fertilization of, 94; flower of spotted, 93; shape of, 94
Origin of cell, 74; of man from single stock, 242
Ornosaurus, 306
Ornithorhynchus, 215
Orohippus, 325
Orthocerata, 161, 162
Orthognathi, 245
Osmunlis, 250
Os quadratum in sauropsida, 180
Ostrich, 212, 213; African, 213; American, 213
Otter, 231
Ourang outang, 237
Ova, 178
Oval cells, 60-62
Ovary, 87, 88, 98
Oviparous animals, 178
Ovoviviparous animals, 178
Ovule, 84-91, 98
Ox, 220, 221, 224, 225; rumination of, 227; stomach of, 225, 226
Oyster, 159

P

Pachydermata, 286
Pacific Islands, 250
Pain area and rain area, 393
Paleolithic, age, 257; skulls, 298
Paleotherium, 286, 287, 306
Paleozoic epoch, 263, 264, 275; fossils of, 265, 275
Palestine, 42, 43; climate of, 44; conquest of, 41; fauna of, 50; flora of, 50; winter in, 46
Palm tree, 50, 52, 55, 58, 59, 96, 99, 105; growth of, 70; stem of, 69, 70
Pancreas, 176
Papuans, 245, 246, 248
Papyrus, 50
Paradise, account of, 361-363; disappearance of, 364; evolution of man in, 309; expulsion from, 363, 364; site of, 361; submergence of, 366; traditions of, 366
Parallel veins, 56, 95
Paramœcium, 128
Paris, fossils near, 286
Parnassia palustris, 114
Parrots, 210
Passage of Jordan, 32
Pelvic bones, 238; girdle, 166
Penstemon, 114
Perching birds, 210
Periwinkle, 109, 159
Perfection, process of, 375
Perissodactyla, 220, 221
Perm, 277
Permian epoch, 264, 277
Persia, 263
Persian Gulf, 362
Persians, 249, 254

Petals,
Pharynx,
Pheasants,
Phœnicians, Semites, 254
Pigs,
Pine, 273, 276, 279, 306; ovules of, 87; pollen grains of, 91, scales of, 84, 87
Pinguicula, 114
Pinnigrade animals, 231
Pison, 361-363
Pistils, 91
Pith, 61, 62, 66, 67
Pith of flowers, 88, 89
217; teeth of, 218
44; of Sharon, 44
231
cellular, 71, 76; difference between animals and, 103, 115, 116; of, 81; digestion in, 111; distribution in time of animals and, 255; exogenous, 58, 114; fertilization of, by insects, 114; glutinous secretion in, 111, 112; growth of, 96, 98; leaf type of, 57; male element of, 97; male organ of, 78; mutual relation of countries and, 51; nutrition of 96; by flies, 113; relation of animals to, 301-305; reproduction of, 72; sensibility in, 110; sleep in, 109; structure of, 50, 51; tissue of, 100; twining, 107; vascular, 70, 71, 76
Platyrhina, 236
Pleistocene epoch, 264, 288
Plesiosaurus, 280, 283, 306
Pliocene epoch, 264, 326; climate of, 283
Pliohippus, 323, 326
Polar men, 247, 248, 251
Pole cat, 231
Pollen, 86, 88, 94, 97, 107; cells, 84, 86, 87; grains, 84, 86, 87, 89, 91, 97; tube, 89
Polygastrica, 128
Polynesia, 286
Polypetalæ, 95
Polyps, 139, 140, 142, 155
Polyzoa, 155, 156
Pomegranate, 50
Porpoises, 229
Position of formations, determination of age by, 267
Post-diluvial
103, 122, 123
Power,
396
Prevention and
Prey birds 230
351
Primeval
Primrose, flower of China, 88

Proboscidea, 218, 228
Process of degradation, 374 ; of perfection, 375
Productions of countries, 50
Prognathi, 245
Progression, mode of, of amphioxus, 182 ; of cephalopoda, 160 ; of periwinkle, 159 ; of snail, 159, 160 ; of whelks, 159
Progression of life history of the earth, 301-307
Promised land, 35, 42, 45
Proteus, 191, 192, 193
Prothallium, 80, 82
Protista, 119 ,149
Protohippus, 323, 326
Protoplasm, 63-68, 72, 78, 96, 97, 116, 119, 120, 122, 123, 129, 131, 262 ; differentiation of, in amœba, 123, 127 ; in the body, 124 ; in infusoria, 126
Protozoa, 132, 133, 135, 149
Pseudopodia, 122, 124-127, 135
Pterodactyl, 197, 198, 200, 280, 281, 284, 306 ; link between reptile and bird, 204
Public life of Joseph, 20
Pupa stage, 154
Pyramids, the, 126 ; use of, 12-26
Pyrenees, 284

Q.

QUADRANGULAR cells, 60-62
Quadrate bone, 180
Quadrumana, 218, 235 ; thumb of, 236
Quaternary epoch, 264, 288 ; evidences of man in, 265

R.

RABBIT, 228, 233
Races of man, 244
Radiata, 147
Radius, 168, 169
Rain area and pain area, 393
Rain and rheumatism, 392
Rain, effect on flowers of, 108 ; protection of flowers from, 108
Rameses II., 26, 27
Raptores, 211, 212
Rasores, 210
Rat, 228, 232
Rays, 280 ; medullary, 61
Reaping in Egypt, 14
Recent epoch, 264
Record, geological, imperfection of, 325, 327 ; Mosaic, 337
Red Indians, 245-251
Red Sea, 260-262
Reefs, coral, 139-142
Reflex action, 175
Reformatory for children, 379
Reindeer, 288
Relation of plants and animals, 301-307
Relative ages of formations, 266

Religion and development, 401
Religion of Egyptians, 26
Reproduction, 118; of algæ, 73 ; of fungi, 73 ; of hydra, 134 ; of infusoria, 128 ; of molluscoida, 155 ; in mosses, 79 ; sexual, 178 ; of sponges, 130-133 ; of trees, 72 ; of vertebrata, 178
Reptilia, 180, 192-199, 201-208, 265, 273
Resemblances to ancestors, 372
Respiration, 121-123, 149, 150 ; external, 151 ; internal, 153 ; in birds, 203, 204
Respiratory sac of ascidians, 153
Respiratory system, of myxinoids, 185 ; of oyster, 159 ; of periwinkle, 159 ; of reptiles, 193 ; of snails, 159 ; of whelks, 159
Rhea, 213
Rheumatism and rain, 392
Rhinoceros, 220-223, 288
Rings in wood, 69
Rocks, 266-270, 274 ; nummulitic, 262
Rodentia, 218, 228, 231-233
Romans, the, 249, 254
Rome, 254, 256
Root-leaves, 55
Roots, 73, 106 ; adaptation in, 107 ; adventitious, 105 ; function of, 106, 107
Rose of Sharon, 47
Rudimentary digestive cavity, 127
Ruminants, 221, 224-227, 286
Running, birds, 212, 213 ; footmen, 8
Russia, 250, 277

S.

SAC, embryo, 86, 90
Sahara, 247, 252, 262
Salamander, 194
Saliva, 175
Salt water lake, 139, 141
Sandworm, 151
Sarracenia, 113
Saurians, 278, 280, 285
Sauropsida, 179, 180, 194, 200 ; structure of, in reptiles and birds, 200-208
Saxons, 254
Scale, of cypress, 89 ; of Scotch fir, 87
Scandinavia, 250
Scandinavians, 249, 254
Scansores, 210
Scapulæ, 167, 173
Sclaves, 249, 254
Scotch fir, staminal scale of, 87
Scotch heath, 275
Scotland in glacial period, 291
Scratching birds, 210
Scripture, literal interpretation of, impossible, 357-359 ; our interpretation of, 355 ; St. Paul's teaching of, 355 ; use of, 354
Sea anemone, 137
Sea cows, 229
Sea fir, 275

INDEX. 413

Seals, 231
Sea lilies, 275
Sea mats, 155
Sea mosses, 155
Sea weed, 62, 70, 265, 273, 274; white, 155
Sea urchins, 143, . . . , 306
Secondary 278
Section, of . . . . . ; of monocotyledon, 59
Seeds, 90; arrangement of, 52; growth of, 90; difference between spores and, 84
Selachei, 185
Selection, artificial, 333; natural, 332, 334; Darwin on, 336
Semitic tribes, 249, 253, 254; Phœnicians, 254
Sensitive plants, 110
Sensory nerve, 174
Sepal, 84
Septa of actinozoa, 138
Sertularians, 275
Seti, 27
Sexual reproduction, 178
Shape of Egypt, 9
Shark, 185, 188, 308
Sharon, 50; plain of, 44; rose of, 47
Sheep, 227
Sheffield tools, 256
Shell-fish, 159
Shells of foraminifera, 125
Shepherd kings, 21
Sheppey, fossils in Isle of, 288
Shoulder girdle, 165, 166
Siege of Jericho, 35
Sigillaria, 275
Silica, spicules of, 124
Silk-worm, 45
Silurian epoch, 264, 274, 275
Sirenia, 218, 228, 229
Skull, 165, 175; of man, 239, 240, 244; neolithic, 298; paleolithic, 298; of sauropsida, 180
Sleep in plants, 109
Sloths, 218
Snails, 159, 160
Snakes, 195, 196; horned, 11
Solomon, 4, 228
South Sea Islands, 256, 332
Spain, 253
Special creation, 318, 319
Species, nature of, 369
Sperm cells, 97
Spermatozoa, 178; cells, 178
Spermatozoids, 78, 83, 84, 97
Spermatozoon, 97
Spicules of silica, 124
Spies, return of, 30
Spiders, 280
Spinal cord, 174, 175
Spine, 165
Spindle-shaped cells, 62, 68
Spitzbergen, fossils in, 288

Sp . . . , 129; buds . . 131; cilia in, . .
. . . .
. . 31; 11 . . . .
. . . . of, 32 . . . .
ova 131 . . . .
p . . cells in, ...
. . -133; spermatozoa
Spores, 80, 97, 98; cases, 81; difference between seeds and, 84; propagation by, 77, 78, 80
Spotted orchis, 93
Stalk, 57
Stamens, 86, 92; irritable, 91; of barbery, 91; of nettle, 91
Staminodes, 114
Star-fish, 144, 145, 147, 275, 306
Star of Bethlehem, 47
Stems, 57, 73; acrogenous, 60; cells of, 60; endogenous, 59; exogenous, 58, 59; growth of, 105; hairs on, 114; microscopic structure of, 60-65; of palm, 69; vegetable tissue of, 69; vessels of, 60
Sternum, 173
Still-haired men, 247, 248
Stigma, 88, 89, 91, 94, 107
Stigmaria, 275, 276
Stomach, 176
Stomata, 104
Stone age, 256-259, 352, 364; in Egypt, 260
Stone lilies, 146, 147
Stone of fruit, 67
. . . . Mrs. Beecher, 380
. . . . 209
. . . . 138
. . . .
. . . . for . . . .
Strepsirhina, 236
Structure, of . . . . . . 190; . . . . . .
oxus, 182; . . . . . 200 . . . .
teryx, ...
230; . . . .
. . . . 209; . . . . . .
204; . . . . 84; . . . .
. . . . ; of . . . .
. . . . 188, 189; . . . .
. . . . 214 of . . . .
of myxinoids, ...
51; of proboscidea, ...
of pterodactyl, 204; . . . .
. . . . . birds, 213; . . . .
. . . . 185, 186; . . . .
teeth, . . . ; . . . .
196; . . . .
with . . . .
. . . .
. . . .
. . . . 89
. . . .
. . . 239
. . . .
Sun, ... Joshua's command to, 37-39

414　INDEX.

Sun-dew, 111
Sunflower, 107
Survival of the good, 381
Swine, 220, 221, 224, 225
Swimming birds, 210
Swimming-bladder of fish, 188
Syrian desert, 42
Syrian hills, 53
Syncoryne, 136

T.

TADPOLES, 192, 193
Tail, heterocercal, 186
Tape-worm, 147, 148
Tapir, 220, 221, 228, 286, 325; intermediate position of, 223
Tartars, 245, 249, 250
Tasmania, 246
Teeth, 176; classification by, 218, 245; structure of, 219; kinds of, 219; of carnivora, 230; of hyracoidea, 228; of insectivora, 234; of mammals, 218, 219; of man, 245, 360; of proboscidea, 228; of rodents, 233
Teleostian fish, 306
Teleostei, 186, 187
Tennyson, 379
Tentacles, contractile, 138
Tertiary epoch, 264, 284
Thames, the, plants of, 286
Thigh bone, 168; of bird, 208; of crocodile, 208; of dinosaur, 208
Thumb, of catarhina, 237; of man, 235; of quadrumana, 235; of platyrhina, 236; of strepsirhina, 236
Tibia, 168, 169
Tigris, 362
Tin, use of, in weapons, 258
Tissue, 71; animal, 177; of bark, 60; cellular, 69; formation of vegetable, 67; functional activity of, 177; of plants, 100; structure of, 73; of stems, 61; vegetable formation of, 67; waste, 178; woody, 67
Tombs, Egyptian, 19
Tools, man's first, 257
Tortoises, 196, 197
Tours in the East, 7
Transformation of energy, 161
Tree, the age of, 58; almond, 47, 56; bark of, 57, 58; beech, 69; fig, 50, 284; growth of, 50, 96; maple, 69; myrtle, 284; nutrition of, 96; oak, 57, 58, 68, 71, 284; olive, 45, 50; palm, 50, 57-59, 105; reproduction in, 72; structure of, 50; walnut, 284; willow, 57
Trias epoch, 264, 278; footprints in, 279; lycopods in, 279
Trias formation, 204
Tribute, 14
Trilobites, 153, 274, 275
Tropic of Capricorn, 247

Tubal Cain, 364
Tubes of leaves, 105
Tuft-haired men, 245
Tunicata, 117, 156-158
Turkey, 250
Turks, 249
Turtle, 280
Twigs, 68, 105; growth of, 62-66
Twining plants, 107

U.

ULNA, 168, 169
Ulotrichi, 245, 247, 248, 252
Ungulata, 217, 220-224
Union of Great Britain with France, 294, 296
Universe, future of the, 340-342
Upper Nile, 252

V.

VACUOLES, contractile, 123
Valley, the Egyptian, 260; Jordan, 33; Nile, 260
Van Diemen's Land, 246
Vascular plants, 70, 71; buds of, 76
Vegetable kingdom, the, 231; distinction between the animal and, 117; relations of, 303
Veined leaves, 55, 56
Venation of leaf, 53, 57
Venus' fly-trap, 112
Vermes, 147
Vertebrata, 154, 158, 162-165, 178, 179, 214; Huxley on, 179; link between mollusca and, 162, 180, 182, 183; reproduction in, 178, 180
Vertebral column, 163, 164, 180, 183-185
Vessels, 62, 73; blood, 176, 177; bundles of, 69, 70; formation of, 68; of stems, 60; tubular, 61, 62, 68
Viviparous animals, 178
Viper, horned, 11
Vulture, 211, 212

W.

WADING birds, 209
Walnut, 284, 288
Walrus, 231
War in Egypt, 22
Warm-blooded animals, 203
Waste, nitrogenous, 178; of tissue, 178
Water-newt, gills of, 193
Waters of Marah, 29
Water vascular system, 143, 144
Waxy surface, 114
Weapons, man's first, 257; his first use of copper in, 257; of iron in, 259; of tin in, 258

Weasels, 231
Weather, and death-rate, 391; influences of, on intellect and temper, 395
Weir Mitchell, Dr., 392, 393
Well, artesian, 29
Whales, 229; fossil, 285
Wheat, 50, 51
Whelk, 150
Will, the, power of, 380
Wisdom of Solomon, 4
Woman, creation of, 353, 354
Woodlouse, 274
Wood, rings in, 69
Woodpeckers, 210
Woody cells, 68; tissue, 61

Woolly-haired men, 245, 247-249
Work versus growth, 398
Worms, 147, 274
Wrist, bones of, 170, 171

Y.

Year, length of, fixed by Egyptians 26
Yew, flower of, 84

Z.

Zambesi, 363

THE END.

LONDON:
R. CLAY, SONS, AND TAYLOR,
BREAD STREET HILL.

BEDFORD STREET, COVENT GARDEN, LONDON,
February, 1881.

Macmillan & Co.'s Catalogue of Works in Mathematics and Physical Science; including Pure and Applied Mathematics; Physics, Astronomy, Geology, Chemistry, Zoology, Botany; and of Works in Mental and Moral Philosophy and Allied Subjects.

MATHEMATICS.

Airy.—Works by Sir G. B. Airy, K.C.B. ....
ELEMENTARY TREATISE ON PARTIAL DIFFERENTIAL EQUATIONS. Designed for the Use of Students in the Universities. With Diagrams. New Edition. .... 5s. 6d.
ON THE ALGEBRAICAL AND NUMERICAL THEORY OF ERRORS OF OBSERVATIONS AND THE COMBINATION OF OBSERVATIONS. Second Edition. Crown 8vo. 6s. 6d.
UNDULATORY THEORY OF OPTICS. Designed for the Use of Students in the University. New Edition. .... 6s. 6d.
ON SOUND AND ATMOSPHERIC VIBRATIONS. With the Mathematical Elements of Music. Designed for the Use of Students of the University. Second Edition, Revised and Enlarged. Crown 8vo. 9s.

A TREATISE ON MAGNETISM. Designed for the Use of Students in the University. Crown 8vo. 9s. 6d.

Alexander.—ELEMENTARY APPLIED MECHANICS. By Thomas Alexander, C.E., Professor of Engineering in the Imperial College of Engineering, Tokei, Japan. Crown 8vo. 4s. 6d.

5,000.2.81.]   A

Ball (R. S., A.M.).—EXPERIMENTAL MECHANICS. A Course of Lectures delivered at the Royal College of Science for Ireland. By ROBERT STAWELL BALL, A.M., Professor of Applied Mathematics and Mechanics in the Royal College of Science for Ireland (Science and Art Department). Royal 8vo. Cheaper Issue. 10s. 6d.

"*We have not met with any book of the sort in English. It elucidates instructively the methods of a teacher of the very highest rank. We most cordially recommend it to all our readers.*"—Mechanics' Magazine.

Bayma.—THE ELEMENTS OF MOLECULAR MECHANICS. By JOSEPH BAYMA, S.J., Professor of Philosophy, Stonyhurst College. Demy 8vo. 10s. 6d.

Boole.—Works by G. BOOLE, D.C.L, F.R.S., Professor of Mathematics in the Queen's University, Ireland :—

A TREATISE ON DIFFERENTIAL EQUATIONS. Third Edition. Edited by I. TODHUNTER. Crown 8vo. 14s.

A TREATISE ON DIFFERENTIAL EQUATIONS. Supplementary Volume. Edited by I. TODHUNTER. Crown 8vo. 8s. 6d.

THE CALCULUS OF FINITE DIFFERENCES. Third Edition. Edited by J. F. MOULTON, late Fellow of Christ's College, Cambridge. Crown 8vo. 10s. 6d.

Cheyne.—AN ELEMENTARY TREATISE ON THE PLANETARY THEORY. With a Collection of Problems. By C. H. H. CHEYNE, M.A., F.R.A.S. Second Edition. Crown 8vo. 6s. 6d.

Clausius.—THE MECHANICAL THEORY OF HEAT. By R. CLAUSIUS. Translated by WALTER R. BROWNE, M.A., late Fellow of Trinity College, Cambridge. Crown 8vo. 10s. 6d.

Clifford.—THE ELEMENTS OF DYNAMIC. An Introduction to the study of Motion and Rest in Solid and Fluid Bodies. By W. K. CLIFFORD, F.R.S., Professor of Applied Mathematics and Mechanics at University College, London. Part I.—Kinematic. Crown 8vo. 7s. 6d.

Cumming.—AN INTRODUCTION TO THE THEORY OF ELECTRICITY. With numerous Examples. By LINNÆUS CUMMING, M.A., Assistant Master at Rugby School. Crown 8vo. 8s. 6d.

Cuthbertson.—EUCLIDIAN GEOMETRY. By F. CUTHBERTSON, M.A., Head Mathematical Master of the City of London School. Extra fcap. 8vo. 4s. 6d.

Everett.—UNITS AND PHYSICAL CONSTANTS. By J. D. Everett, M.A., D.C.L., F.R.S., Professor of Natural Philosophy, Queen's College, Belfast. Extra fcap. 8vo. 4s. 6d.

Ferrers.—Works by the Rev. N. M. Ferrers, M.A., F.R.S., Master and Fellow of Gonville and Caius College, Cambridge:—

AN ELEMENTARY TREATISE ON TRILINEAR CO-ORDINATES, the Method of Reciprocal Polars, and the Theory of Projectors. Third Edition, revised. Crown 8vo. 6s. 6d.

SPHERICAL HARMONICS AND SUBJECTS CONNECTED WITH THEM. Crown 8vo. 7s. 6d.

Frost.—Works by Percival Frost, M.A., late Fellow of St. John's College, Mathematical Lecturer of King's Coll. Cambridge:—

THE FIRST THREE SECTIONS OF NEWTON'S PRINCIPIA. With Notes and Illustrations. Also a Collection of Problems, principally intended as Examples of Newton's Methods. Third Edition. 8vo. 12s.

AN ELEMENTARY TREATISE ON CURVE TRACING. 8vo. 12s.

SOLID GEOMETRY. Being a New Edition, revised and enlarged, of the Treatise by Frost and Wolstenholme. Vol. I. 8vo. 16s.

Godfray.—Works by Hugh Godfray, M.A., Mathematical Lecturer at Pembroke College, Cambridge:—

A TREATISE ON ASTRONOMY, for the Use of Colleges and Schools. 8vo. 12s. 6d.

AN ELEMENTARY TREATISE ON THE LUNAR THEORY, with a Brief Sketch of the Problem up to the time of Newton. Second Edition, revised. Crown 8vo. 5s. 6d.

Green (George).—MATHEMATICAL PAPERS OF THE LATE GEORGE GREEN, Fellow of Gonville and Caius College, Cambridge. Edited by N. M. Ferrers, M.A., Fellow and Master of Gonville and Caius College. 8vo. 15s.

Hemming.—AN ELEMENTARY TREATISE ON THE DIFFERENTIAL AND INTEGRAL CALCULUS. For the Use of Colleges and Schools. By G. W. Hemming, M.A., Fellow of St. John's College, Cambridge. Second Edition, with Corrections and Additions. 8vo. 9s.

Jackson.—GEOMETRICAL CONIC SECTIONS. An Elementary Treatise in which the Conic Sections are defined as the Plane Sections of a Cone, and treated by the Method of Projections. By J. STUART JACKSON, M.A., late Fellow of Gonville and Caius College. Crown 8vo. 4s. 6d.

Kelland and Tait.—AN INTRODUCTION TO QUATERNIONS. With numerous Examples. By P. KELLAND, M.A., F.R.S., and P. G. TAIT, M.A., Professors in the department of Mathematics in the University of Edinburgh. Crown 8vo. 7s. 6d.

Kempe.—HOW TO DRAW A STRAIGHT LINE. A Lecture on Linkages. By A. B. KEMPE, B.A. Illustrated. Crown 8vo. 1s. 6d.
[*Nature Series.*]

Merriman.—ELEMENTS OF THE METHOD OF LEAST SQUARES. By MANSFIELD MERRIMAN, Professor of Civil and Mechanical Engineering, Lehigh University, Bethlehem, Penn., U.S.A. Crown 8vo. 7s. 6d.

Morgan.—A COLLECTION OF PROBLEMS AND EXAMPLES IN MATHEMATICS. With Answers. By H. A. MORGAN, M.A., Sadlerian and Mathematical Lecturer of Jesus College, Cambridge. Crown 8vo. 6s. 6d.

Newton's Principia.—4to. 31s. 6d.
It is a sufficient guarantee of the reliability of this complete edition of Newton's Principia that it has been printed for and under the care of Professor Sir William Thomson and Professor Blackburn, of Glasgow University.

Parkinson.—Works by S. PARKINSON, D.D., F.R.S., Fellow and Tutor of St. John's College, Cambridge.
  A TREATISE ON OPTICS. Third Edition, revised and enlarged. Crown 8vo. cloth. 10s. 6d.
  A TREATISE ON ELEMENTARY MECHANICS. For the Use of the Junior Classes at the University and the Higher Classes in Schools. With a Collection of Examples. Fifth Edition, revised. Crown 8vo 9s. 6d.

Phear.—ELEMENTARY HYDROSTATICS. With Numerous Examples. By J. B. PHEAR, M.A., Fellow and late Assistant Tutor of Clare Coll. Cambridge. Fourth Edition. Cr. 8vo. cloth. 5s. 6d.

Pirie.—LESSONS ON RIGID DYNAMICS. By the Rev. G. PIRIE, M.A., Fellow and Tutor of Queen's College, Cambridge. Crown 8vo. 6s.

Puckle.—AN ELEMENTARY TREATISE ON CONIC SECTIONS AND ALGEBRAIC GEOMETRY. With numerous Examples and Hints for their Solution. By G. HALE PUCKLE, M.A. Fouth Edition, enlarged. Crown 8vo. 7s. 6d.

Rayleigh.—THE THEORY OF SOUND. By LORD RAYLEIGH, F.R.S., formerly Fellow of Trinity College, Cambridge. 8vo. Vol. I. 12s. 6d.; Vol. II. 12s. 6d. [Vol. III. *In preparation.*

Reuleaux.—THE KINEMATICS OF MACHINERY. Outlines of a Theory of Machines. By Professor F. REULEAUX. Translated and edited by A. B. W. KENNEDY, C.E., Professor of Civil and Mechanical Engineering, University College, London. With 450 Illustrations. Medium 8vo. 20s.

Routh.—Works by EDWARD JOHN ROUTH, M.A., F.R.S., late Fellow and Assistant Tutor of St. Peter's College, Cambridge; Examiner in the University of London.

AN ELEMENTARY TREATISE ON THE DYNAMICS OF THE SYSTEM OF RIGID BODIES. With numerous Examples. Third Edition, enlarged. 8vo. 21s.

STABILITY OF A GIVEN STATE OF MOTION, PARTICULARLY STEADY MOTION. The Adams' Prize Essay for 1877. 8vo. 8s. 6d.

Tait and Steele.—DYNAMICS OF A PARTICLE. With numerous Examples. By Professor TAIT and Mr. STEELE. Fourth Edition, revised. Crown 8vo. 12s.

Thomson.—PAPERS ON ELECTROSTATICS AND MAGNETISM. By Professor SIR WILLIAM THOMSON, F.R.S. 8vo. 18s.

Todhunter.—Works by I. TODHUNTER, M.A., F.R.S., of St. John's College, Cambridge:—

"*Mr. Todhunter is chiefly known to students of mathematics as the author of a series of admirable mathematical text-books, which possess the rare qualities of being clear in style and absolutely free from mistakes, typographical or other.*"—Saturday Review.

A TREATISE ON SPHERICAL TRIGONOMETRY. New Edition, enlarged. Crown 8vo. 4s. 6d.

PLANE CO-ORDINATE GEOMETRY, as applied to the Straight Line and the Conic Sections. With numerous Examples. New Edition. Crown 8vo. 7s. 6d.

A TREATISE ON THE DIFFERENTIAL CALCULUS. With numerous Examples. New Edition. Crown 8vo. 10s. 6d.

A TREATISE ON THE INTEGRAL CALCULUS AND ITS APPLICATIONS. With numerous Examples. New Edition, revised and enlarged. Crown 8vo. 10s. 6d.

Todhunter—*continued.*

EXAMPLES OF ANALYTICAL GEOMETRY OF THREE DIMENSIONS. New Edition, revised. Crown 8vo. cloth. 4s.

A TREATISE ON ANALYTICAL STATICS. With numerous Examples. New Edition, revised and enlarged. Crown 8vo. cloth. 10s. 6d.

A HISTORY OF THE MATHEMATICAL THEORY OF PROBABILITY, from the Time of Pascal to that of Laplace. 8vo. 18s.

RESEARCHES IN THE CALCULUS OF VARIATIONS, Principally on the Theory of Discontinuous Solutions: An Essay to which the Adams' Prize was awarded in the University of Cambridge in 1871. 8vo. 6s.

A HISTORY OF THE MATHEMATICAL THEORIES OF ATTRACTION, and the Figure of the Earth, from the time of Newton to that of Laplace. Two vols. 8vo. 24s.

AN ELEMENTARY TREATISE ON LAPLACE'S, LAME'S, AND BESSEL'S FUNCTIONS. Crown 8vo. 10s. 6d.

Wilson (W. P.).—A TREATISE ON DYNAMICS. By W. P. WILSON, M.A., Fellow of St. John's College, Cambridge, and Professor of Mathematics in Queen's College, Belfast. 8vo. 9s. 6d.

Wolstenholme.—MATHEMATICAL PROBLEMS, on Subjects included in the First and Second Divisions of the Schedule of Subjects for the Cambridge Mathematical Tripos Examination. Devised and arranged by JOSEPH WOLSTENHOLME, late Fellow of Christ's College, sometime Fellow of St. John's College, and Professor of Mathematics in the Royal Indian Engineering College. New Edition, greatly enlarged. 8vo. 18s.

Young.—SIMPLE PRACTICAL METHODS OF CALCULATING STRAINS ON GIRDERS, ARCHES, AND TRUSSES. With a Supplementary Essay on Economy in suspension Bridges. By E. W. YOUNG, Associate of King's College, London, and Member of the Institution of Civil Engineers. 8vo. 7s. 6d.

PHYSICAL SCIENCE.

Airy (G. B.).—POPULAR ASTRONOMY. With Illustrations. By Sir G. B. AIRY, K.C.B., Astronomer Royal. New Edition. fcap. 8vo. 4s. 6d.

Balfour.—A TREATISE ON COMPARATIVE EMBRYOLOGY. By F. M. BALFOUR, M.A., F.R.S., Fellow and Lecturer of Trinity College, Cambridge. With Illustrations. In Two Volumes. 8vo. Vol. I. 18s. [*Vol. II. in the Press.*

Bastian.—Works by H. CHARLTON BASTIAN, M.D., F.R.S., Professor of Pathological Anatomy in University College, London, &c. :—

THE BEGINNINGS OF LIFE : Being some Account of the Nature, Modes of Origin, and Transformations of Lower Organisms. In Two Volumes. With upwards of 100 Illustrations. Crown 8vo. 28s.

"*It is a book that cannot be ignored, and must inevitably lead to renewed discussions and repeated observations, and through these to the establishment of truth.*"—A. R. Wallace *in* Nature.

EVOLUTION AND THE ORIGIN OF LIFE. Crown 8vo. 6s. 6d.

"*Abounds in information of interest to the student of biological science.*"—Daily News.

Blake.—ASTRONOMICAL MYTHS. Based on Flammarion's "The Heavens." By John F. BLAKE. With numerous Illustrations. Crown 8vo. 9s.

Blanford (H. F.).—RUDIMENTS OF PHYSICAL GEOGRAPHY FOR THE USE OF INDIAN SCHOOLS. By H. F. BLANFORD, F.G.S. With numerous Illustrations and Glossary of Technical Terms employed. New Edition. Globe 8vo. 2s. 6d.

Blanford (W. T.).—GEOLOGY AND ZOOLOGY OF ABYSSINIA. By W. T. BLANFORD. 8vo. 21s.

Brodie.—IDEAL CHEMISTRY. A LECTURE. By Sir B. C. BRODIE, Bart., D.C.L., F.R.S., Professor of Chemistry in the University of Oxford. Crown 8vo. 2s.

Brunton.—PHARMACOLOGY AND THERAPEUTICS ; or Medicine Past and Present. The Goulstonian Lectures delivered before the Royal College of Physicians in 1877. By T. LAUDER BRUNTON, M.D., F.R.C.P., F.R.S., Assistant Physician and Lecturer on Materia Medica and Therapeutics at St. Bartholomew's Hospital. Crown 8vo. 6s.

Bosanquet.—AN ELEMENTARY TREATISE ON MUSICAL INTERVALS AND TEMPERAMENT. With an Account of an Enharmonic Harmonium exhibited in the Loan Collection of Scientific Instruments, South Kensington, 1876; also of an Enharmonic Organ exhibited to the Musical Association of London, May, 1875. By R. H. Bosanquet, Fellow of St. John's College, Oxford. 8vo. 6s.

Challenger.—Report on the Scientific Results on the Voyage of H.M.S. "Challenger," during the Years 1873-76. Under the command of Captain Sir GEORGE NARES, R.N., F.R.S., and Captain FRANK TURLE THOMSON, R.N. Prepared under the Superintendence of Sir C. WYVILLE THOMSON, Knt., F.R.S., &c. Regius Professor of Natural History in the University of Edinburgh; Director of the Civilian Scientific Staff on board. With Illustrations. Published by order of Her Majesty's Government. Volume I. Zoology. Royal. 37s. 6d.

> Part. I. Report on the Brachiopoda, 2s. 6d.
> II. Report on the Pennatulida, 4s.
> III. Report on the Ostracoda, 15s.
> IV. Report on the Bones of Cetacea, 2s.
> V. The Development of the Green Turtle, 4s. 6d.
> VI. Report on the Shore Fishes, 10s.

Clifford.—SEEING AND THINKING. By the late Professor W. K. CLIFFORD, F.R.S. With Diagrams. Crown 8vo. 3s. 6d.
[*Nature Series.*

Coal: ITS HISTORY AND ITS USES. By Professors GREEN, MIALL, THORPE, RÜCKER, and MARSHALL, of the Yorkshire College, Leeds. With Illustrations. 8vo. 12s. 6d.
> "*It furnishes a very comprehensive treatise on the whole subject of Coal from the geological, chemical, mechanical, and industrial points of view, concluding with a chapter on the important topic known as the 'Coal Question.'*"— Daily News.

Cooke (Josiah P., Jun.).—FIRST PRINCIPLES OF CHEMICAL PHILOSOPHY. By JOSIAH P. COOKE, Jun., Ervine Professor of Chemistry and Mineralogy in Harvard College. Third Edition, revised and corrected. Crown 8vo. 12s.

Cooke (M. C.).—HANDBOOK OF BRITISH FUNGI, with full descriptions of all the Species, and Illustrations of the Genera. By M. C. COOKE, M.A. Two vols. crown 8vo. 24s.
> "*Will maintain its place as the standard English book, on the subject of which it treats, for many years to come.*"—Standard.

Crossley.—HANDBOOK OF DOUBLE STARS, WITH A CATALOGUE OF 1,200 DOUBLE STARS AND EXTENSIVE LISTS OF MEASURES. FOR THE USE OF AMATEURS. By E. CROSSLEY, F.R.A.S., J. GLEDHILL, F.R.A.S., and J. M. WILSON, F.R.A.S. With Illustrations. 8vo. 21s.

CORRECTIONS TO THE HANDBOOK OF DOUBLE STARS. 8vo. 1s.

Dawkins.—Works by W. BOYD DAWKINS, F.R.S., Professor of Geology at Owens College, Manchester.

CAVE-HUNTING : Researches on the Evidence of Caves respecting the Early Inhabitants of Europe. With Coloured Plate and Woodcuts. 8vo. 21s.

"*The mass of information brought together, with the judicious use he has made of his materials, will be found to invest his book with much of new and singular value.*"—Saturday Review.

EARLY MAN IN BRITAIN, AND HIS PLACE IN THE TERTIARY PERIOD. With Illustrations. 8vo. 25s.

Dawson (J. W.).—ACADIAN GEOLOGY. The Geological Structure, Organic Remains, and Mineral Resources of Nova Scotia, New Brunswick, and Prince Edward Island. By J. WILLIAM DAWSON, M.A., LL.D., F.R.S., F.G.S., Principal and Vice-Chancellor of M'Gill College and University, Montreal, &c. With a Geological Map and numerous Illustrations. Third Edition, with Supplement. 8vo. 21s. Supplement, separately, 2s. 6d.

Fiske.—DARWINISM; AND OTHER ESSAYS. By JOHN FISKE, M.A., LL.D., formerly Lecturer on Philosophy in Harvard University. Crown 8vo. 7s. 6d.

Fleischer.—A SYSTEM OF VOLUMETRIC ANALYSIS. By Dr. E. FLEISCHER. Translated from the Second German Edition by M. M. Pattison Muir, F.R.S.E., with Notes and Additions. Illustrated. Crown 8vo. 7s. 6d.

Flückiger and Hanbury.—PHARMACOGRAPHIA. A History of the Principal Drugs of Vegetable Origin met with in Great Britain and India. By F. A. FLÜCKIGER, M.D., and D. HANBURY, F.R.S. Second Edition, revised. 8vo. 21s.

Forbes.—THE TRANSIT OF VENUS. By GEORGE FORBES, B.A., Professor of Natural Philosophy in the Andersonian University of Glasgow. With numerous Illustrations. Crown 8vo. 3s. 6d.
[*Nature Series.*

Foster.—A TEXT-BOOK OF PHYSIOLOGY. By MICHAEL FOSTER, M.D., F.R.S., Prælector in Physiology, and Fellow of Trinity College, Cambridge. With Illustrations. Third Edition, revised 8vo. 21s.

"*After a careful perusal of the entire work, we can confidently recommend it, both to the student and the practitioner as being one of the best text-books on Physiology extant.*"—The Lancet.

Foster and Balfour.—ELEMENTS OF EMBRYOLOGY By MICHAEL FOSTER, M.D., F.R.S., and F. M. BALFOUR, M.A., Fellow of Trinity College, Cambridge. With numerous Illustrations. Part I. Crown 8vo. 7s. 6d.

Galloway.—THE STEAM ENGINE AND ITS INVENTORS. A Historical Sketch. By ROBERT L. GALLOWAY, Mining Engineer. With numerous Illustrations. Crown 8vo. 10s. 6d.

Galton.—Works by FRANCIS GALTON, F.R.S. :—
METEOROGRAPHICA, or Methods of Mapping the Weather Illustrated by upwards of 600 Printed Lithographic Diagrams. 4to. 9s.

HEREDITARY GENIUS: An Inquiry into its Laws and Consequences. Demy 8vo. 12s.
The Times *calls it "a most able and most interesting book."*

ENGLISH MEN OF SCIENCE; THEIR NATURE AND NURTURE. 8vo. 8s. 6d.
"*The book is certainly one of very great interest.*"—Nature.

Gamgee.—A TEXT-BOOK OF THE PHYSIOLOGICAL CHEMISTRY OF THE ANIMAL BODY. By ARTHUR GAMGEE, M.D., F.R.S., Professor of Physiology in Owens College, Manchester. With Illustrations. In Two Vols. Medium 8vo. Vol. I. 18s. [*Vol. II in the Press.*

Geikie.—Works by ARCHIBALD GEIKIE, LL.D., F.R.S., Murchison Professor of Geology and Mineralogy at Edinburgh :—
ELEMENTARY LESSONS IN PHYSICAL GEOGRAPHY. With numerous Illustrations. Fcap. 8vo. 4s. 6d. Questions, 1s. 6d.
OUTLINES OF FIELD GEOLOGY. With Illustrations. Crown 8vo. 3s. 6d.
PRIMER OF GEOLOGY. Illustrated. 18mo. 1s.
PRIMER OF PHYSICAL GEOGRAPHY. Illustrated. 18mo. 1s.
TEXT-BOOK OF GEOLOGY. 8vo. [*In the Press.*

Gray.—STRUCTURAL BOTANY, OR ORGANOGRAPHY ON THE BASIS OF MORPHOLOGY. To which are added the .... and a Glossary of Botanical ...... By ASA GRAY, LL.D., &c. Professor of Natural History (Botany) in Harvard University. With numerous Illustrations. 8vo. 10s. 6d.

Green.—A SHORT GEOGRAPHY OF THE BRITISH ISLANDS. By JOHN RICHARD GREEN and ALICE STOPFORD GREEN. With Maps. Fcap. 8vo. 3s. 6d.

The Times says:—"The .... so far as real instruction is concerned, is .... could be desired.... Its great merit, in addition to ...s scientific arrangement and the attractive style so familiar to the readers of Green's 'Short History' is that the facts are so presented as to compel the careful student to think for himself..... The work may be read with .... and profit by anyone; we trust that it will gradually .... into the higher forms of our schools. With this .... has guide, an intelligent teacher might make geography what .... is—one of the most interesting and widely-instructive studies."

Guillemin.—THE FORCES OF NATURE: A Popular Introduction to the Study of Physical Phenomena. By AMÉDÉE GUILLEMIN. Translated from the French by MRS. NORMAN LOCKYER; and Edited, with Additions and Notes, by J. NORMAN LOCKYER, F.R.S. Illustrated by Coloured Plates, and 455 Woodcuts. Third and cheaper Edition. Royal 8vo. 21s.

"*Translator and Editor have done justice to their .... The text has all the force and flow of original .... faithfulness to the author's meaning with purity .... in regard to idiom; while the historical precision .... pervading the work throughout, speak of the .... supervision which has been given to every scientific .... can well exceed the clearness and delicacy of the .... cuts. Altogether, the work may be said to have no parallel, either in point of fulness or attraction, as a popular manual of physical science.*"—Saturday Review.

THE APPLICATIONS OF PHYSICAL FORCES. By A. GUILLEMIN. Translated from the French by MRS. LOCKYER, and Edited with Notes and Additions by J. N. LOCKYER, F.R.S. With Coloured Plates and numerous Illustrations. New and Cheaper Edition. Imperial 8vo. cloth, cxii ... 21s.

"*A book which we can heartily recommend, both on account of the width and soundness of its contents, and also because of the excellence of its print, its illustrations, and external appearance.*"—Westminster Review.

Hanbury.—SCIENCE PAPERS: chiefly Pharmacological and Botanical. By DANIEL HANBURY, F.R.S. Edited, with Memoir, by J. INCE, F.L.S., and Portrait engraved by C. H. JEENS. 8vo. 14s.

Henslow.—THE THEORY OF EVOLUTION OF LIVING THINGS, and Application of the Principles of Evolution to Religion considered as Illustrative of the Wisdom and Beneficence of the Almighty. By the Rev. GEORGE HENSLOW, M.A., F.L.S. Crown 8vo. 6s.

Hooker.—Works by Sir J. D. HOOKER, K.C.S.I., C.B., F.R.S., M.D., D.C.L.:—

THE STUDENT'S FLORA OF THE BRITISH ISLANDS. Second Edition, revised and improved. Globe 8vo. 10s. 6d.
"*Certainly the fullest and most accurate manual of the kind that has yet appeared. Dr. Hooker has shown his characteristic industry and ability in the care and skill which he has thrown into the characters of the plants. These are to a great extent original, and are really admirable for their combination of clearness, brevity, and completeness.*"—Pall Mall Gazette.

PRIMER OF BOTANY. With Illustrations. 18mo. 1s. New Edition, revised and corrected.

Hooker and Ball.—JOURNAL OF A TOUR IN MAROCCO AND THE GREAT ATLAS. By Sir J. D. HOOKER, K.C.S.I., C.B., F.R.S., &c., and JOHN BALL, F.R.S. With Appendices, including a Sketch of the Geology of Marocco. By G. MAW, F.L.S., F.G.S. With Map and Illustrations. 8vo. 21s.
"*This is, without doubt, one of the most interesting and valuable books of travel published for many years.*"—Spectator.

Huxley and Martin.—A COURSE OF PRACTICAL INSTRUCTION IN ELEMENTARY BIOLOGY. By T. H. HUXLEY, LL.D., Sec. R.S., assisted by H. N. MARTIN, B.A., M.B., D.Sc., Fellow of Christ's College, Cambridge. Crown 8vo. 6s.
"*This is the most thoroughly valuable book to teachers and students of biology which has ever appeared in the English tongue.*"—London Quarterly Review.

Huxley (Professor). LAY SERMONS, ADDRESSES, AND REVIEWS. By T. H. HUXLEY, LL.D., F.R.S. New and Cheaper Edition. Crown 8vo. 7s. 6d.
> I (1) ... ness of ... Black and ... —(3) A ... and ... it:—(4) ... (5) On the ... of the Natural History Sciences:—(6) On the Study Zoology:—(7) On the Physical Basis of Life:—(8) The ... of Positivism:—(9) On a Piece of Chalk:—(10) ... poraneity and Persistent ... (12) The Origin of ... "... of Species."—(14) On ... ... of using One's Reason ...

ESSAYS SELECTED FROM "LAY SERMONS, ADDRESSES, AND REVIEWS." Second Edition. Crown 8vo. 1s.

CRITIQUES AND ADDRESSES. 8vo. 10s. 6d.
> Contents:—1. Administrative Nihilism. 2. The School Boards: what they can do, and what they may do. 3. On Medical Education. 4. Yeast. 5. On the Formation of Coal. 6. On Coral and Coral Reefs. 7. On the Methods and Results of Ethnology. 8. On some Fixed Points in British Ethnology. 9. Palæontology and the Doctrine of Evolution. 10. Biogenesis and Abiogenesis. 11. Mr. Darwin's Critics. 12. The Genealogy of Animals. 13. Bishop Berkeley on the Metaphysics of Sensation.

LESSONS IN ELEMENTARY PHYSIOLOGY. With numerous Illustrations. New Edition. Fcap. 8vo. 4s. 6d.
> "Pure gold throughout."—Guardian. "Unquestionably the ... and most complete elementary treatise on this subject that ... in any language."—Westminster Review.

AMERICAN ADDRESSES: with a Lecture on the Study of Biology. 8vo. 6s. 6d.

PHYSIOGRAPHY: An Introduction to the Study of Nature. With Coloured Plates and numerous Woodcuts. New and Cheaper Edition. Crown 8vo. 6s.
> "It would be hardly possible to place a more useful or ... book in the hands of learners and teachers, or ... calculated to make physiography a favourite subject ... schools."—Academy.

INTRODUCTORY PRIMER. 18mo. 1s.

Jellet (John H., B.D.).—A TREATISE ON THE THEORY OF FRICTION. By JOHN H. JELLET, B.D., Senior Fellow of Trinity College, Dublin; President of the Royal Irish Academy. 8vo. 8s. 6d.

SCIENTIFIC CATALOGUE.

Jones.—Works by FRANCIS JONES, F.R.S.E., F.C.S., Chemical Master in the Grammar School, Manchester.
THE OWENS COLLEGE JUNIOR COURSE OF PRACTICAL CHEMISTRY. With Preface by Professor ROSCOE. New Edition. 18mo. With Illustrations. 2s. 6d.
QUESTIONS ON CHEMISTRY. A Series of Problems and Exercises in Inorganic and Organic Chemistry. 18mo. 3s.

Kingsley.—Works By CHARLES KINGSLEY, Canon of Westminster.
GLAUCUS: OR, THE WONDERS OF THE SHORE. New Edition, with numerous Coloured Plates. Crown 8vo. 6s.
SCIENTIFIC LECTURES AND ESSAYS. Crown 8vo. 6s.
SANITARY AND SOCIAL LECTURES AND ESSAYS. Crown 8vo. 6s.
MADAM HOW AND LADY WHY; or, Lessons in Earth-Lore for Children. Illustrated. Crown 8vo. 6s.

Landauer.—BLOWPIPE ANALYSIS. By J. LANDAUER. Authorised English Edition, by JAMES TAYLOR and W. E. KAY, of the Owens College, Manchester. With Illustrations. Extra fcap. 8vo. 4s. 6d.

Langdon.—THE APPLICATION OF ELECTRICITY TO RAILWAY WORKING. By W. E. LANGDON, Member of the Society of Telegraph Engineers. With numerous Illustrations. Extra fcap. 8vo. 4s. 6d.

"*There is no officer in the telegraph service who will not profit by the study of this book.*"—Mining Journal.

Lankester.—DEGENERATION. A Chapter in Darwinism. By Professor E. RAY LANKESTER, F.R.S., Fellow of Exeter College, Oxford. With Illustrations. Crown 8vo. 2s. 6d. (Nature Series).

Lockyer (J. N.).—Works by J. NORMAN LOCKYER, F.R.S.—
ELEMENTARY LESSONS IN ASTRONOMY. With numerous Illustrations. New Edition. Fcap. 8vo. 5s. 6d.

"*The book is full, clear, sound, and worthy of attention, not only as a popular exposition, but as a scientific 'Index.'*"—Athenæum.

THE SPECTROSCOPE AND ITS APPLICATIONS. By J. NORMAN LOCKYER, F.R.S. With Coloured Plate and numerous Illustrations. Second Edition. Crown 8vo. 3s. 6d. [*Nature Series.*

Lockyer (J.N.)—*continued.*

CONTRIBUTIONS TO SOLAR PHYSICS. By J. Norman Lockyer, F.R.S. I. A Popular Account of Inquiries into the Physical Constitution of the Sun, with especial reference to Recent Spectroscopic Researches. II. Communications to the Royal Society of London and the French Academy of Sciences, with Notes. Illustrated by 7 Coloured Lithographic Plates and 175 Woodcuts. Royal 8vo. cloth, price 1s. 6d.

"*The book may be taken ... the present state of science in ... the ... of spectroscopic analysis. ... Even ... derive much information from it.*"—Daily News.

PRIMER OF ASTRONOMY. With Illustrations. 18mo. 1s.

Lockyer and Seabroke. STAR-GAZING; PAST AND PRESENT. An Introduction to Instrumental Astronomy. By J. N. Lockyer, F.R.S. Expanded from Shorthand Notes of a Course of Royal Institution Lectures with the assistance of G. M. Seabroke, F.R.A.S. With numerous Illustrations. Royal 8vo. 21s.

"*A book of great interest and utility to the astronomical student.*" — Athenæum.

Lubbock.—Works by Sir John Lubbock, M.P., F.R.S., D.C.L.:

THE ORIGIN AND METAMORPHOSES OF INSECTS. With numerous Illustrations. Second Edition. Crown 8vo. 3s. 6d.
[*Nature Series.*

"*As a summary of the phenomena of insect metamorphoses his little book is of great value, and will be read with interest and profit by all students of natural history. The whole chapter on the origin of insects is most interesting and valuable. The illustrations are numerous and good.*"—Westminster Review.

ON BRITISH WILD FLOWERS CONSIDERED IN RELATION TO INSECTS. With Numerous Illustrations. Second Edition. Crown 8vo. 4s. 6d.
[*Nature Series.*

SCIENTIFIC LECTURES. With Illustrations. 8vo. 8s. 6d.
Contents:—*Flowers and Insects—Plants and Insects—The Habits of Ants—Introduction to the Study of Prehistoric Archæology, &c.*

Macmillan (Rev. Hugh).—For other Works by the same Author, see Theological Catalogue.

HOLIDAYS ON HIGH LANDS; or, Rambles and Incidents in search of Alpine Plants. Globe 8vo. cloth. 6s.

FIRST FORMS OF VEGETATION. Second Edition, corrected and enlarged, with Coloured Frontispiece and numerous Illustrations. Globe 8vo. 6s.

The first edition of this book was published under the name of "Footnotes from the Page of Nature; or, First Forms of Vegetation. Probably the best popular guide to the study of mosses, lichens, and fungi ever written. Its practical value as a help to the student and collector cannot be exaggerated."—Manchester Examiner.

Mansfield (C. B.).—Works by the late C. B. MANSFIELD :—
A THEORY OF SALTS. A Treatise on the Constitution of Bipolar (two-membered) Chemical Compounds. Crown 8vo. 14s.

AËRIAL NAVIGATION. The Problem, with Hints for its Solution. Edited by R. B. MANSFIELD. With a Preface by J. M. LUDLOW. With Illustrations. Crown 8vo. 10s. 6d.

Mayer.—SOUND : a Series of Simple, Entertaining, and Inexpensive Experiments in the Phenomena of Sound, for the Use of Students of every age. By A. M. MAYER, Professor of Physics in the Stevens Institute of Technology, &c. With numerous Illustrations. Crown 8vo. 3s. 6d. [*Nature Series.*

Mayer and Barnard.—LIGHT. A Series of Simple, Entertaining, and Useful Experiments in the Phenomena of Light, for the use of Students of every age. By A. M. MAYER and C. BARNARD. With Illustrations. Crown 8vo. 2s. 6d. [*Nature Series.*

Miall.—STUDIES IN COMPARATIVE ANATOMY. No. 1, The Skull of the Crocodile. A Manual for Students. By L. C. MIALL, Professor of Biology in Yorkshire College. 8vo. 2s. 6d. No. 2, The Anatomy of the Indian Elephant. By L. C. MIALL and F. GREENWOOD. With Plates. 5s.

Miller.—THE ROMANCE OF ASTRONOMY. By R. KALLEY MILLER, M.A., Fellow and Assistant Tutor of St. Peter's College, Cambridge. Second Edition, revised and enlarged. Crown 8vo. 4s. 6d.

Mivart (St. George).—Works by ST. GEORGE MIVART, F.R.S. &c., Lecturer in Comparative Anatomy at St. Mary's Hospital:—
ON THE GENESIS OF SPECIES. Second Edition, to which notes have been added in reference and reply to Darwin's "Descent of Man." With numerous Illustrations. Crown 8vo. 9s.

"In no work in the English language has this great controversy been treated at once with the same broad and vigorous grasp of facts, and the same liberal and candid temper."—Saturday Review.

Mivart (St. George)—*continued*
THE COMMON FROG. With Numerous .... Crown 8vo. 3s. 6d. (Nature Series.)
"*It is an able monogram of the Frog, and .... It throws valuable crosslights over wide portions of animated nature. Would that such works were more plentiful.*"—Quarterly Journal of Science.

Moseley.—NOTES BY A NATURALIST ON THE "CHALLENGER," being an account of various .... the voyage of H.M.S. "Challenger" .... years 1872–76. By H. N. MOSELEY, M.A. .... of the Scientific Staff of the "Challenger." .... Plates, and Woodcuts. 8vo. 21s.
"*This is .... book, descriptive of a .... been published since Mr. Darwin's .... appeared, now more years ago. That it is worthy to be placed alongside that record of the impressions, speculations, and .... mind, is, we do not doubt, the highest praise which .... would desire for his book, and we do not hesitate to .... such praise is its desert.*"—Nature.

Muir.—PRACTICAL CHEMISTRY FOR MEDICAL STUDENTS. Specially arranged for the first M. B. Course. By M. M. PATTISON MUIR, F.R.S.E. Fcap. 8vo. 1s. 6d.

Murphy.—HABIT AND INTELLIGENCE: a Series of Essays on the Laws of Life and Mind. By JOSEPH JOHN MURPHY. Second Edition, thoroughly revised and mostly re-written. With Illustrations. 8vo. 16s.

Nature.—A WEEKLY ILLUSTRATED JOURNAL OF SCIENCE. Published every .... Price 6d. Monthly Parts, 2s. and 2s. 6d.; Half-yearly V......... 15s. Cases for binding Vols. 1s. 6d.
"*This able and well-edited Journal, which posts up the science of the day .... and promises to be of signal service to students and .... Scarcely any expressions that we can employ .... exaggerate our sense of the moral and theological value of the work.*"—British Quarterly Review.

Newcomb.—POPULAR ASTRONOMY. By SIMON NEWCOMB, LL.D., Professor U.S. Naval Observatory. With 112 Engravings and .... of the Stars. 8vo. 18s.
"*As affording a .... reliable foundation for more advanced reading, Professor .... s 'Popular Astronomy' is deserving of strong .... *"—Nature.

Oliver.—Works by DANIEL OLIVER, F.R.S., F.L.S., Professor of Botany in University College, London, and Keeper of the Herbarium and Library of the Royal Gardens, Kew :—

Oliver—*continued.*
LESSONS IN ELEMENTARY BOTANY. With nearly Two Hundred Illustrations. New Edition. Fcap. 8vo. 4s. 6d.
FIRST BOOK OF INDIAN BOTANY. With numerous Illustrations. Extra fcap. 8vo. 6s. 6d.
"*It contains a well-digested summary of all essential knowledge pertaining to Indian Botany, wrought out in accordance with the best principles of scientific arrangement.*"—Allen's Indian Mail.

Pasteur.—STUDIES ON FERMENTATION. The Diseases of Beer; their Causes and Means of Preventing them. By L. Pasteur. A Translation of "Études sur la Bière." With Notes, Illustrations, &c. By F. Faulkner & D. C. Robb, B.A. 8vo. 21s.

Pennington.—NOTES ON THE BARROWS AND BONE CAVES OF DERBYSHIRE. With an account of a Descent into Elden Hole. By Rooke Pennington, B.A., LL.B., F.G.S. 8vo. 6s.

Penrose (F. C.)—ON A METHOD OF PREDICTING BY GRAPHICAL CONSTRUCTION, OCCULTATIONS OF STARS BY THE MOON, AND SOLAR ECLIPSES FOR ANY GIVEN PLACE. Together with more rigorous methods for the Accurate Calculation of Longitude. By F. C. Penrose, F.R.A.S With Charts, Tables, &c. 4to. 12s.

Perry.—AN ELEMENTARY TREATISE ON STEAM. By John Perry, B.E., Whitworth Scholar; Fellow of the Chemical Society, Lecturer in Physics at Clifton College. With numerous Woodcuts, Numerical Examples, and Exercises. New Edition. 18mo. 4s. 6d.
"*Mr. Perry has in this compact little volume brought together an immense amount of information, new told, regarding steam and its application, not the least of its merits being that it is suited to the capacities alike of the tyro in engineering science or the better grade of artisan.*"—Iron.

Pickering.—ELEMENTS OF PHYSICAL MANIPULATION. By E. C. Pickering, Thayer Professor of Physics in the Massachusetts Institute of Technology. Part I., medium 8vo. 10s. 6d. Part II., 10s. 6d.
"*When finished 'Physical Manipulation' will no doubt be considered the best and most complete text-book on the subject of which it treats.*"—Nature.

Prestwich.—THE PAST AND FUTURE OF GEOLOGY. An Inaugural Lecture, by J. Prestwich, M.A., F.R.S., &c., Professor of Geology, Oxford. 8vo. 2s.

Radcliffe.—PROTEUS; OR UNITY IN NATURE. By C. B. Radcliffe, M.D., Author of "Vital Motion as a mode of Physical Motion. Second Edition. 8vo. 7s. 6d.

Rendu.—THE THEORY OF THE GLACIERS OF SAVOY. By M. le Chanoine Rendu. Translated by A. Wells, Q.C., late President of the Alpine Club. To which are added, the Original Memoir and Supplementary Articles by Professors Tait and Ruskin. Edited with Introductory remarks by George Forbes, B.A., Professor of Natural Philosophy in the Andersonian University, Glasgow. 8vo. 7s. 6d.

Roscoe.—Works by Henry E. Roscoe, F.R.S., Professor of Chemistry in the Victoria University, the Owens College, Manchester :—

LESSONS IN ELEMENTARY CHEMISTRY, INORGANIC AND ORGANIC. With . . . . and Chromolitho of the . . . and of the Alkalis and Alkaline Earths. New . . . 8vo. 4s. 6d.

CHEMICAL PROBLEMS, adapted to the above by Professor Thorpe. Fifth Edition, with Key. 2s.
"*We unhesitatingly pronounce it the best of all our elementary treatises on Chemistry.*"—Medical Times.

PRIMER OF CHEMISTRY. Illustrated. 18mo. 1s.

Roscoe and Schorlemmer.—A TREATISE ON CHEMISTRY. With numerous . . . By Professors Roscoe and Schorlemmer. Vol. I. and II. Inorganic Chemistry.

    Vol. I., The Non-metallic Elements. 8vo. 21s
    Vol. II., Part I. Metals. 8vo. 18s.
    Vol. II., Part II. Metals. 8vo. 18s.
    Vol. III., Organic Chemistry. [*In the press.*

"*Regarded as a treatise on the Non-metallic Elements, there can be no doubt that this volume is incomparably the most satisfactory one of which we are in possession.*"—Spectator.

"*It would be difficult to praise the work too highly. . . . which we noticed in the first volume are . . . The arrangement is clear and scientific; . . . research are fairly represented and judiciously . . . th. style throughout is singularly lucid.*"—Lancet.

Rumford (Count).—THE LIFE AND . . . . . . OF BENJAMIN THOMPSON, ... Notices of his Daughter. By George . . . . Five Vols. 8vo. 4l. 14s. 6d.

Schorlemmer.—A MANUAL OF THE CHEMISTRY OF THE CARBON COMPOUNDS OR ORGANIC CHEMISTRY. By C. SCHORLEMMER, F.R.S., Professor of Chemistry in the Victoria University, the Owens College, Manchester. 8vo. 14s.
"*It appears to us to be as complete a manual of the metamorphoses of carbon as could be at present produced, and it must prove eminently useful to the chemical student.*"—Athenæum.

Shann.—AN ELEMENTARY TREATISE ON HEAT, IN RELATION TO STEAM AND THE STEAM ENGINE. By G. SHANN, M.A. With Illustrations. Crown 8vo. 4s. 6d.

Smith.—HISTORIA FILICUM: An Exposition of the Nature, Number, and Organography of Ferns, and Review of the Principles upon which Genera are founded, and the Systems of Classification of the principal Authors, with a new General Arrangement, &c. By J. SMITH. A.L.S., ex-Curator of the Royal Botanic Garden, Kew. With Thirty Lithographic Plates by W. H. FITCH, F.L.S. Crown 8vo. 12s. 6d.
"*No one anxious to work up a thorough knowledge of ferns can afford to do without it.*"—Gardener's Chronicle.

South Kensington Science Lectures.
Vol. I.—Containing Lectures by Captain ABNEY, F.RS., Professor STOKES, Professor KENNEDY, F. J. BRAMWELL, F.R.S., Professor G. FORBES, H. C. SORBY, F.R.S., J. T. BOTTOMLEY, F.R.S.E., S. H. VINES, B.Sc., and Professor CAREY FOSTER. Crown 8vo. 6s.
Vol. II.—Containing Lectures by W. SPOTTISWOODE, P.R.S., Prof. FORBES, H. W. CHISHOLM, Prof. T. F. PIGOT, W. FROUDE, F.R.S., Dr. SIEMENS, Prof. BARRETT, Dr. BURDEN-SANDERSON, Dr. LAUDER BRUNTON, F.R.S., Prof. MCLEOD, Prof. ROSCOE, F.R.S., &c. Crown 8vo. 6s.

Spottiswoode.—POLARIZATION OF LIGHT. By W. SPOTTISWOODE, President of the Royal Society. With numerous Illustrations. Third Edition. Cr. 8vo. 3s. 6d. (Nature Series.)
"*The illustrations are exceedingly well adapted to assist in making the text comprehensible.*"—Athenæum. "*A clear, trustworthy manual.*"—Standard.

Stewart (B.).—Works by BALFOUR STEWART, F.R.S., Professor of Natural Philosophy in the Victoria University, the Owens College, Manchester:—
LESSONS IN ELEMENTARY PHYSICS. With numerous Illustrations and Chromolithos of the Spectra of the Sun, Stars, and Nebulæ. New Edition. Fcap. 8vo. 4s. 6d.
The Educational Times calls this the beau-idéal of a scientific textbook, clear, accurate, and thorough.
PRIMER OF PHYSICS. With Illustrations. New Edition, with Questions. 18mo. 1s.

Stewart and Tait.—THE ... UNIVERSE: or, ... By BALFOUR ... Edition. ... 6s.

"... is ... well ... attention ... and religious ... It is ... sober inquiry, on scientific grounds, into the possibilities a ... existence."—*Guardian.*

Stone.—ELEMENTARY LESSONS ON SOUND. By Dr. W. H. STONE, Lecturer on Physics at St. Thomas' Hospital. With Illustrations. Fcap. 8vo. 3s. 6d.

Tait.—LECTURES ... IN ... of ... in the ... before ... 9s.

Tanner.—Works by HENRY TANNER, F.C.S., Professor of Agri- ... University College, Aberystwith, ... in ... Agriculture under the Government ... of Science.

FIRST PRINCI... OF AGRICULTURE. 18mo. 1s.

THE ABBOTT'S FARM; OR PRACTICE WITH SCIENCE. Crown 8vo. 3s. 6d.

Taylor.—SOUND AND MUSIC: A ... tise on the Physical ... including the Chief Acoustical ... of ... holtz. By SEDLEY TAYLOR, M.A., late ... Col. ledge, Cambridge. Large crown 8vo. 8s. 6d.

"*In no previous scientific treatise do we remember so ... and so richly illustrated a description of forms of ... of wave-motion in fluids.*"—*Musical Standard.*

Thomson.— ... by SIR WYVILLE THOMSON, K.C.B., F.R.S. THE DEPTHS ... THE SEA: An Account ... Results of ... Cruises of H.M ... "Lightning ... Summers of ... scientific direction of Dr. Carpenter, ... F.R.S., and Sir ... Thomson, ... Illustrations and ... Maps and ... Second ... Royal 8vo. cloth, gilt. ... 6d.

The Athenæum *says:* ... *book is full* ... *and is a ... the art ... It is*

high merit. ... operations will of course make a point of reading this work

Thomson—*continued.*

who wish to be pleasantly introduced to the subject, and rightly to appreciate the news which arrives from time to time from the 'Challenger,' should not fail to seek instruction from it."

THE VOYAGE OF THE "CHALLENGER."—THE ATLANTIC. A Preliminary account of the Exploring Voyages of H.M.S. "Challenger," during the year 1873 and the early part of 1876. With numerous Illustrations, Coloured Maps & Charts, & Portrait of the Author, engraved by C. H. JEENS. 2 Vols. Medium 8vo. 45s.

The Times says:—"It is right that the public should have some authoritative account of the general results of the expedition, and that as many of the ascertained data as may be accepted with confidence should speedily find their place in the general body of scientific knowledge. No one can be more competent than the accomplished scientific chief of the expedition to satisfy the public in this respect. . . . The paper, printing, and especially the numerous illustrations, are of the highest quality. . . . We have rarely, if ever, seen more beautiful specimens of wood engraving than abound in this work. . . . Sir Wyville Thomson's style is particularly attractive; he is easy and graceful, but vigorous and exceedingly happy in the choice of language, and throughout the work there are touches which show that science has not banished sentiment from his bosom."

Thudichum and Dupré.—A TREATISE ON THE ORIGIN, NATURE, AND VARIETIES OF WINE. Being a Complete Manual of Viticulture and Œnology. By J. L. W. THUDICHUM, M.D., and AUGUST DUPRÉ, Ph.D., Lecturer on Chemistry at Westminster Hospital. Medium 8vo. cloth gilt. 25s.

"*A treatise almost unique for its usefulness either to the wine-grower, the vendor, or the consumer of wine. The analyses of wine are the most complete we have yet seen, exhibiting at a glance the constituent principles of nearly all the wines known in this country.*" —Wine Trade Review.

Wallace (A. R.).—Works by ALFRED RUSSEL WALLACE.
CONTRIBUTIONS TO THE THEORY OF NATURAL SELECTION. A Series of Essays. New Edition, with Corrections and Additions. Crown 8vo. 8s. 6d.

The Saturday Review *says:* "*He has combined an abundance of fresh and original facts with a liveliness and sagacity of reasoning which are not often displayed so effectively on so small a scale.*"

THE GEOGRAPHICAL DISTRIBUTION OF ANIMALS, with a study of the Relations of Living and Extinct Faunas as Elucidating the Past Changes of the Earth's Surface. 2 vols. 8vo. with Maps, and numerous Illustrations by Zwecker, 42s.

Wallace (A. R.)—*continued.*

The ... "Altogether ... a wonderful and fascinating story ... objections ... to theories founded upon it. Mr. Wallace has ... to add to its interest by any adornments of style; he ... a simple and clear statement of intrinsically interesting facts, ... what he considers to be legitimate inductions from them. ... ought to be grateful to him for having undertaken so toilsome a task. The work, indeed, is a credit to all concerned—the author, the publishers, the artist—unfortunately now no more—of the attractive illustrations—last but by no means least, Mr. Stanford's map-designer."

ISLAND LIFE; OR, THE PHENOMENA AND CAUSES OF INSULAR FAUNAS AND FLORAS, including a revision and attempted ... the problem of geological climates. With Maps. ...

"*Island Life* is a work to be accepted almost without reservation from beginning to end ... Whoever reads his book must be charmed with it."—St. James's Gazette. "The work throughout abounds with interest ... It may be read with equal pleasure by those who are already acquainted with the general principles of distribution and by those who wish for the first time to learn something about modern biological geography."—Athenæum. "The result of his work he has already given us in more than one form; and his new volume on *Island Life* contains his ... views on the subject set forth in a clear and popular manner ... should make them accessible to many readers who would not venture on the perusal of his more strictly scientific expositions ... Mr. Wallace has written nothing more clear, more masterly, or more convincing than this delightful volume."—Fortnightly Review.

TROPICAL NATURE: with other Essays. 8vo. 12s.

"*Nowhere amid the many descriptions of the tropics that have ... given is to be found a summary of the past history ... phenomena of the tropics which gives that which is ... of the phases of nature in them more clearly, shortly, and impressively.*"—Saturday Review.

Warington.—THE WEEK OF CREATION; OR, THE COSMOGONY OF GENESIS CONSIDERED IN ITS RELATION TO MODERN SCIENCE. By GEORGE WARINGTON, Author of "The Historic Character of the Pentateuch Vindicated." Crown 8vo. 4s. 6d.

Wilson.—RELIGIO CHEMICI. By the late GEORGE WILSON, M.D., F.R.S.E., Regius Professor of Technology in the University of Edinburgh. With a Vignette beautifully engraved after a design by Sir NOEL PATON. Crown 8vo. 8s. 6d.

Wilson (Daniel).—CALIBAN: a Critique on Shakespeare's "Tempest" and "Midsummer Night's Dream." By DANIEL WILSON, LL.D., Professor of History and English Literature in University College, Toronto. 8vo. 10s. 6d.

"*The whole volume is most rich in the eloquence of thought and imagination as well as of words. It is a choice contribution at once to science, theology, religion, and literature.*"—British Quarterly Review.

Wright.—METALS AND THEIR CHIEF INDUSTRIAL APPLICATIONS. By C. ALDER WRIGHT, D.Sc., &c., Lecturer on Chemistry in St. Mary's Hospital School. Extra fcap. 8vo. 3s. 6d.

Wurtz.—A HISTORY OF CHEMICAL THEORY, from the Age of Lavoisier down to the present time. By AD. WURTZ. Translated by HENRY WATTS, F.R.S. Crown 8vo. 6s.

"*The discourse, as a résumé of chemical theory and research, unites singular luminousness and grasp. A few judicious notes are added by the translator.*"—Pall Mall Gazette. "*The treatment of the subject is admirable, and the translator has evidently done his duty most efficiently.*"—Westminster Review.

SCIENCE PRIMERS FOR ELEMENTARY SCHOOLS.

Under the joint Editorship of Professors HUXLEY, ROSCOE, and BALFOUR STEWART.

Introductory. By Professor HUXLEY, F.R.S. 18mo 1s.

Chemistry.—By H. E. ROSCOE, F.R.S., Professor of Chemistry in the Victoria University the Owens College, Manchester. With numerous Illustrations. 18mo. 1s. New Edition. With Questions.

Physics.— By BALFOUR STEWART, F.R.S., Professor of Natural Philosophy in the Victoria University the Owens College, Manchester. With numerous Illustrations. 18mo. 1s. New Edition. With Questions.

Physical Geography. — By ARCHIBALD GEIKIE, F.R.S., Murchison Professor of Geology and Mineralogy at Edinburgh. With numerous Illustrations. New Edition with Questions. 18mo. 1s.

Geology.—By Professor GEIKIE, F.R.S. With numerous Illustrations. New Edition. 18mo. cloth. 1s.

Science Primers for Elementary Schools.

Physiology — By M. FOSTER, M.D., F.R.S. With numerous Illustrations. New Edition. 18mo. 1s.

Astronomy. — By J. NORMAN LOCKYER, F.R.S. With numerous Illustrations. New Edition. 18mo. 1s.

Botany. — By Sir J. D. HOOKER, K.C.S.I., C.B., F.R.S. With numerous Illustrations. New Edition. 18mo. 1s.

Logic. — By Professor STANLEY JEVONS, LL.D., M.A., F.R.S. New Edition. 18mo. 1s.

Political Economy. — By Professor STANLEY JEVONS, LL.D., M.A., F.R.S. 18mo. 1s.

Others in preparation.

ELEMENTARY SCIENCE CLASS-BOOKS.

Agriculture. — ELEMENTARY LESSONS IN AGRICULTURAL SCIENCE. By H. TANNER, F.C.S., Professor of Agricultural Science, University College, Aberystwith.
[*In preparation.*

Astronomy. — By the ASTRONOMER ROYAL. POPULAR ASTRONOMY. With Illustrations. By Sir G. B. AIRY, K.C.B., Astronomer Royal. New Edition. 18mo. 4s. 6d.

Astronomy. — ELEMENTARY LESSONS IN ASTRONOMY. With Coloured Diagram of the Spectra of the Sun, Stars, and Nebulæ, and numerous Illustrations. By J. NORMAN LOCKYER, F.R.S. New Edition. Fcap. 8vo. 5s. 6d.
QUESTIONS ON LOCKYER'S ELEMENTARY LESSONS IN ASTRONOMY. For the Use of Schools. By JOHN FORBES ROBERTSON. 18mo, cloth limp. 1s. 6d.

Botany. — LESSONS IN ELEMENTARY BOTANY. By D. OLIVER, F.R.S., F.L.S., Professor of Botany in University College, London. With nearly Two Hundred Illustrations. New Edition. Fcap. 8vo. 4s. 6d.

Chemistry. — LESSONS IN ELEMENTARY CHEMISTRY, INORGANIC AND ORGANIC. By HENRY E. ROSCOE, F.R.S., Professor of Chemistry in the Victoria University, Owens College, Manchester. With numerous Illustrations and Chromo-Litho of the Solar Spectrum, and of the Alkalies and Alkaline Earths. New Edition. Fcap. 8vo. 4s. 6d.

Elementary Science Class-books—*continued*.

A SERIES OF CHEMICAL PROBLEMS, prepared with Special Reference to the above, by T. E. THORPE, Ph.D., Professor of Chemistry in the Yorkshire College of Science, Leeds. Adapted for the preparation of Students for the Government, Science, and Society of Arts Examinations. With a Preface by Professor ROSCOE. New Edition, with Key. 18mo. 2s.

Practical Chemistry.—THE OWENS COLLEGE JUNIOR COURSE OF PRACTICAL CHEMISTRY. By FRANCIS JONES, F.R.S.E., F.C.S., Chemical Master in the Grammar School, Manchester. With Preface by Professor ROSCOE, and Illustrations. New Edition. 18mo. 2s. 6d.

Chemistry.—QUESTIONS ON. A Series of Problems and Exercises in Inorganic and Organic Chemistry. By F. JONES, F.R.S.E., F.C.S. 18mo. 3s.

Electricity and Magnetism.—By Professor SYLVANUS THOMPSON, of University College, Bristol. With Illustrations.
[*In preparation.*

Physiology.—LESSONS IN ELEMENTARY PHYSIOLOGY. With numerous Illustrations. By T. H. HUXLEY, F.R.S., Professor of Natural History in the Royal School of Mines. New Edition. Fcap. 8vo. 4s. 6d.

QUESTIONS ON HUXLEY'S PHYSIOLOGY FOR SCHOOLS. By T. ALCOCK, M.D. 18mo. 1s. 6d.

Political Economy.—POLITICAL ECONOMY FOR BEGINNERS. By MILLICENT G. FAWCETT. New Edition. 18mo. 2s. 6d.

Logic.—ELEMENTARY LESSONS IN LOGIC; Deductive and Inductive, with copious Questions and Examples, and a Vocabulary of Logical Terms. By W. STANLEY JEVONS, LL.D., M.A., F.R.S. New Edition. Fcap. 8vo. 3s. 6d.

Physics.—LESSONS IN ELEMENTARY PHYSICS. By BALFOUR STEWART, F.R.S., Professor of Natural Philosophy in the Victoria University the Owens College, Manchester. With numerous Illustrations and Chromo-Litho of the Spectra of the Sun, Stars, and Nebulæ. New Edition. Fcap. 8vo. 4s. 6d.

Anatomy.—LESSONS IN ELEMENTARY ANATOMY. By ST. GEORGE MIVART, F.R.S., Lecturer in Comparative Anatomy at St. Mary's Hospital. With upwards of 400 Illustrations. Fcap. 8vo. 6s. 6d.

Elementary Science Class-books—continued.

Mechanics.—AN ELEMENTARY TREATISE. By A. B. W. KENNEDY, C.E., ... Mechanics in University College, London. With ... ... [*In preparation*.

Steam.—AN ELEMENTARY TREATISE. By JOHN PERRY, B.E., Whitworth Scholar; Fellow of the Chemical Society, Lecturer in Physics at Clifton College. With numerous Woodcuts and Numerical Examples and Exercises. New Edition. 18mo. 4s. 6d.

Physical Geography.—ELEMENTARY LESSONS IN PHYSICAL GEOGRAPHY. By A. GEIKIE, F.R.S., Murchison Professor of Geology, ... Edinburgh. With numerous Illustrations. Fcap. 8vo. 4s. 6d.
QUESTIONS ON THE SAME. 1s. 6d.

Psychology.—ELEMENTARY LESSONS IN PSYCHOLOGY. By G. CROOM ROBERTSON, Professor of Mental Philosophy, &c., University College, London. [*In preparation*.

Geography.—CLASS-BOOK OF GEOGRAPHY. By C. B. CLARKE, M.A., F.G.S. New Edition, with eighteen coloured Maps. Fcap. 8vo. 3s.

Moral Philosophy.—AN ELEMENTARY TREATISE. By Professor E. CAIRD, of Glasgow University. [*In preparation*.

Natural Philosophy.—NATURAL PHILOSOPHY FOR BEGINNERS. By I. TODHUNTER, M.A., F.R.S. Part I. The Properties of Solid and Fluid Bodies. 18mo. 3s. 6d. Part II. Sound, Light, and Heat. 18mo. 3s. 6d.

The Economics of Industry.—By A. MARSHALL, M.A., late Principal of University College, Cheltenham, and MARY P. MARSHALL, late Lecturer at Newnham Hall, Cambridge. Extra fcap. 8vo. 2s. 6d.
"*The book is of sterling value, and will be of great use to students and teachers.*"—Athenæum.

Sound.—AN ELEMENTARY TREATISE. By Dr. W. H. STONE. With Illustrations. 18mo. 3s. 6d.

Easy Lessons in Science.—Edited by Professor W. F. BARRETT.
  I. HEAT. By C. A. MARTINEAU. Illustrated. Extra fcap. 8vo. 2s. 6d.
  II. LIGHT. By Mrs. W. AWDRY. Illustrated. Extra fcap. 8vo. 2s. 6d.
  Others in Preparation.

MANUALS FOR STUDENTS.

Crown 8vo.

Cossa.—GUIDE TO THE STUDY OF POLITICAL ECONOMY. By Dr. LUIGI COSSA, Professor of Political Economy in the University of Pavia. Translated from the Second Italian Edition. With a Preface by W. STANLEY JEVONS, F.R.S. Crown 8vo. 4s. 6d.

Dyer and Vines.—THE STRUCTURE OF PLANTS. By Professor THISELTON DYER, F.R.S., assisted by SYDNEY VINES, B.Sc., Fellow and Lecturer of Christ's College, Cambridge. With numerous Illustrations. [*In preparation.*

Fawcett.—A MANUAL OF POLITICAL ECONOMY. By Right Hon. Henry FAWCETT, M.P. New Edition, revised and enlarged. Crown 8vo. 12s.

Fleischer.—A SYSTEM OF VOLUMETRIC ANALYSIS. Translated, with Notes and Additions, from the second German Edition, by M. M. PATTISON MUIR, F.R.S.E. With Illustrations. Crown 8vo. 7s. 6d.

Flower (W. H.).—AN INTRODUCTION TO THE OSTEOLOGY OF THE MAMMALIA. Being the Substance of the Course of Lectures delivered at the Royal College of Surgeons of England in 1870. By Professor W. H. FLOWER, F.R.S., F.R.C.S. With numerous Illustrations. New Edition, enlarged. Crown 8vo. 10s. 6d.

Foster and Balfour.—THE ELEMENTS OF EMBRYOLOGY. By MICHAEL FOSTER, M.D., F.R.S., and F. M. BALFOUR, M.A. Part I. crown 8vo. 7s. 6d.

Foster and Langley.—A COURSE OF ELEMENTARY PRACTICAL PHYSIOLOGY. By MICHAEL FOSTER, M.D., F.R.S., and J. N. LANGLEY, B.A. Fourth Edition. Crown 8vo. 6s.

Hooker (Dr.)—THE STUDENT'S FLORA OF THE BRITISH ISLANDS. By Sir J. D. HOOKER, K.C.S.I., C.B., F.R.S., M.D., D.C.L. New Edition, revised. Globe 8vo. 10s. 6d.

Huxley.—PHYSIOGRAPHY. An Introduction to the Study of Nature. By Professor HUXLEY, F.R.S. With numerous Illustrations, and Coloured Plates. New and cheaper Edition. Crown 8vo. 6s.

Manuals for Students—*continued.*

Huxley and Martin.—A COURSE OF PRACTICAL IN-
STRUCTION IN ELEMENTARY BIOLOGY. By Professor
HUXLEY, F.R.S., assisted by H. N. MARTIN, M.B., D.Sc. New
Edition, revised. Crown 8vo. 6s.

Huxley and Parker.—ELEMENTARY BIOLOGY. PART
II. By Professor HUXLEY, F.R.S., assisted by T. J. PARKER.
With Illustrations. [*In preparation.*

Jevons.—MANUALS. By Professor W. STANLEY JEVONS, LL.D.,
M.A., F.R.S. :—
THE PRINCIPLES OF SCIENCE. A Treatise on Logic and
Scientific Method. New and Revised Edition. Crown 8vo. 12s. 6d.
STUDIES IN DEDUCTIVE LOGIC. A Manual for Students.
Crown 8vo. 6s.

Kennedy.—MECHANICS OF MACHINERY. By A. B. W.
KENNEDY, M. Inst. C.E., Professor of Engineering and
Mechanical Technology in University College, London. With
Illustrations. Crown 8vo. [*In the Press.*

Kiepert.—A MANUAL OF ANCIENT GEOGRAPHY. From
the German of Dr. H. KIEPERT. Crown 8vo. [*Immediately.*

Oliver (Professor).—FIRST BOOK OF INDIAN BOTANY.
By Professor DANIEL OLIVER, F.R.S., F.L.S., Keeper of the
Herbarium and Library of the Royal Gardens, Kew. With
numerous Illustrations. Extra fcap. 8vo. 6s. 6d.

Parker and Bettany.—THE MORPHOLOGY OF THE
SKULL. By Professor PARKER and G. T. BETTANY. Illustrated. Crown 8vo. 10s. 6d.

Tait.—AN ELEMENTARY TREATISE ON HEAT. By Professor TAIT, F.R.S.E. Illustrated. [*In the Press.*

Thomson.— ZOOLOGY. By Sir C. WYVILLE THOMSON,
F.R.S. Illustrated. [*In preparation.*

Tylor—ANTHROPOLOGY: An Introduction to the Study of Man
and Civilization. By E. B. TYLOR, M.A., F.R.S. Illustrated.
[*In the Press.*

Other volumes of these Manuals will follow.

SCIENTIFIC TEXT-BOOKS.

Balfour.—A TREATISE ON COMPARATIVE EMBRYOLOGY. With Illustrations. By F. M. Balfour, M.A., F.R.S., Fellow and Lecturer of Trinity College, Cambridge. In 2 vols. 8vo. Vol. I. 18s. now ready. [*Vol. II. in the Press.*

Ball (R.S., A.M.)—EXPERIMENTAL MECHANICS. A Course of Lectures delivered at the Royal College of Science for Ireland. By R. S. Ball, A.M., Professor of Applied Mathematics and Mechanics in the Royal College of Science for Ireland. Royal 8vo. 10s. 6d.

Clausius.—MECHANICAL THEORY OF HEAT. By R. Clausius. Translated by Walter R. Browne, M.A., late Fellow of Trinity College, Cambridge. Crown 8vo. 10s. 6d.

Cotterill.—A TREATISE ON APPLIED MECHANICS. By James Cotterill, M.A., F.R.S., Professor of Applied Mechanics at the Royal Naval College, Greenwich. With Illustrations. 8vo. [*In preparation.*

Daniell.—A TREATISE ON PHYSICS FOR MEDICAL STUDENTS. By Alfred Daniell. With Illustrations. 8vo. [*In preparation.*

Foster.—A TEXT-BOOK OF PHYSIOLOGY. By Michael Foster, M.D., F.R.S. With Illustrations. Third Edition, revised. 8vo. 21s.

Gamgee.—A TEXT-BOOK OF THE PHYSIOLOGICAL CHEMISTRY OF THE ANIMAL BODY. Including an account of the chemical changes occurring in Disease. By A. Gamgee, M.D., F.R.S., Professor of Physiology in the Victoria University and Owens College, Manchester. 2 vols. 8vo. With Illustrations. Vol. I. 18s. [*Vol. II. in the Press.*

Gegenbaur.—ELEMENTS OF COMPARATIVE ANATOMY. By Professor Carl Gegenbaur. A Translation by F. Jeffrey Bell, B.A. Revised with Preface by Professor E. Ray Lankester, F.R.S. With numerous Illustrations. 8vo. 21s.

Geikie.—TEXT-BOOK OF GEOLOGY. By Archibald Geikie, F.R.S., Professor of Geology in the University of Edinburgh. With numerous Illustrations. 8vo. [*In the Press.*

Scientific Text-Books—*continued.*

Gray.—STRUCTURAL BOTANY, OR ORGANOGRAPHY ON THE BASIS OF MORPHOLOGY. To which are added the principles of Taxonomy and Phytography, and a Glossary of Botanical Terms. By Professor ASA GRAY, LL.D. 8vo. 10s. 6d.

Newcomb.—POPULAR ASTRONOMY. By S. NEWCOMB, LL.D., Professor U.S. Naval Observatory. With 112 Illustrations and 5 Maps of the Stars. 8vo. 18s.
"*It is unlike anything else of its kind, and will be of more use in circulating a knowledge of ——— than nine-tenths of the books which have appeared on the ——— of late years.*"—Saturday Review.

Reuleaux.—THE KINEMATICS OF MACHINERY. Outlines of a Theory of Machines. By Professor F. REULEAUX. Translated and Edited by Professor A. B. W. KENNEDY, C.E. With 450 Illustrations. Medium 8vo. 21s.

Roscoe and Schorlemmer.—INORGANIC CHEMISTRY. A Complete Treatise on Inorganic Chemistry. By Professor H. E. ROSCOE, F.R.S., and Professor C. SCHORLEMMER, F.R.S. With numerous Illustrations. Medium 8vo. Vol. I.—The Non-Metallic Elements. 21s. Vol. II.—Metals.—Part I. 18s. Vol. II. Part II.—Metals. 18s.
ORGANIC CHEMISTRY. A complete Treatise on Organic Chemistry. By Professors ROSCOE and SCHORLEMMER. With numerous Illustrations. Medium 8vo. [*In the Press.*

Schorlemmer.—A MANUAL OF THE CHEMISTRY OF THE CARBON COMPOUNDS, OR ORGANIC CHEMISTRY. By C. SCHORLEMMER, F.R.S., Professor of Chemistry, the Victoria University the Owens College, Manchester. With Illustrations. 8vo. 14s.

Thorpe and Rücker.—A TREATISE ON CHEMICAL PHYSICS. By Professor THORPE, F.R.S., and Professor RÜCKER, of the Yorkshire College of Science. Illustrated. 8vo. [*In preparation.*

WORKS ON MENTAL AND MORAL PHILOSOPHY, AND ALLIED SUBJECTS.

Aristotle.—AN INTRODUCTION TO ARISTOTLE'S RHETORIC. With Analysis, Notes, and Appendices. By E. M. COPE, Trinity College, Cambridge. 8vo. 14s.

ARISTOTLE ON FALLACIES; OR, THE SOPHISTICI ELENCHI. With a Translation and Notes by EDWARD POSTE, M.A., Fellow of Oriel College, Oxford. 8vo. 8s. 6d.

ARISTOTLE.—The Metaphysics, Book I. Translated into English Prose, with Marginal Analysis, and Summary of each Chapter. By a Cambridge Graduate. Demy 8vo. 5s.

Balfour.—A DEFENCE OF PHILOSOPHIC DOUBT: being an Essay on the Foundations of Belief. By A. J. BALFOUR, M.P. 8vo. 12s.

"*Mr. Balfour's criticism is exceedingly brilliant and suggestive.*"—Pall Mall Gazette.

"*An able and refreshing contribution to one of the burning questions of the age, and deserves to make its mark in the fierce battle now raging between science and theology.*"—Athenæum.

Birks.—Works by the Rev. T. R. BIRKS, Professor of Moral Philosophy, Cambridge:—

FIRST PRINCIPLES OF MORAL SCIENCE; or, a First Course of Lectures delivered in the University of Cambridge. Crown 8vo. 8s. 6d.

This work treats of three topics all preliminary to the direct exposition of Moral Philosophy. These are the Certainty and Dignity of Moral Science, its Spiritual Geography, or relation to other main subjects of human thought, and its Formative Principles, or some elementary truths on which its whole development must depend.

MODERN UTILITARIANISM; or, The Systems of Paley, Bentham, and Mill, Examined and Compared. Crown 8vo. 6s. 6d.

SUPERNATURAL REVELATION; or, First Principles of Moral Theology. 8vo. 8s.

Boole.—AN INVESTIGATION OF THE LAWS OF THOUGHT, ON WHICH ARE FOUNDED THE MATHEMATICAL THEORIES OF LOGIC AND PROBABILITIES. By GEORGE BOOLE, LL.D., Professor of Mathematics in the Queen's University, Ireland, &c. 8vo. 14s.

Butler.—LECTURES ON T... ...LOSOPHY. By W... ...Philosophy in the Author's MSS., with N... THOMPSON, M.A., Master of Greek in the University revised by the Editor. 8vo.

Caird.—AN INTRODUCTION TO THE PHILOSOPHY OF RELIGION. By JOHN CAIRD, D.D. Principal and Vice-Chancellor of the University of ... ore of ... Chaplains for Scotland. 8vo.

Caird.— ... PHILOSOPHY OF ... By E. CAIRD, M.A. ... the University of Glasgow. 8vo. 18s.

Calderwood.—Works by the Rev. HENRY CALDERWOOD, M.A., LL.D., Professor of Moral Philosophy in the University of Edinburgh:—

PHILOSOPHY OF THE INFINITE: A Treatise on Man's Knowledge of the Infinite Being, in answer to Sir W. Hamilton and Dr. Mansel. Cheaper Edition. 6d.

"*A book of great ability . . . . stle, and may be easily understood by even not versed in such discussions.*"—British Quarterly

A HANDBOOK OF MORAL PHILOSOPHY. S Crown 8vo. 6s.

"*It is, we feel convinced, the best on the subject, and morally, and does infinite to its author. "A and l work, great in a to suggest / His be an assistance students own University of Edinburgh.*"

THE RELATIONS OF MIND AND BRAIN. 8vo. 12s.

"*It should be of real service as a clear exposition and a searching criticism of cerebral psychology.*"—Westminster Review.

"*Altogether his work is probably the best combination to be found at present in England of exposition and criticism on the subject of physiological psychology.*"—The Academy.

Clifford.—LECTURES AND ESSAYS. Professor W. K. CLIFFORD, F.R.S. Edited by and FREDERICK POLLOCK, with Introduction . Two Portraits. 2 vols. 8vo. 25s.

Clifford—*continued.*

> "*The* Times *of October 22nd says:*—"*Many a friend of the author on first taking up these volumes and remembering his versatile genius and his keen enjoyment of all realms of intellectual activity must have trembled, lest they should be found to consist of fragmentary pieces of work, too disconnected to do justice to his powers of consecutive reading, and too varied to have any effect as a whole. Fortunately these fears are groundless. . . . It is not only in subject that the various papers are closely related. There is also a singular consistency of view and of method throughout. . . . It is in the social and metaphysical subjects that the richness of his intellect shows itself, most forcibly in the rarity and originality of the ideas which he presents to us. To appreciate this variety it is necessary to read the book itself, for it treats in some form or other of all the subjects of deepest interest in this age of questioning.*"

Fiske.—OUTLINES OF COSMIC PHILOSOPHY, BASED ON THE DOCTRINE OF EVOLUTION, WITH CRITICISMS ON THE POSITIVE PHILOSOPHY. By JOHN FISKE, M.A., LL.B., formerly Lecturer on Philosophy at Harvard University. 2 vols. 8vo. 25s.

> "*The work constitutes a very effective encyclopædia of the evolutionary philosophy, and is well worth the study of all who wish to see at once the entire scope and purport of the scientific dogmatism of the day.*"—Saturday Review.

Harper.—THE METAPHYSICS OF THE SCHOOL. By the Rev. THOMAS HARPER (S.J.). In 5 vols. 8vo. Vol. I. 8vo. 18s.
[*Vol II. in the press.*

Herbert.—THE REALISTIC ASSUMPTIONS OF MODERN SCIENCE EXAMINED. By T. M. HERBERT, M.A., late Professor of Philosophy, &c., in the Lancashire Independent College, Manchester. 8vo. 14s.

> "*Mr. Herbert's work appears to us one of real ability and importance. The author has shown himself well trained in philosophical literature, and possessed of high critical and speculative powers.*"—Mind.

Jardine.—THE ELEMENTS OF THE PSYCHOLOGY OF COGNITION. By ROBERT JARDINE, B.D., D.Sc., Principal of the General Assembly's College, Calcutta, and Fellow of the University of Calcutta. Crown 8vo. 6s. 6d.

Jevons.—Works by W. STANLEY ...

THE ...
Scientific ...
8vo. 12s.
"*No one in future can ... has been done in the ... England without having ... book.*"—Spectator.

THE SUBSTITUTION OF SIMILARS, ... of
Reasoning. Derived from a Modification of ...
Fcap. 8vo. 2s. 6d.

ELEMENTARY LESSONS IN ... AND
INDUCTIVE. With ... of
Logical Terms.

STUDIES IN ... Students.
Crown 8vo. 6s.

PRIMER OF LOGIC. New Edition. 18mo. 1s.

M'Cosh.—Works by JAMES M'COSH, LL.D., ...
College, New Jersey, U.S.
"*He certainly shows himself skilful in that ... to psychology, in that inductive science of the ... is the fine side of English philosophy. His philosophy as ... is worthy of attention.*"—Revue de Deux Mondes.

THE METHOD OF THE DIVINE ... , Physical
and Moral. Tenth Edition. 8vo. 1
"*This work is distinguished ... based upon a thorough ... knowledge of its present ... by ... a deeper and more unfettered ... cussion of the ... ques- tions. The ... and dreaminess of German speculation since ... the onesidedness and narrowness of the ... and positivism which have so prevailed in England.*"—Dr. Ulrici, in "Zeitschrift fur Philosophie."

THE INTUITIONS OF THE MIND. A New Edition. 8vo.
cloth. 10s. 6d.
"*The undertaking to adjust the claims of the sensational and in- tuitional philosophies, and of the* à posteriori *and* à priori *methods, is accomplished in this work with a great amount of* — Westminster Review. "*I value it for its ... with English Philosophy, which has not ... neglect the great German works. I admire the ... , as well as comprehensiveness, of the author's ... of Berlin.*

M'Cosh—*continued.*

AN EXAMINATION OF MR. J. S. MILL'S PHILOSOPHY: Being a Defence of Fundamental Truth. Second edition, with additions. 10s. 6d.

"*Such a work greatly needed to be done, and the author was the man to do it. This volume is important, not merely in reference to the views of Mr. Mill, but of the whole school of writers, past and present, British and Continental, he so ably represents.*"—Princeton Review.

THE LAWS OF DISCURSIVE THOUGHT: Being a Text-book of Formal Logic. Crown 8vo. 5s.

"*The amount of summarized information which it contains is very great; and it is the only work on the very important subject with which it deals. Never was such a work so much needed as in the present day.*"—London Quarterly Review.

CHRISTIANITY AND POSITIVISM: A Series of Lectures to the Times on Natural Theology and Apologetics. Crown 8vo. 7s. 6d.

THE SCOTTISH PHILOSOPHY FROM HUTCHESON TO HAMILTON, Biographical, Critical, Expository. Royal 8vo. 16s.

THE EMOTIONS. Crown 8vo. 9s.

Masson.—RECENT BRITISH PHILOSOPHY: A Review with Criticisms; including some Comments on Mr. Mill's Answer to Sir William Hamilton. By DAVID MASSON, M.A., Professor of Rhetoric and English Literature in the University of Edinburgh. Third Edition, with an Additional Chapter. Crown 8vo. 6s

"*We can nowhere point to a work which gives so clear an exposition of the course of philosophical speculation in Britain during the past century, or which indicates so instructively the mutual influences of philosophic and scientific thought.*"—Fortnightly Review.

Maudsley.—Works by H. MAUDSLEY, M.D., Professor of Medical Jurisprudence in University College, London.

THE PHYSIOLOGY OF MIND; being the First Part of a Third Edition, Revised, Enlarged, and in great part Re-written, of "The Physiology and Pathology of Mind." Crown 8vo. 10s. 6d.

THE PATHOLOGY OF MIND. Revised, Enlarged, and in great part Re-written. 8vo. 18s.

BODY AND MIND: an Inquiry into their Connexion and Mutual Influence, specially with reference to Mental Disorders. An Enlarged and Revised edition. To which are added, Psychological Essays. Crown 8vo. 6s. 6d.

Maurice.—Works ... the Rev ... CK ... MAURICE, M.A., ...

CA

SOCIAL MORALITY. ... Lectures ...
University of Cambridge. N ... Edition. ...
10s. 6d.

"*Whilst reading it we ... by
and prejudice, the large ... the
ness to recognize and
extant in the world,
We gain new
perhaps, ... of so
noble ... a*

THE CONSCIENCE : ' ... Casuistry, delivered in the University of Cambridge. ... and Cheaper Edition. Crown 8vo. 5s.
*The Saturday Review says: "We rise from ...
of all that is selfish and mean, and with a ... that
there is such a thing as goodness after all."*

MORAL AND METAPHYSICAL PHI ... Vol. I.
Ancient Philosophy from the First to the ...
Vol. II. the Fourteenth Century and the ...
a glimpse into the Nineteenth Century. ...
Preface. 2 Vols. 8vo. 25s.

Morgan.—ANCIENT ... of
Human Progress, from ...
By LEWIS H. MORGAN, ... the ... of
Sciences. 8vo. 16s.

Murphy.—THE SCIENTIFIC BASES OF ...
JOSEPH JOHN MURPHY, Author of "Habit ...
8vo. 14s.

"*The book is not without ... ; the
work of the best apologists of the last century,
force and clearness, but still with commendable
tact; and with an intelligent feeling for the changed
the problem."*—Academy.

Paradoxical Philosophy.—A Sequel to " ...
verse." Crown 8vo. 7s. 6d.

Picton.—THE MYSTERY OF MATTER ...
ESSAYS. By J. ALLANSON PICTON, ...
and the Old Faith." Cheaper issue with ...
8vo. 6s.

Picton—*continued.*

    CONTENTS :—*The Mystery of Matter—The Philosophy of Ignorance—The Antithesis of Faith and Sight—The Essential Nature of Religion—Christian Pantheism.*

Sidgwick.—THE METHODS OF ETHICS. By HENRY SIDGWICK, M.A., Prælector in Moral and Political Philosophy in Trinity College, Cambridge. Second Edition, revised throughout with important additions. 8vo. 14s.

  A SUPPLEMENT to the First Edition, containing all the important additions and alterations in the Second. 8vo. 2s.

  "*This excellent and very welcome volume. . . . Leaving to metaphysicians any further discussion that may be needed respecting the already over-discussed problem of the origin of the moral faculty, he takes it for granted as readily as the geometrician takes space for granted, or the physicist the existence of matter. But he takes little else for granted, and defining ethics as 'the science of conduct,' he carefully examines, not the various ethical systems that have been propounded by Aristotle and Aristotle's followers downwards, but the principles upon which, so far as they confine themselves to the strict province of ethics, they are based.*"—Athenæum.

Thornton.—OLD-FASHIONED ETHICS, AND COMMON-SENSE METAPHYSICS, with some of their Applications. By WILLIAM THOMAS THORNTON, Author of "A Treatise on Labour." 8vo. 10s. 6d.

  The present volume deals with problems which are agitating the minds of all thoughtful men. The following are the Contents:—I. Ante-Utilitarianism. II. History's Scientific Pretensions. III. David Hume as a Metaphysician. IV. Huxleyism. V. Recent Phase of Scientific Atheism. VI. Limits of Demonstrable Theism.

Thring (E., M.A.).—THOUGHTS ON LIFE-SCIENCE. By EDWARD THRING, M.A. (Benjamin Place), Head Master of Uppingham School. New Edition, enlarged and revised. Crown 8vo 7s. 6d.

Venn.—THE LOGIC OF CHANCE: An Essay on the Foundations and Province of the Theory of Probability, with especial reference to its logical bearings, and its application to Moral and Social Science. By JOHN VENN, M.A., Fellow and Lecturer of Gonville and Caius College, Cambridge. Second Edition, re-written and greatly enlarged. Crown 8vo. 10s. 6d.

  "*One of the most thoughtful and philosophical treatises on any subject connected with logic and evidence which has been produced in this or any other country for many years.*"—Mill's Logic, vol. ii. p. 77. Seventh Edition.

NATURE SERIES.

THE SPECTROSCOPE AND ITS APPLICATIONS. By J. N. LOCKYER, F.R.S. With Illustrations. *Second Edition.* Crown 8vo. 3s. 6d.

THE ORIGIN AND METAMORPHOSES OF INSECTS. By Sir JOHN LUBBOCK, M.P., F.R.S. With Illustrations. 3s. 6d. *Second Edition.*

THE TRANSIT OF VENUS. By G. FORBES, B.A., Professor of Natural Philosophy in ... With numerous Illustrations. Crown ...

THE COMMON FROG. By ST. GEORGE MIVART, F.R.S. Illustrated. 3s. 6d.

POLARISATION OF LIGHT. By W. SPOTTISWOODE, LL.D., President of the Royal Society. Illustrated. *Second* ... Crown 8vo. 3s. 6d.

ON BRITISH WILD FLOWERS CONSIDERED IN RELATION TO INSECTS. By Sir JOHN LUBBOCK. Illustrated. *Second Edition.* Crown 8vo. 4s. 6d.

THE SCIENCE OF WEIGHING AND MEASURING. By H. W. CHISHOLM, Warden of the ... 4s. 6d.

HOW TO DRAW A STRAIGHT LINE: A LECTURE on Linkages. By A. B. KEMPE, B.A. Illustrated. Crown 8vo. 1s. 6d.

LIGHT: A Series of ... Useful Experiments in the ... By ALFRED M. ... Crown 8vo. 2s. 6d.

SOUND: A Series of Simple, En... pensive ... in the ... M. MAYER. ... With numerous ...

SEEING AND THINKING. By Prof. W. K. CLIFFORD, F.R.S. With Diagrams. Crown 8vo. 3s. 6d.

DEGENERATION. A Chapter in Darwinism. By Professor E. RAY LANKESTER, F.R.S. Crown 8vo. 2s. 6d.

(*Others to follow.*)

MACMILLAN AND CO., LONDON.

Published every Thursday, price 6d.; Monthly Parts 2s. and 2s. 6d., Half-Yearly Volumes, 15s.

NATURE:

AN ILLUSTRATED JOURNAL OF SCIENCE.

NATURE expounds in a popular and yet authentic manner, the GRAND RESULTS OF SCIENTIFIC RESEARCH, discussing the most recent scientific discoveries, and pointing out the bearing of Science upon civilisation and progress, and its claims to a more general recognition, as well as to a higher place in the educational system of the country.

It contains original articles on all subjects within the domain of Science; Reviews setting forth the nature and value of recent Scientific Works; Correspondence Columns, forming a medium of Scientific discussion and of intercommunication among the most distinguished men of Science, Serial Columns, giving the gist of the most important papers appearing in Scientific Journals, both Home and Foreign; Transactions of the principal Scientific Societies and Academies of the World, Notes, &c.

In Schools where Science is included in the regular course of studies, this paper will be most acceptable, as it tells what is doing in Science all over the world, is popular without lowering the standard of Science, and by it a vast amount of information is brought within a small compass, and students are directed to the best sources for what they need. The various questions connected with Science teaching in schools are also fully discussed, and the best methods of teaching are indicated.

LONDON: R. CLAY, SONS, AND TAYLOR, PRINTERS

www.ingramcontent.com/pod-product-compliance
Lightning Source LLC
Chambersburg PA
CBHW051850300426
44117CB00006B/339